Chasing the Game

Chasing the Game

Sporting Trails from Jo'burg to Jamaica

Peter Davies

ZEBRA

To my parents,

without whom no game-chasing

would have been possible.

ZEBRA

Published by Zebra Press
a division of Struik Publishers (Pty) Ltd
(a member of the Struik Publishing Group (Pty) Ltd)
32 Thora Crescent, Wynberg, Sandton

Reg. No.: 54/00965/07

First published in September 1997

Editor Tamsin Shelton
DTP Marlene Willoughby-Smith
Cover design Neels Bezuidenhout
Cover photograph Rob Till
Maps Tony Keeling

Reproduction by Disc Express cc, Johannesburg
Printed and bound by Creda Press (Pty) Ltd, PO Box 200, Thornton 7485

ISBN 1 86872 069 1

Contents

Introduction

THE IDEA FOR THIS BOOK came while I sat sipping Zywiec lager one night at an open-air pub called the Beer Cave in downtown Warsaw. In my experience, most creative journalistic ideas are helped along by frequently consulting the 'bottled think tank', and the beer in Poland certainly proved obliging.

Not that I'm in any way being facetious about journalism. This book has been crafted in the noble and painstaking tradition of the five 'W's' of sports reporting: who, what, when, why and whisky.

No? Okay then: wine, women, whingeing, Wintergreen and WetOnes? Something like that.

Anyway, the spark for writing a sports travelogue was ignited by a conversation I had with a broadcaster I met that evening in Warsaw. I was dressed in a Bafana Bafana replica soccer shirt, and as I rose to leave the Beer Cave, a voice belonging to the only black face I encountered in Poland shouted, 'Hey, South Africa!'

I wandered over and ended up talking to the owner of this face, Brian Scott, for the rest of the evening. He was from Guyana but had studied journalism in Poland and was now something of a household name in his adopted country. Scott had watched South Africa win the African Cup of Nations and was in the Beer Cave for a final interview for the job of hosting a weekly television programme. But as soon as he learned I'd been to the cricket World Cup a few months earlier, he ignored his interrogator, and we sat huddled over more Zywiec lagers debating the merits of Carl Hooper cover drives and Allan Donald outswingers until a hefty, tattooed bouncer made it plain we should move on. The TV exec? He couldn't speak English, so just sat nodding vacantly at us for four hours.

This cricketing conversation in Poland, of all places, got me thinking about the universality of sport. How sport can be a passport to the planet for a lucky few – the handful of players good enough to make it and those of us less talented individuals who earn a living by hanging on an athlete's every exclamation.

As editor of a sports magazine, and later in a freelance role, I was finding myself in an increasing number of exotic locations, metaphorically clinging on to the shirt tails of South African and other international sports teams as they disappeared through airport departure gates, across hotel lobbies and beyond nightclub doors.

One minute I'd be trawling through what was left of my brain for a slurred explanation of the rudiments of rugby to a weaving Pittsburgh Steelers fan the night before Super Bowl. The next I'd be bawling 'LADU-U-UMA' at the top of my lungs in a Marrakesh hotel bar, as Shoes Moshoeu riveted home that game-settling goal in the African Cup of Nations semifinal against Ghana. It was all new and exciting for us wide-eyed South African journalists as the planet unfolded gloriously in the post-apartheid era.

But I didn't want to write a book solely about sport, a grave, statistics-driven, how-I-felt-when-I-scored-my-first-century tome to be lapped up only by the anorak sector of the sports community. What you're about to read is essentially a cocktail comprising one tot sport and one tot travel diary, mixed with many parts subjective musing. You won't get a definitive Berlitz-style travel guide, though I do believe being a sports journalist gives one an in-built edge in sniffing out some of the better places on earth to swig beer. (Hint: give Paris a wide berth, unless you're happy parting with R50 for a glass of lukewarm lager.) Neither am I here to earnestly reveal the exclusive scoop behind the truth masking the real reason why Francois Pienaar was dumped, nor the pre-game dietary habits of Joost van der Westhuizen.

As I discovered on my voyages, there's a pretty massively huge, great big colossal world out there beyond the Limpopo, and it doesn't all revolve around the latest Currie Cup try-scoring stats. I wanted to attempt to get this across. Paul Simon once sang of the 'Boy in the Bubble', a child whose damaged immune system meant he had to exist inside a sterile plastic igloo. During the dim days of apartheid, we South Africans were similarly isolated from the real world.

In the same way, sport, for some, has become a safe little virtual-world where regular life is merely the time ticked off between one Saturday afternoon and the next. Little else matters.

This is reflected in much of the contemporary sporting lexicon. Writers constantly allude to apparent life-threatening events. 'Hansie tragically run out.' 'Own-goal disaster for Fish.' 'Calamity as Joubert pulls hamstring.'

Tragedy is when a box-car full of miners gets concertinaed in a 300-metre free fall at Western Deep gold mine, not when James Small fumbles with the tryline gaping. Disaster is when a batch of Alexandra shacks slides into the Jukskei River after a Gauteng cloudburst. Not when Jonty Rhodes is left out of the Test side. For my money, words like disaster and tragedy should never enter into sport.

Unless, of course, you're discussing England's cricket team.

But sport can be a serious business that goes beyond the mere chalk lines of a pitch. If you don't believe this, try jesting with a Springbok rugby fan after his side has just lost. Only don't send me the hospital bills.

Sport invades some lives completely and can turn the most cogent of minds to slush. Remember those Tupac Amaru rebels who held Japanese Embassy guests hostage in Peru for four months? The siege ended late one afternoon when the rebels were surprised by the Peruvian army. These 'freedom fighters' intended to form the next Peruvian government, yet what were they doing when they were attacked? Playing soccer in the ballroom.

Sport can drive nations to war. El Salvador and Honduras once took up arms after a disputed goal in a World Cup tie. In recent times, members of the West Indies and Australian cricket sides appear hell-bent on wrapping stumps round each other's necks. And everyone knows the tweezer-lipped relationship between the All Black and Springbok rugby teams, peri-peri prawns notwithstanding.

Yet sport also seems to be a powerful tool for bringing together divergent peoples. Witness our rugby World Cup win and the African Cup of Nations triumph. Both Band-Aids over scratched-raw wounds of real-life South Africa. In sport, language and culture pose no barriers. I remember once spending 20 minutes discussing Russian football with a Soviet seaman at leisure in the bars of Maputo. Neither of us could speak the other's language. Yet through mimes and gestures we concluded that Dynamo Tbilisi were not the side they once were, that South Africa should surely rule the football world in the twenty-first century, and that Lev Yashin was the greatest goalkeeper of all time. When we parted, I promised to visit him in his one-bedroomed government apartment if I were ever in Georgia. And I think he even offered me his daughter's hand in marriage.

My attitude to writing about sport is not to take things too solemnly; to entertain as well as inform. To poke a little fun, and to root out, like a pig with a nose for truffles, the oddball aspect of life on sport's interstates, ringroads and dirt tracks. Might as well have some enjoyment while toiling away over a hot laptop. After all, much as we scribes might want to think of ourselves as Yoda-like founts of wisdom, every fan in the country is a closet sports reporter. Their views are just as valid as those of us out there pretending to be working for a living. Ultimately, sport boils down to opinion. If you live in Cape Town, Francois Pienaar is an over-rated, flash money-grabber who got what he deserved. But if you live in Gauteng, he's a martyr on a scale not known since Chris Hani. No amount of mushy back-page dissertations from 'Our Rugby Correspondent' will change those views.

At parties and other functions, you tend to get one of two reactions when you reveal that you earn your living chasing the game. Type A is a fellow sports nut who expects you to be able to recite each FA Cup Final goalscorer since World War II, then to list, alphabetically, all those Grey College old boys who have played rugby for the Springboks. If you fail to match the fluency of Dustin Hoffman's idiot savant character in *Rainman*, this type will look upon you as a fraud.

Type B is generally a smug individual who smiles patronisingly and may even go so far as to enquire what you're going to do with your life when you finally grow up. At this point it's nice to showboat a little. I thus reveal that I too know what the capital of Finland is, and that I'm as concerned as the next man what will happen to this country when Nelson Mandela ambles off into the sunset. I'm then regarded as if I'm one of those dowdy-looking birds that inhabit Papua New Guinea and with one flourish of their tail-feathers reveal themselves to be rainbow-hued birds of paradise.

The travel writing component of my life came as a natural extension of the job I was doing as a professional follower of ball games. At times, when in exotic destinations, the update on the star flyhalf's knee niggle is the highlight of your day. And that's when the vast world beyond the hotel lobby becomes so irresistible that even the free pizza delivery service and the in-house satellite system lose their gloss.

So I began wandering beyond the practice fields toward elegant temples, down cute winding boulevards and into dishevelled bars in search of pithy truths regarding the heart and soul of nations. Not to mention cheap beer and a good prawn curry.

I ended up writing travel pieces for newspapers and magazines. Things mushroomed. Travel agents called offering trips to places like Morocco. For merely jotting thousand-word articles.

Now here's where some craggy newspaper editors may complain that ethics are in jeopardy. That the scrupulous objectivity we journalists aspire to might conceivably become tainted. That the lure of free travel might seduce us into omitting from our articles quite how bad Casablancan plumbing really is, just so that we can score another trip.

But newspaper editors can rest assured that we impressionable ambassadors will not tarnish their publications with our tame holiday musings. Press travel junkets are designed so that even dim-bulb writers with inch-thick axle grease on their world-view antennae can do minimal damage. We're led off single file to only the most photogenic, sanitised parts of nations. Places where indigenous dancers gyrate for our pleasure, where hotel staff smile at us 24 hours a day and where in-house craftsmen press little wooden trinkets in our palms for souvenirs. The real world is kept at arm's length. If the United States Tourist Board was organising a journalists' recce to New York's Port Authority bus station, they'd find a way of passing off the bag ladies as night-shift cleaners at tea, and the purple-nosed drunks as participants in a cross-cultural wine-tasting tournament.

That's not to say that in travel writing scrupulous honesty doesn't always win the day. If the hotel is billed as a twinkling five-star sanctuary but more closely resembles a street corner shebeen at midnight, then you are obliged to say so. If the catering induces vomiting, spare no savaging adjective. Should iguanas frolic in the jacuzzi, chide mercilessly. After all, we travel writers have a duty to uphold the stainless traditions of our art. Unless, of course, we can persuade the management to write off the minibar bill and give us another free go at para-sailing.

The best thing about travel writing, naturally, is that you get to scribble what you like, get paid for doing so, and everything's for free. Intuitive readers will detect a similarity with sports writing, and I'm not here to pour scorn on that observation.

Also, travel people have this great way of asking you to join them on a planetary romp. They'll phone up and say, 'Would you be at all interested in coming along next week to Cancun, Mexico? I know it's short notice and that you're extremely busy. Unfortunately first class is full, so we'll only be flying business. And the deluxe hotel is quite a distance from the beach – at least a 30-second walk. But we've got front row tickets to Pavarotti's concert at Chichen Itza and the watersports are on the house. If you're not doing anything, please let us know.'

It's as if Uma Thurman has shed her silk bathrobe, foamed up the hot-tub, poured chilled Veuve Clicquot into crystal flutes, then pleaded in tones to melt gold, 'If you're not doing anything really pressing in the next hour, might you see your way clear to joining me in here?'

So what have I learnt in three years of earth roaming in pursuit of sport? What bonds of culture-fair bonhomie have I forged in the global village? Which heart-gladdening notions confirming man's inherent goodness have I absorbed?

Here's my list:

Never touch the hotel minibar.
Always settle the price before getting into the cab.
And if you're in India, take the tuk-tuk instead.
Leave be the Mekong whisky in Bangkok.
And the Black Death vodka in Poland.
Not to mention most of Kingston, Jamaica after dark.
There are more gorgeous blonde señoritas in Buenos Aires than in Sweden and Camps Bay combined.
That Bangkok go-go dancer wants more than a Singha beer when she comes preening beside you. Whoops, where'd my money-belt go?
No matter how vital the match, there are always spare tickets to be found.
Should you drink your beer outside a Parisian pub, it will cost you more than if you sit indoors.
Americans are the friendliest, fattest, most naive people on the planet.
The spectacular Lake Malawi sunsets defy description.
As does Malawian public transport.
An accent and a business card are sure-fire tickets to impressing impressionable girls from California to Cracow. Especially in America: 'Hey, that sure was neat. Say that again, will ya? You're from South Africa, huh. Ain't that near Australia?'

Peter Davies
Chembe Lodge
Cape Maclear
Malawi

AFRICA
CÔTE d' IVOIRE
GHANA
Accra
TOGO
BENIN
Lomé
NIGERIA
Atlantic Ocean

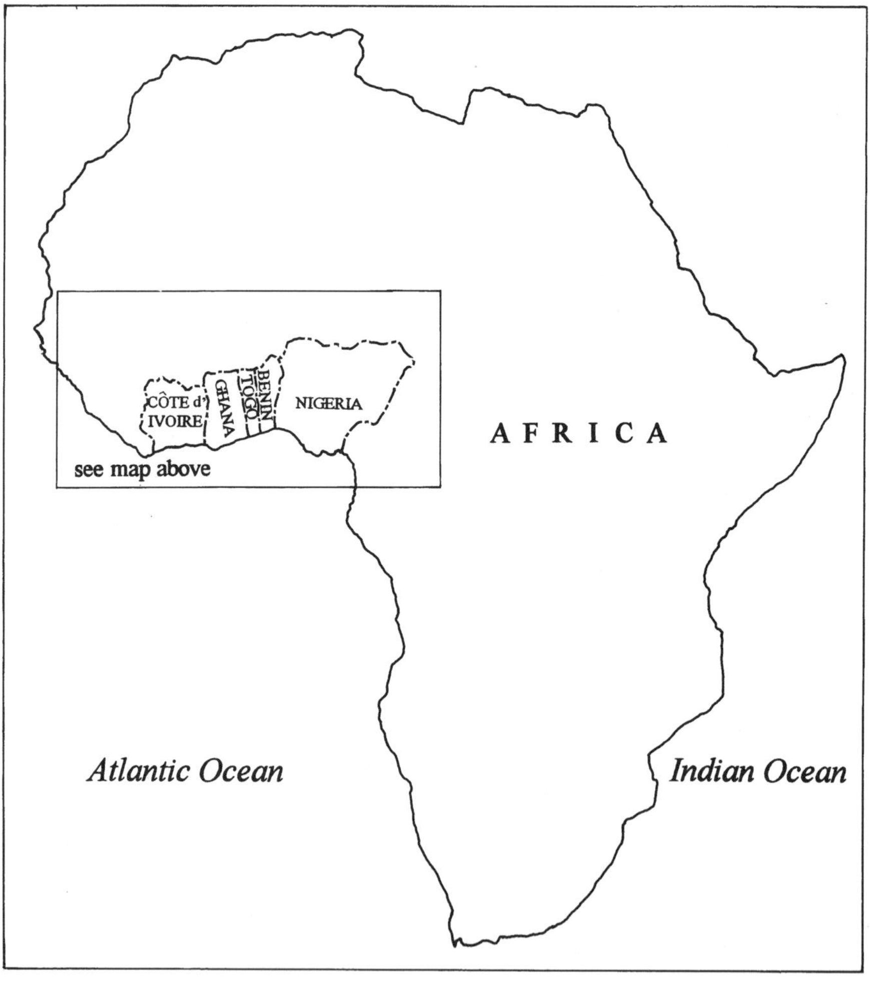
CÔTE d' IVOIRE
GHANA
TOGO
BENIN
NIGERIA
see map above
AFRICA
Atlantic Ocean
Indian Ocean

CHAPTER ONE

Togo and Talismans

I DON'T KNOW whether Togo possesses a Society for the Prevention of Cruelty to Animals, or whatever the French equivalent of that noble institution is. If it does, it's not doing its job properly. If it doesn't, might I suggest it stays that way, lest some sensitively disposed, newly qualified animal lover be traumatised for life?

Togo and neighbouring Benin are known as the fetish and voodoo capitals of the world, and this ancient animist practice requires skeletons and corpses, skulls and cadavers. Mounds of them. Generations of Togolese jungle creatures lose their lives to provide powerful medicines and potent protective charms.

The fetish and voodoo market of Akodessewa lies just outside the Togolese capital of Lomé, and the first thing that assails you there is a ripe stench lingering in the heat. The source of this reek is a vivid array of tables stretching out under the sun. It could be a scene from any Sunday morning fleamarket anywhere in the world, but instead of wood carvings, candles and assorted goods, the market at Akodessewa offers up the heads of animals for sale. Row upon row of rotting skulls ferment in the humid tropical air, the skin shrunk tight and clinging leather-like to the bones. Flies flourish among the grinning jaws and facial cavities of crocodile, warthog, antelope, hyena, viper, shark, frog. Also for sale are withered monkey hands, whole carcasses of chameleons, ducks and owls. All are displayed in a manner enticing to fetish browsers. A visit to Akodessewa voodoo market is like invading an anti-vivisectionist's most pulse-quickening nightmare.

There are also heads of furry animals on display, mouths agape, eternally snarling. These beasts are smaller than a jungle predator and possess matted black and golden fur.

'What are these?' I asked the youthful proprietor of the stall.
'C'est un chien,' he replied.
Next time you take a dish of meat chunks out to Rover or Rex, offer up a silent prayer for his pals in West Africa.

When I said I was off to Togo one fine autumn morning, I was met with a volley of questions, the most common of which was 'Say where?'

Some thought of Tonga in the South Pacific and asked me to pass on regards to the monarch of those islands, who has had the distinction of being the fattest ruler in the world (he's now on a well-publicised diet). Others were sure that I was heading for Otago in New Zealand's South Island. The particularly witless believed that the Japanese capital was my next port of call.

For the record, Togo is a snippet of moist, green and humid land on the West African coast. It invades the continent like an ingrowing finger, and lies wedged between Ghana and Benin. The South African soccer team had been sent to this former French colony to play a crucial World Cup soccer qualifier against Zaïre. The game was supposed to have been played in Kinshasa, but the civil war that was looming in that vast, stricken land meant that the tie had to be conducted at a neutral venue. When FIFA decided upon Togo as the location, it sent football officials scurrying for their atlases.

With hindsight, should South Africa ever again have to play at a neutral venue in Africa, those officials will surely be pleading to return to this small, engaging nation.

Lomé is a neat city by African standards. A pleasant-looking lagoon bisects it, the pavements are fastidiously swept each morning, a sense of orderliness prevails and gardens are kempt and flourishing. The traffic lights also feature an innovation that the Togolese might wish to patent. Supplementing the main robot is a miniature set of red, orange and green lights at pedestrian eye-level, which seems a fine and logical idea for a nation where those on foot far outnumber those in vehicles. Humidity is high in Lomé, but a cool ocean breeze stirs around noon and usually tugs at the palm trees until four in the afternoon, making the stifling conditions more manageable. The stretch of beach that forms Togo's coastline is only 56 kilometres long but features eye-catching golden-brown sands and a sea with a vicious undertow. No one swims off the coast because, if they did, chances are the currents would ensure their next stop would be Recife, Brazil.

The South African soccer side's previous experience of life in a former French colony had been in Congo three weeks earlier. They had not experienced hospitality. Their original Pointe-Noire hotel quarters had been so unappealing they had moved out speedily. The team's training ground had been an uneven sandpit, and when the side had tried to move their practice to the stadium, Congolese soldiers had jammed AK-47 barrels under South African nostrils. Journalists, who as we know occupy the lowest rung of the sporting ladder, had been forced to sleep in the lobby of the hotel for the weekend.

It was thus understandable that it was a somewhat apprehensive Bafana Bafana squad and attendant coterie of reporters, officials, trainers, gurus and marketing suits that disembarked from the charter plane at the trim Lomé airport. The team's arrival meant that the customs officials were too occupied with shaking the hands of anyone believed to be connected with Bafana Bafana to scrutinise travel documents thoroughly. Mark Fish was the man they wanted. 'Hey, Poisson, ça va?' they shouted when they recognised the Italian-based defender. Doctor Khumalo, who had been left out of the national side for the last few games, was also in demand. As was Phil Masinga, back from self-imposed exile. So personally had the lanky striker taken the barbs of criticism from the boo-boys back home that he'd vowed never to play for his country again. It took that one awful performance in Congo for coach Clive Barker to ask Masinga to reconsider. The former Leeds striker didn't let his confident coach down.

The South Africans soon banished all concerns about their Togo base. An air-conditioned bus had been laid on to transport the players 9 kilometres to their hotel. In Congo, an air-conditioned vehicle would have been a bus with the windshield missing. Two other minibuses had been obtained for the rest of the group, and the entire roster of Bafanas were soon snugly lodged at the 35-storey-high Sofitel Deuxième Février hotel. This building dominates the Lomé skyline like the Eiffel Tower broods over Paris, and was to prove as agreeable as most four-star hotels in South Africa. The rooms offered a superb bird's-eye view of the Municipal Stadium at which the match was to be played. If Clive Barker had wanted to spy on the Zaïreans at training, all he had to do was order a BB lager from room service, put his feet up on the balcony and catch the action from his superb sixteenth-floor vantage point of the compact ground. This technique was put to use on the day of the big game, with the hotel coming to a standstill as maids, waiters, scullery workers and receptionists all crammed into the rooms overlooking the stadium.

The Hôtel Deuxième Février also featured an unexpected touch of familiarity for South African sports lovers. Flick on the TV, and who would materialise into focus but Darren Scott and Naas Botha discussing the upcoming Super 12 games on M-Net's Supersport. It was weird to step outside your hotel in the middle of Togo, blither your way in bad French to try to extract a decent restaurant recommendation from a taxi driver, then disappear back to your room to catch a few overs of the Standard Bank Cricket Cup Final as you dressed. I once asked the chambermaid if she knew what this peculiar game was as I sprawled on the bed watching Pat Symcox bowling to Herschelle Gibbs. She stared at the screen for a few seconds before venturing, 'Tennis?'

M-Net has made huge inroads into Africa. Almost 30 countries north of the Limpopo River have access to the pay channel. It's clear, however, that M-Net has little patience with those customers beyond South African borders who forget to pay their monthly fees. A large advert in one of Ghana's newspapers reminded customers that if they didn't pay their subscription dues by the twenty-sixth of each month, their signal would be cut.

I had driven to Togo from neighbouring Ghana and arrived a day or two ahead of the South African team's charter plane. There's a direct connection between Johannesburg and Accra, and I was in for a surprise after stepping from the excellent Ghana Airways flight. At customs, a uniformed official shot a derisive glance at my visa-smeared, stamp-riddled passport and announced I couldn't enter his country.

'We have a big stamp here in Ghana,' he reasoned. 'There is no space for us to put it.'

Various experiences in Africa have taught me not to argue in such a situation, no matter how vividly the red rag dances before my eyes. I apologised for this situation, which I agreed was indeed catastrophic and, in fact, almost beyond belief. I then asked through clenched teeth if he could not perhaps squeeze the stamp over a previous, outdated visa. What about that silly United States smudge over there?

Not possible. The Ghanaian entry stamp evidently needs to stand proud and solitary on a virginal page. The matter was finally resolved in the time-honoured fashion of African travel: $10 changed hands.

A hired vehicle was secured to whisk us the 200 or so kilometres between Accra and Lomé. The beach highway started out promisingly. An efficiently manned tollbooth suggested excellent roads ahead, and this proved true for about a quarter of the journey. At the turnpike, hawkers fought fiercely to capture their bit of the market, thrusting dog leads, biscuits, batteries, sweets and fruit at the car windows. We bought a packet of apples, which, on closer inspection, bore that little Cape sticker identifying it as some of Elgin's finest produce. The South African invasion of the continent is under way in earnest.

Wildly coloured minibuses and bush taxis with customised logos barrelled past us as the road degenerated into a series of ruts and potholes. The West African coastal road between Lagos in Nigeria and Abidjan in Côte d'Ivoire is one of the most heavily used in Africa, and these bush taxis ferry people along its length with their bright slogans like 'God Knows We Worry', 'Bright Heaven Hallelujah', and, given the speed of some of these vehicles, the potentially prophetic 'Six Feet Under'. Our journey to Lomé was most memorable, though, for the musical accompaniment. Before we started out, our driver had stopped at a roadside kiosk in Accra to buy a selection of Ghanaian cassettes. His stereo system, however, was one of those hi-tech items that requires a security code to disarm the loud bleep that otherwise sounds out at short intervals. The driver, unhappily, didn't know the security code, so we were forced to drive for three and a half hours to the accompaniment of full-blast Ghanaian folk songs punctuated by a jarring ping every three seconds. By the time we reached the Togolese border, I was ready to take an axe to the speakers.

I was hanging around in Togo with Sue Destombes, of the sports marketing company that handles all the arrangements for Bafana Bafana. Sue is usually sent headlong into Africa two or three days ahead of the squad's arrival to ensure that all arrangements are in place. Detail is the key word. Every obstacle must be anticipated and smoothed. The players' dietary requirements were in hand, as Sue was flying in their own Southern Sun cook – the amiable Jeff the Chef – with his hundreds of pre-cooked, shrink-wrapped pastas, spaghetti bolognaise and other dishes to minimise the chance of food poisoning. Vast amounts of water and Powerade would also be brought in on the team plane.

In addition, Sue had to hire three buses from the Togolese, a five-ton truck to haul the television equipment and enough local muscle to load and off-load this considerable baggage. She also had to keep track of the exchange rate while negotiating a price for these vehicles, as there was no shortage of fly-by-nighters eager to cash in on the Bafana Bafana visit. One guy purporting to be head programmer of Togo Radio offered a bus for hire at the cost of $4 000 a day.

Accommodation was the most vital link in the land arrangements chain. The choice of hotel rooms in which the team were to stay had been precisely communicated, but on arrival in Lomé it was found that the players had been allocated lodgings on higher floors than requested. The renovations under way at the top of the hotel would have disturbed them. Sue insisted this must change. It did.

Diplomacy and protocol also had to be heeded. There were rumours that the Togolese president wanted to meet the South Africans. The president of Togo's son is known in that country as a huge Bafana Bafana supporter. He has all the South African kit and has even named his son Bafana. Time had been set aside for Saturday afternoon, the day before the game. It later became apparent that the president wanted the team to journey to his remote village. He didn't venture to Lomé that often. This would mean a flight to the interior, and hasty amendments to schedules were made. As it turned out, the visit never went ahead.

Television rights was another point that threatened to become an issue. The SABC, which was broadcasting the game, had already paid Zaïre for the coverage rights, as the Zaïreans were the original home team. Now, a third country was involved, and Togo officials were requiring documentary proof of the SA–Zaïre agreement, otherwise they wouldn't permit the game to be televised.

I tagged along to this TV meeting at the home of the Togo Football Federation president, General Seyi Memene. General Memene is also the minister of the interior and overall second in command of the country. With a Togolese journalist who had been hired as interpreter and general smoother-of-paths, Sue and I arrived at the minister's substantial city compound and were vetted by three separate sets of bodyguards before being ushered in to sit at an outdoor lapa-like meeting place. At last the general emerged with a bevy of advisers. Although he would appear to wear a number of hats in Togo, the general is not too keen on shoes. He shed these at his earliest convenience. While his minions dashed around fetching bottles of French champagne for us to quaff, he scratched contemplatively at the corns on his feet. The coverage problems were swiftly resolved amid hearty doses of the pink stuff. The amiable manner of this meeting set the tone for the rest of the South Africans' stay in Togo.

Later that evening, photographer Duif du Toit, soccer writer Gavin Barker and I put faith in my tenuous command of the French language and set forth in search of a typical Togolese night out. We were dropped among the teeming hawker stalls near the beachfront. The moon was absent from a black night sky, and the only light in the dusty collection of streets came from candles brightening the vendors' scant wares. We stopped for a drink at a tiny backstreet shebeen called Dolau's Restaurant. Rickety tables and chairs were hurriedly brought for us to sit out in the street. Around us, workers were refuelling after a day of toil. *Fufu*, a type of pap, only softer, was the food of choice and vast 650-mililitre bottles of Eku beer were being drunk. Palm wine was also available. This delicacy is made by tapping the higher reaches of the tree, then leaving the liquid to ferment in a calabash. In the early stages, the liquid is transparent and sweet and is called female wine. Later it becomes browner and more fermented – male palm wine.

Throngs of prostitutes were available too. Young women with alcohol-breath and vacant eyes would bump against us and try to drape themselves around us as we ventured down the streets. Some had toddlers slung on their hips. These ladies were chased away by store owners but the more persistent hung around our table while we drank. This finally prompted a loud, violent quarrel between a local who had decided to become our guide and protector, and ended with the women slinking off muttering into the shadows.

Our white skins had swiftly identified us as part of the Bafana Bafana entourage. We were greeted as brothers and with the now familiar questions 'Ou est Doctor Khumalo? Ou est Mark Fish?' The knowledge and affection that most Togolese possessed for the South African football team was astonishing. The patrons at Dolau's came up, shook our hands and faithfully pledged allegiance to the South African cause that Sunday. One stout old mama, who introduced herself as the president of the Togo Football Supporters' Club, told us she was bringing a party of 40 women to the big game to bellow for the Bafana. 'One woman equals a thousand supporters,' she explained.

Another Bafana lover sat down with us and identified himself as Jean Akpo Kofu. Like David Copperfield producing a rabbit from a hat, he suddenly whipped out a large South African flag from under his shirt and pronounced himself jack, queen and king of all Bafana Bafana fans. To prove this, he recited the entire South African Cup of Nations winning side in 20 seconds flat.

While we knocked back Ekus, another prostitute materialised and loitered. When she was told to leave by our protectors, she began braiding Duif's hair. In two minutes his shaggy mane had been transformed into a neat plait. We drained another beer and were then escorted by a growing band of personal guides, guardians and advisers to a seafood restaurant on the beachfront – Auberge Provençale – run by an elderly French expatriate with a resigned, wrinkled face and a long white ponytail. The restaurant wouldn't have been out of place in the *arrondissements* of Paris. It offered succulent prawns and a great steak Béarnaise. At the gates of this smart establishment, our new-found mates from the streets were quickly hounded away. Segregation in Africa is still very much alive. We ate and drank in a degree of luxury for two hours then left the restaurant. Still waiting patiently outside were our drinking pals from Dolau's, now eager to show us the best disco in Lomé – the Privilège Fine Disco at the Palm Beach Hotel. It was 1.30 in the morning, but we were on a roll.

The Privilège was glitzy and hi-tech. Beers were $4 a bottle. We got talking to a group of Dutch travellers who turned out to be police officers. Their assignment had been to escort Togolese illegal immigrants from Holland back to their country of origin. The Privelège was also home to another multitude of Bafana admirers and a teeming array of hookers. We managed to side-step the insistent advances of the sex sellers long enough to achieve intimacy instead with more Togolese beer, and we eventually staggered outside at around 5 am. The taxi driver who'd dropped us among the street hawkers ten hours earlier was waiting calmly in the car park. We were back at the hotel in time to catch the last few minutes of the early-morning Super 12 encounter on Supersport.

To get to the Akodessewa voodoo market you drive along the well-surfaced Boulevard de la République beach road in the direction of Benin, past the palm trees and sand stretching out to the ocean. Then continue past the Hôtels de la Paix and Sarakawa and turn left a couple of streets further down, heading inland for a kilometre and a half along a sand road. Beyond is a tavern on the right-hand side that is named the Bafana Bar, South African connection intended, and advertises Guinness stout. A sharp right turn later, and there you are, smack in the middle of animal heads, fly-encrusted pelts and writhing boa constrictors.

While this part of West Africa is said to be the voodoo HQ of the planet, Haiti is the accepted Hollywood home of such phenomena. But the Haitians, of course, are descendants of West African slaves, who were transported across the Atlantic centuries ago and ended up in various parts of the Caribbean. Also popular with movie bosses is the notion that voodoo is entirely concerned with chicken slaughtering, unexplained blood dripping from ceilings and wide-eyed dolls with pins stuck in them. The voodoo market in Togo, I'm happy to report, has more to do with natural healing and spiritual guardianship than with marketing revenge dolls so that spurned Hollywood starlets can stick pins in pudgy effigies of studio execs who have overlooked them for the next season of *Beverley Hills 90210*.

I do have to say, however, that there is an element of commercialism about Akodessewa. For one thing the *guérisseur*, or fetish headman, Guedenon Benoit, gave me his business card.

It also appears you can negotiate the magnitude of your good fortune. Let me explain.

I was invited into a low, darkened hut festooned with carvings, feathers, horns and skins and ordered to sit on a little bench where mosquitoes whined around my ears. As soon as I entered, I was told to give the *guérisseur* my name so that he could bless me and call on the ancestors to bestow luck and health. This he did by clattering an iron bar against a sculpted mound of earth that my flash camera later revealed as a humanesque hump rather in the shape of R2D2, the *Star Wars* android.

The headman then declared, through the market's translator, that he had six essential powers to offer me that day. The first charm was a wooden item shaped like a tiny caveman's club. This was for happy and trouble-free travelling. Around the wood was entwined a smaller, sharpened stake that fitted into the main club like a cork in a bottle. Before a lengthy journey, uncork this small stake, tell the charm where you are headed, and ask it for protection. Then re-cork the charm, stow it in your pocket and sally forth, whistling confidently.

The next talisman was a shiny, brown ebony seed, essential for good memory. Before retiring at night, put this seed in your left hand, splash it with three drops of fresh water and stow it under your pillow. It's also a great cure for headaches, so should its existence become well known, this talisman will surely have the world's hangover cure market in a flurry.

The principle was similar for the third icon, which was a pair of sticks wrapped tight by a small piece of grass and sealed with a darkened resin. When you wish to attract undying devotion from a girl, put this trinket in your left hand and scatter three drops of perfume on it. From that day onward, the girl will agree with everything you say. This was probably the most fanciful fetish of them all.

A small clay figure that looked a little like a Gummi Bear with a Mohican haircut was next paraded before me. This figure is known in the local language as 'Ledda', and his job is to protect dwellings. For his powers to be unleashed, it is vital to give Ledda a cigarette once a year. The hole that forms his mouth is the perfect size for just such an offering. The *guérisseur* confirmed that, if your house was a smoke-free zone, Ledda's capabilities would be just as potent if you fed him a single tot of alcohol per annum.

The last amulet, the *guérisseur* assured me, was to ensure that men could enjoy sport ten times a night. At first I lost this explanation a little in the translation and thought the fix was for particularly active ten-pin bowlers or action cricketers. Later I deduced that the voodoo chief was talking sex. He was telling me that the piece of bark I held in my hand gave me the power to 'make sport' all night.

'You cut a small, small piece, clean it very good and put it in water for two hours,' he explained. 'Then you take a small drink from the cup. You leave it for half an hour, then go and see your wife. Your power will come – quick quick.'

I could choose from these five trinkets plus a good luck charm necklace. I selected the two wooden charms, the house protector and the ebony seed. I then had to put the charms in a tortoise shell bowl, shout my name out three times and give the shell to the *guérisseur*. He blessed the chosen items three times, returned them to me, and I then had to push the shell against my stomach three more times before the powers could begin exerting their influence.

The crucial moment had arrived. We had to ask the spirits what would be a fair price to pay for the formidable arsenal of luck-spawning gewgaws I had acquired. The *guérisseur* threw some cowry shells into the tortoise bowl and finally divined a price of $30. I was about to pay up quite happily when the translator, sensing hesitation, whispered that the fetish expert would be prepared to accept $20.

Not wanting the spirits to think I was a cheapskate, I handed over the original price, and the *guérisseur* guaranteed that the good luck I'd experience over the next few days would now be doubly powerful. He added that I needn't worry about the next day's game – South Africa would score two goals.

Blinking back into the sunshine, I stumbled straight into a throng of teenagers who had heard that there were white faces worth toying with at the market. Three of the kids wore lengthy, live pythons as necklaces. The python is a holy creature in many West African countries. Killing it is taboo. It is also a symbol of fidelity in marriage. According to one local, if someone secretly kills a python and his wife gives birth after this murder, the child will not be able to walk or talk.

One teenager had three chameleons crawling on his chin. Another had a grey rat the size of a dassie shinning up and down his arms and an anxious monkey darting between his shoulders. The kids homed in on me. I took a backward step. Their faces split with white, toothy grins. 'Petit cadeau, petit cadeau,' they chimed. I willingly handed over a few dollar bills. A small present is a pittance to pay for the comfort of not having chameleons, rats and boas thrust in your face. That jungle animal display is as convincing an argument for extracting money from tourists as a hijacker with an AK-47 is for handing over the keys to your car.

While in Togo, I shared a room with the South African team translator, Isaac Pognon, who holds a master's degree in English from Benin University. He was busy finishing an advanced course of translation and interpreting at Wits. Isaac spoke English, Spanish, French and had a basic knowledge of Portuguese to add to his multitude of African tongues. One night I asked how he, as a sophisticated, modern African, viewed the role fetishism and voodoo played in today's society. For instance, what would villagers want with crocodile jaws or viper heads?

'Crocodiles symbolise power,' he said. 'Somebody from the village will buy those dead crocodile heads and use the lips and mouth to make a very powerful *bo*.' *Bo* is the Beninese word that can be equated to South African muti or Nigerian juju.

'If you want protection from your enemies you use a viper's head mixed with other ingredients to make *bo* for the protection of your family and your house. If you bury the viper's head at the entrance of your home, then anyone entering with bad intentions towards you or your family will be bitten by a live snake. This is not a myth, this happens. Those monkey hands you saw today. Those are used when you leave your country to look for a job. If you are involved in any enterprise or project, you won't come unstuck in the same way a monkey never misses a branch when it jumps from tree to tree.'

To influence rainfall, said Isaac, you would buy the head of a tortoise. If the mouth is pointing at the sky, it will rain pretty soon. Turn the head face down, and the rain will cease.

'I have seen it many times in my life. I was taught Christian ideologies, but little by little I have noticed how powerful this *bo* can be. My father once took me to a village in Benin to bury one of his best friends. It started raining. In our culture, if your father is being buried and it rains, this means you are not a decent family. So the elders took this powder made from the tortoise and sprinkled it on the boundaries around the mourners. It then rained everywhere except in this circle. I couldn't believe it, but I witnessed it.'

This was getting interesting. Was there any *bo* with which I could anoint my car to ward off Gauteng criminals?

'There is a *bo* we make with a certain animal's head that, if you have it with you, there is no way a bullet can penetrate you. Again I have witnessed this. But I can't reveal the secret. It is handed down and if I was to tell anyone, I would be betraying my ancestors.'

The vital World Cup game was played on Sunday, April 27, 1997 – South Africa's Freedom Day as well as Togo's Independence Day. It was a good day for a double celebration. I walked the 300 metres from the hotel to the stadium with plenty of time to spare. No press passes were needed. A white skin and a camera were all the identification required to distinguish me as a journalist. I had my money-belt with my newly-acquired fetishes safely nestled against my T-shirt.

Songs like 'Give My Love to Africa' blared over the public address system at the ground. Further evidence of South African penetration into the rest of Africa came in the form of SAA dishing out little South African flags to the locals, and the kids selling drinks in the stadium all wearing Castle Lager caps and T-shirts.

Despite the public outpouring of affection for South Africa, the crowd was not large, 6 000 at most. The tickets on sale were between $15 and $30 and thus beyond the means of most people.

There was a hint of drama as the pre-match band marched past the dignitaries box, which had been freshly painted for the occasion. The drum-major executed a snappy eyes right to receive the minister's salute and unfortunately tripped over the television cable.

The South African side knew that victory was the only result worth contemplating in Togo. Defeat would render qualification for the 1998 World Cup Finals remote. Clive Barker had dropped defensive stalwart Neil Tovey, to the surprise of many. He'd also recalled Phil Masinga and prodigal son Doctor Khumalo.

Bafana Bafana were on a mission and their early raids on the Zaïrean goal bristled with intent. They had the ball in the net after three minutes, only for it to be disallowed for offside. Looking around the main stand, I spotted the old 'one woman is a thousand supporters' lady nearby. True to her word, she was surrounded by friends and decked out in full Sunday finery. She sported two SAA South African flags in her hat band. The balconies of the nearby high-rises were chockful of spectators enjoying a perfect, free aerial view of the field.

There were plenty of Zaïrean supporters too, and many of my neighbours had radios glued to their ears, following the progress of Togo in their own World Cup match against Cameroon. By half-time the Togolese were 3–0 down, and the locals, admitting defeat, gave their full attention to roaring on the Bafana.

Doctor Khumalo repaid his coach's faith by opening the scoring in the twenty-third minute, but South Africa's defence, which had looked creaky from the outset, conceded a goal soon afterwards. At half-time it seemed the Zaïreans were the stronger side. As the second half wore on, the South African bench looked increasingly tense. Twice Neil Tovey stripped off his tracksuit and limbered up. Twice he sat down again. The two fullbacks were neglecting their defensive duties, and holes were opening up so large you could drive a bus through them. It was being left to new skipper Lucas Radebe to avert disaster.

Finally, with 18 minutes left, came one of those glorious moments that occasionally illuminate a sporting contest. Khumalo received the ball to the right of the Zaïrean penalty area. He teased the opposing fullback by dummying a cross three times, before curling over a ball that Masinga met with the full force of his head to bury the ball in the back of the net. The goal was made by Khumalo and finished by Masinga, the two players most roundly criticised by press and public alike. It was a sweet moment, and Clive Barker would have been fully justified in teaming up with Masinga, two-stepping up to the nearest TV camera and delivering one-fingered salutes to the watching masses. What he *did* do was race forward and plant a huge kiss on his redeemed striker's forehead.

Still the drama wasn't done. The South African defence almost threw it away in the last minute, when an innocuous shot found its way past André Arendse in goal and struck the upright before bobbling safely behind the goal-line. The final whistle blew moments later.

The pitch was invaded and Doctor Khumalo, who was mobbed by the locals, had to be escorted by truncheon-wielding soldiers back to the dressing room. The South Africans were ecstatic. Cans of Castle were popped and sprayed around the small room. Clive Barker was bellowing at the top of his lungs 'Are we too old? I said are we too old?' at anyone who cared to listen. Eric Tinkler and Mark Fish sank back in the corners with content, weary expressions. For Masinga it had been a fairytale comeback and he knew it.

'I think this has lifted up my self-esteem, because after what happened at home my self-belief was very, very low. I really wanted to play. Clive believes in me. He won't put me on the bench, he will play me. I knew if I came for the game, Clive would select me to play. I'm also glad for Doctor because he didn't go to Zambia, then he went to Congo and didn't play. I think he must be happy to come back like that.'

Barker's instincts are uncanny. He has more than a few critics when it comes to tactics, but he has fostered a powerful family spirit within the South African team. And if players are happy, results often take care of themselves. There was a similar atmosphere cultivated by Kitch Christie when the Springboks won rugby's World Cup. Like Christie, Barker is also prepared to back his beliefs. He had taken a massive risk by choosing Khumalo and Masinga. They had rewarded him with the goals. Like the fetish man said: South Africa will score twice. I reached into my money-belt and patted my new charms appreciatively.

The players had to run a gauntlet of cheering locals back to the team bus. Soldiers beat the over-enthusiastic fans away with sticks and carved a path for the squad. Walking back to the hotel in a buoyant mood, I came across two youngsters keeping the crowds entertained with pythons around heads, underneath jerseys and down trousers. There was a mini-riot near the entrance to the hotel as locals tried to touch the returning Bafana players. Two kids came up and congratulated me on the South African win. They asked if I spoke French. One then took me by the hand and led me onward to the hotel. At this point security guards decided to break up the multitudes and waded into the crowd, truncheons ablur. I was almost knocked off my feet before somehow being spat unscathed into the hotel lobby.

I flicked on Supersport back in my room and ordered a Castle lager from room service. Reaching into my money-belt to pay for the drink, I noticed the zip was open. Further inspection revealed that all my cash, around R1 500, had been removed with the precision of a surgeon's scalpel. My credit card remained and my good luck fetishes lay unmolested. I thought of the clamour outside the hotel but concluded that those sweet-faced kids had done the job. I hadn't felt a thing. Use the cash well, guys. Good luck charms – what happened?

An hour after the game, the South African players congregated at the pool – potential bait for the massive vulture-like fruit bats that swooped low over the water each dusk. Jeff the Chef tossed cans of Castle into the water from his formidable stock. The players formed a circle in the pool and chatted noisily about the game as the sun dipped. France '98 beckoned. Clive Barker led the festivities and basked contentedly under the spray when Eric Tinkler decided to run amuck with the garden hose.

Later that night, the team's chartered jet rocked and sang its way back to Johannesburg via Brazzaville. Gavin Lane and Mark Fish were in particularly good voice, and Jeff the Chef's beer supply was speedily exhausted. As the plane touched down at Johannesburg International early next morning, Eric Tinkler noticed the Air France jumbo on the tarmac.

'There's our plane, boys,' he said.

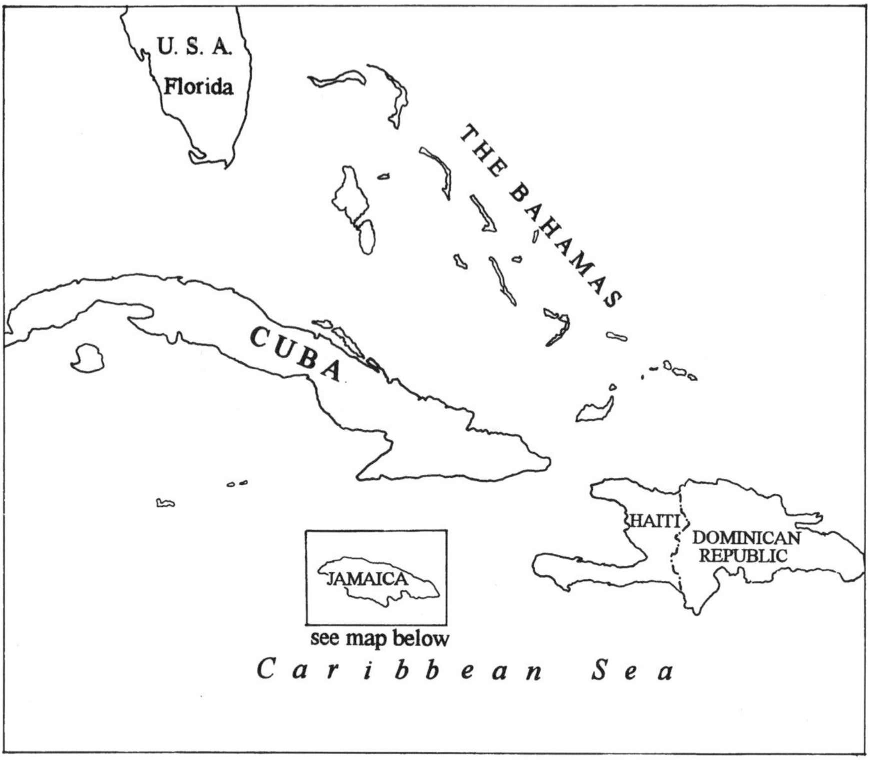
U. S. A.
Florida
THE BAHAMAS
CUBA
HAITI
DOMINICAN REPUBLIC
JAMAICA
see map below
Caribbean Sea

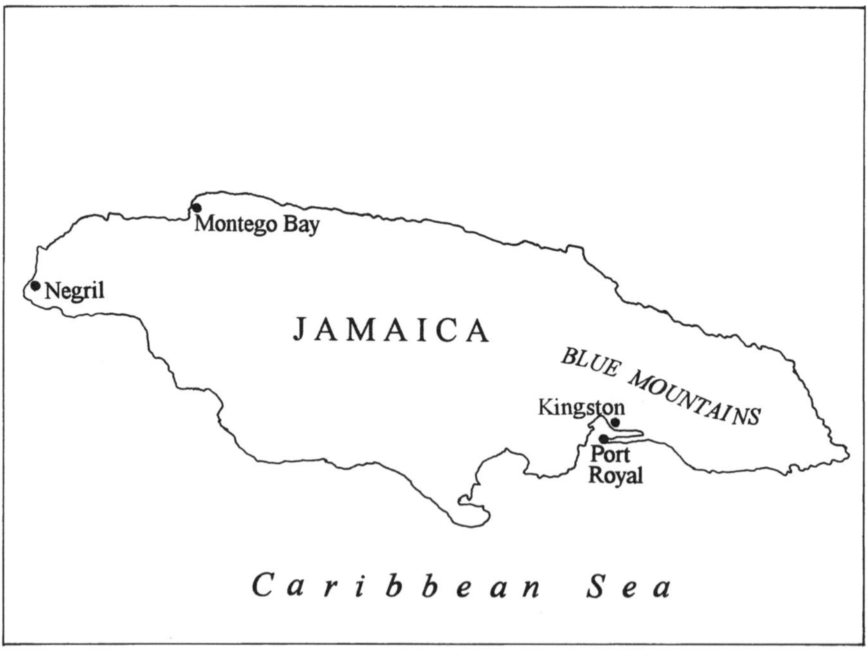
Montego Bay
Negril
JAMAICA
BLUE MOUNTAINS
Kingston
Port Royal
Caribbean Sea

CHAPTER TWO

Jamaica Me Crazy

JAMAICA IS A TINY ISLAND in the Caribbean, best known for its reggae, its rum, its Rastas and its ganja.

But there are a few other fields in which Jamaica regularly makes the headlines. One is crime. Heavy-duty, South African-style crime with hi-tech killings and violent maimings. Tourists are told to avoid the capital, Kingston, in the same way visitors to South Africa are advised to bypass Johannesburg.

The similarities between Jamaica and South Africa don't end there. Both are relatively small nations that have produced a rich crop of world-class sportsmen and women. For instance, the last three Olympic 100-metre champions have all been Jamaicans. Of sorts. Canada's Donovan Bailey, who sprinted to the world record in Atlanta in 1996, was born on the island, and, in fact, three of the four Canadians who won the 4 x 100-metre relay gold in Atlanta are originally from Jamaica. As is Britain's 1992 gold medallist Linford Christie. So too Ben Johnson, who was running in Canadian colours when he was disqualified for drug use after the 1988 final in Seoul. The Jamaicans aren't too quick to number Johnson as one of their own, but they'll swiftly tell you that, had Johnson been an American, there'd have been howls of protest from US officials and stringent efforts made to validate Johnson's gold. To back this up, they point to the example of Butch Reynolds, the American who won the 400-metre gold in Seoul. Soon afterwards Reynolds was exposed as being brimful of artificial stimulants and banned for three years – but not stripped of his gold medal.

Other Jamaican athletes who have made a huge impact on the world stage include Merlene Ottey, one of the most durable sprinters of all time, who's still going strong at the age of 37. Heavyweight boxer Trevor

Berbick, whose place in history is assured as the last man to have beaten the declining Muhammad Ali, is Jamaican. Then, of course, comes a lengthy list of cricketers. Fast bowler Michael 'Whispering Death' Holding, whose velvet tones embellish Channel Nine cricket commentaries, still owns a service station just outside Kingston, and Jimmy Adams, Courtney Walsh, Robert Samuels and Franklyn Rose are just some of the current stars who ply their trade at Sabina Park, the home of cricket in Jamaica.

Recently, another Jamaican sporting team has sprung to prominence, but its fame has been based largely on athletic ineptness, rather than aptitude. On the road to Negril, Jamaica's new hedonistic resort town, is the bar used in the film *Cool Runnings*. This movie detailed the tribulations of the Jamaican bobsleigh team at the 1988 Calgary Winter Olympics. With snow being a non-existent commodity in the Caribbean, the fact that the Jamaicans had bothered to enter a team for this event hinted at insanity. Nevertheless, the cream of the island's bobsleighers, which numbered exactly four, practised in broiling heat on the island hillsides, hurtling down sheer slopes in home-fashioned karts instead of state-of-the-art sleighs.

The story, unfortunately, failed to deliver a fairytale ending, and the Jamaican Olympians limped home way behind the more fancied teams in Canada. Yet the sheer impudence of the Jamaican Winter Olympics raid so caught the public's imagination that the canny Disney studios had virtually scripted a movie before the team members had even packed away their snowsuits.

During my stop-off at the *Cool Runnings* bar, I read a story in the Jamaican *Gleaner* newspaper announcing that the team leader immortalised in the movie, Dudley Stokes, was plotting another attempt at Olympic glory, this time in the 1998 Nagano Winter Games. It also reported that Stokes and his crew had just finished twenty-first out of 24 teams in a World Cup qualifying event. This result had done nothing to blunt Stokes's ambition to finish in the top ten in Nagano, although he admitted that the Japanese sortie would be his swansong: 'I'll be 36 years old in Nagano. I have two young children at home and this bobsleighing is a very time-consuming thing.'

Stokes and his crew had managed to rustle up sponsorship of $100 000 from a beer company, a hotel chain and the Jamaican Tourist Board to continue chasing their dream. Stokes, a helicopter pilot when not barrelling down hillsides in makeshift toboggans, prefers to regard Jamaica's skimpy practice and competition schedule as an advantage that leaves him fresher than other bobsleigh drivers.

'We also try to compensate for lack of track experience by using mental imagery,' he explained.

Late one night in Kingston I asked a fellow Red Stripe beer drinker why a significant number of Jamaicans have left the island to further their sporting ambitions elsewhere. He spoke of the facilities overseas that were often superior to those in Jamaica. And he also mentioned that unless athletes towed the line with the island's sporting authorities, they got nowhere. 'To make it in sport in Jamaica, it's like smokin' de ganja,' he said. 'De more you suck, de higher you get.'

As a South African in Jamaica, I was vaguely cautious about how I'd be received on the Caribbean's largest English-speaking island. Would I still be ostracised because of lingering resentment against apartheid? Would I be ridiculed over our cricket team? Would my flat-vowelled 'Serth Effrican' accent cause undue embarrassment?

I needn't have worried. For one thing, Jamaicans don't speak English. At least I don't think they do.

Transported by a taxi driver from Montego Bay's Sangster International Airport, I was first introduced to the incomprehensible patois that locals use to talk to each other. The beautiful lilting Jamaican accent can be hard to follow at the best of times, but when islanders converse in the funigalore mixture of English, Spanish and French, it becomes as futile to try to understand as a rap lyric.

The local lingo is celebrated in a number of books available at islandwide souvenir stalls. One of the best is a dictionary of Jamaican English by Ray Chen. He includes a glossary of local vocabulary as well as a fund of rich Jamaican equivalents for well-known English proverbs. Such as:

> 'There is no substitute for experience' = 'Rockstone a ribberbottom doan know sun hot'
> 'Don't try to be someone you're not' = 'When goat laff, everybady see dat im no gat no teeth'
> 'Different strokes for different folks' = 'Lickle bit a ram goat have beard and big bull no hav nun'
> 'Look before you leap' = 'Pig neva know the use a him tail till butcher chop it off'
> 'Don't judge a book by its cover' = 'Yuh shake man hand, yuh no shake him heart'

And my personal favourite:

> 'Those who play with fire burn their fingers' = 'When rat like romp roun puss jaw, one day him gwine en up eena puss jaw'

I needn't have fretted about any hungover attitudes to apartheid either. As a South African, I was greeted like a long-lost, if slightly errant, member of the family.

On my first day in Montego Bay, or Mo' Bay as the locals call the resort town that once transported lard to the colonial powers, I had walked just a few metres down the main tourist strip of Gloucester Road when I was accosted by Rastaman Mike, who wore straggly dreadlocks, red glazed eyes and tatty cut-off jeans.

'Where yo from, mon? Canada?'

'South Africa.'

'You no say? Ah, respect, mon. Respect. We be brothers, mon.'

This was the standard greeting I received in Jamaica whenever I revealed my roots. 'Respect' was the word I heard most often during my stay. Rastaman Mike also gave me the Jamaican handshake, which is a variation on the South African triple grip. Clenched fists on top of each other, then a clash of knuckles and a touching of elbows.

'So where you be going, mon?' asked Mike. 'You wanna get a little high? I have good ganja here.'

It was eight in the morning.

'No, I'm okay right now.'

'What about hash, mon? Coke? Crack? Wassamatter, mon, you doan wanna get high? Wot's wrong wit ya, mon? Ganja be good for you. Better 'n tobacco. Tobacco closes yo' lungs, mon. Ganja clears out de eyeballs.'

Having declined the narcotics, I felt obliged to follow Mike to his tiny souvenir shack set back from the roadside and check out the wood carvings. Inside, he quickly tied a Rasta-coloured bracelet to my wrist. 'My sister makes them to get money for school. For you special price 'cos we be brothers. Only 100 Jamaican dollars.'

Welcome to the emotional hard sell of the average Jamaican stall vendor.

·

I'd arrived in Montego Bay with no lodgings booked, and the all-inclusive resorts that make Jamaica famous are even more famously expensive. Basement prices start at around $200 a night. I was lucky to stumble upon the Ridgeway Guesthouse, which was a snip at $40 a night. To get there you take the road from the airport leading up to the hills, beyond the billboards advertising Red Stripe beer and Irie FM, 'the #1 Reggae

Station in the World', up past the Rotary sign bidding 'Welcome to Montego Bay', left at the traffic roundabout and you're there.

Relva and Brenda Bryan own the Ridgeway, and when I arrived, Brenda was engrossed in *The Bold and the Beautiful*, which flickered from the TV screen on the veranda. I mentioned that we too received this soap programme in South Africa and she was soon quizzing me on the latest plot developments. I wasn't much help. Relva called himself Bryan and he'd worked in the United States and Canada for nearly three decades, fitting pipelines in Saskatchewan at minus 40 degrees and installing cables in redneck country, before returning to his infinitely sunnier roots.

I wasn't the first South African to stay at the Ridgeway. The first group had been a pack of medical interns vacationing from the States. That was four years ago when being a white South African in Jamaica would definitely have been reason to fear grievous bodily harm.

'These guys were 'fraid to say where they were from,' remembered Bryan. 'They went round saying they were British.' The South Africans hired bicycles and pedalled into the island's rural interior. One day they found themselves in the middle of nowhere with night falling fast. They stumbled upon a village where they were forced to ask for shelter. The locals took them in and gave them beds, food and even pyjamas for the night. In the face of such formidable hospitality, the South Africans decided to come clean about their origins.

Montego Bay is set against high green hills that stretch down to enticing white beaches and the sparkling Caribbean beyond. The first day I was there it rained persistently. The gentle misty gusts that drifted down from the hills forced the maniacal, horn-blaring drivers into a more orderly procession through the town's narrow streets. This process was aided by a horse and cart leading a funereal-paced convoy of 50 vehicles past the entrance to Doctor's Cave beach, the frustrated drivers behind almost doing handstands on their hooters. A single attempt at crossing Gloucester Road was all I needed to realise that Jamaican motorists rival Gauteng taxi drivers for speed and road-using eccentricities.

Doctor's Cave is the most famous beach in Mo' Bay. In the Twenties, health-conscious colonial types with time to kill and money to burn sought out the waters, which were said to contain magical healing powers. These days, a hefty lady in a burglar-barred booth takes J$60 (R8) from each patron for the pleasure of using the strip of sand, which seems to be the domain of elderly Germans and Americans, who sit in the shade of the circular turquoise outbuildings, sipping Ting's grapefruit juice.

Jamaica, of course, cultivates the most famous ganja in the world, Jamaica Gold. And in the same way that many tourists visit Amsterdam to ogle sex shows and pose for photos outside houses of ill repute, it appears most travellers who head for these shores come to sample the weed. This despite the fact that dealing in or using marijuana is strictly outlawed on the island. At least that's the theory. But you can't tell me, with tourism being Jamaica's biggest source of income, that a blind eye isn't sometimes turned when a spaced-out whitey with both eyes in the same socket is caught dragging on a sweet-smelling stompie.

It's impossible to dodge the ganja sellers in Montego Bay. One night, I was walking back to the guesthouse when I heard an approaching dull thud-thud-boom sound behind me. I turned to see headlights and a battered, metallic-mauve Dodge squeal to a stop next to me. The window slid down, amplifying the pounding reggae beat. A cloud of blue smoke curled from within. I looked down into the reflector shades of a massive local wearing matted dreadlocks like giant tarantula limbs. He blew a languid smoke-ring out the window and drawled, 'Hey mon, you be looking for a smoke?'

But Jamaica has more pressing problems than hot-tailing it after ganja smokers and dealers. Like crime. The first thing the taxi driver told me at Montego Bay airport was to avoid Kingston.

'Dat be one wicked place, mon,' he said. 'If you go take de taxi in Kingston, you no go near de Trench Town, Spanish Town, Jonestown. Dere dey go fi kill you for nutten. Or dey take you luggage and den dey kill you.'

The driver's name was Matthew Morgan and he had photos of some of his customers taped to his windshield. There was Matthew crushing sugarcane for a German tourist. There was Matthew beaming happily with a couple from Toronto. He had unmixed views on the Jamaican capital, much like a Capetonian will rubbish Johannesburg.

I later heard from Bryan that two tourists had been killed in Jamaica recently, one a reporter from ABC Television and one a backpacker from Canada. The knee-jerk response would have been deep concern, until I remembered I came from Gauteng, where we all have master's degrees in living with the fear of violent crime. Also, the pair who'd been killed had been a trifle negligent, according to Bryan. Both had taken the local ganja salesman back to their rooms so they could smoke their spoils in private. This, said Bryan, was a typical ploy used by the dope peddlers to part tourists from their valuables.

'What you expect if you take a man from the street back to your room? The Canadian, he and his wife took the guy back to the room and got smoked up. This dope guy starts necking with the girl and then there's problems and then suddenly there's a dead guy.' Normally, said Bryan, all that happens is the tourists get glassy-eyed and giggly and start happily signing away their travellers' cheques.

To give an idea of the crime in Kingston, and perhaps to reassure Gauteng dwellers that they are possibly not five points clear at the top of the Violent Crime league table with two games in hand, the following is a typical story from *The Gleaner*, the island's biggest newspaper:

> Two gunmen who yesterday attempted to rob a store along Kingston's busiest area on the Constant Spring Road strip were shot to death by a security guard and police. The two men left their calling cards: an Uzi sub-machine gun and a 9mm pistol with 30 rounds of ammunition. During a tussle at Twin Gates Plaza, the two men tried to disarm the guard of his .38 revolver. One of the gunmen was shot in the stomach. His accomplice, toting two firearms, jumped into a taxi on Molynes Road.
>
> The driver gave *The Gleaner* a brief account of what happened: 'Di gunman just come inna me car with the Uzi and sey fi me drive and bruck all di stoplight dem. Me ask him if him a police and him sey me nuh fi ask him nutten me must just drive. Mi hold on pon the Uzi and de two a we start wrestle fi ti. Same time me see a police car a come wid one policeman innait, the gunman sey me must let go the gun, him nah go shoot me a de policeman he want fi shoot.'
>
> The taxi driver called out to the policeman who shot the gunman during the struggle. The wounded gunman ran into Mandela Town where he was cut down by the policemen's bullets and pronounced dead at the Kingston Public Hospital.

To comfort Gautengers further, check out these Jamaican crime figures from *The Gleaner* of February 28, 1997:

> The gun has been the most lethal weapon used in the 138 violent killings committed across the islands since the start of the year. 95 were slain by gun, 22 stabbed to death and the machete used to kill six. Police records also indicate that drug and gang feuds have been the main motives behind the killings. Most of the 925 murders last year were gang-related. The motives behind the killings show drugs and gangs accounted for 42 murders. This is followed by domestic violence 31, reprisal killings 29 and robbery 18.

Of course the other side of Jamaica, the side more favoured by travel agencies, is that of paradise rediscovered. Of beaches white and soft as talcum powder, of seas blue as a *Hustler* centrefold, of reggae, rum and good times.

Christopher Columbus discovered the island, as the history books will tell you, although Jamaicans want to know how someone can discover a place where people already lived. In fact, Jamaicans say that they discovered Columbus because he was lost at sea at the time. The name Jamaica comes from an Arawak Indian word, *Xaymaca*, which means 'land of wood and water' and is a pretty accurate précis of the island's physical appearance. The Arawaks were essentially a bunch of wimps. In the manner of a latter-day Sandtonite packing for Perth, the peace-loving Arawaks had fled from the war-like Carib tribe in South America and settled in Jamaica. They were thus on hand to greet Columbus when he bumbled upon Discovery Bay in 1494 and promptly claimed the island for Spain. If the Arawaks were unhappy about this development, they weren't saying too much. Plantations were established to supply the ships that plied the Spanish Main between Europe and the Americas, and the Arawaks supplied the bulk of the cheap labour.

Not surprisingly, disease and exploitation by the Spanish led to the demise of the Arawaks, and in the mid-seventeenth century, sturdy slaves were imported from West Africa to take their place. The English accents in West Africa and the Caribbean have huge similarities even today. By the time these slaves had been imported from Ghana, Togo, Benin and the like, the British had taken over Jamaica, and the antics of rampaging pirates like Sir Henry Morgan soon became legendary. The pirates' infamous port of call, Port Royal, became rich with stolen Spanish gold and was known as the 'wickedest city in the world' before it was devastated by an earthquake and hurricanes a few decades later. The history of the island is thus dripping with drama, soaked with romance and pockmarked with tales of derring-do. Latter-day Montego Bay is similarly alluring.

Each night I'd go down to the public beach on Mo' Bay, with its majestic views of the harbour in the distance where massive cruise ships anchored at Freeport Shipping Centre. At around 5 pm, a group of locals would arrive with a soccer ball at a sparsely-grassed park overlooking the beach. A highly competitive two-hour kickaround would ensue. Many of the tackles in these games were two-footed and smacked of intense commitment. Little scuds of dust rose from the bare patches of ground. A guy from Jersey and I were the only whiteys playing. We honkys were more direct. The Jamaicans, like many Africans, took more delight in skinning an opponent twice or three times than in scoring a goal. The games would come to a halt when twilight blanketed the sky. Then we'd all wander down to the sea and flop in the shallows for ten minutes. In the fading light, I'd hear the gentle lapping of the water, see the crabs scuttle on the nearby rocks and watch the planes begin their final approach to Sangster International.

After this refreshing Caribbean dip, I'd stroll back towards town and stop in for a beer or two at Margueritaville's, a three-levelled sports bar jutting out over the ocean. The top level had a bar shack and was the start of 'The Tube', a perspex slide from which one could tumble down three floors and be dumped in the ocean below for R5. Not so great after six strawberry daiquiris. All drinks were paid for in tokens that cost one American dollar each. You can pay for anything in Jamaica with US dollars. Red Stripe cost two tokens, soft drinks one token, dangerous cocktails like Shark Attack four tokens.

At around eight in the evening, Margueritaville's would start filling up and the local band would begin blasting out the reggae. Out across the ocean, the illuminated cruise ships arrowed through the darkness, taking their affluent, well-fed cargo on to the next pampered port-of-call, Ocho Rios. Juicy red $18-lobsters would be brought sizzling from the Margueritaville kitchen and the Red Stripes would start casting their first rosy tints on the evening.

I took a trip to Negril, about 80 kilometres west of Mo' Bay. It soon became obvious that our tour guide had problems distinguishing between left and right. We would be chugging along in the bus and she'd tell us to look out on our left for the Tryall Country Club, where Ernie Els once won the World Championship of Golf. Instead, we'd find ourselves observing skinny cows and a patch of gorse bushes. It took us a while to learn to look the other way.

Negril has mushroomed over the past 25 years as the premier tourism spot in Jamaica. The resort area stretches from Bloody Bay to the lighthouse. Bloody Bay, so named because of the butchering of whales in its waters a century ago, is the eastern end of a length of coastline that includes the longest continuous stretch of white beach in Jamaica. Discovered by the flower children of the Sixties, Negril is a bastion of hedonism. In fact there's even a club there called Hedonism II, a couples-only resort with nudist beaches, toga parties nightly and the like. Most Negril resorts offer similar fare. No building is allowed to tower higher than the tallest palm tree. Resorts have two and sometimes three satellite dishes aimed at the sky, and hairbraiding is big business on the beaches.

I found some more soccer players on the beach here, but they were more reticent than the Montego Bay crowd. I told one I was playing every night in Mo' Bay.

'Okay. You go bring your boys from Mo' Bay. We go mash you. But we no play for nutting. If we go sweat, we must collect. Let's say one tousand dollar for de first tree goals.'

We lunched at the thatched Kuyabu Beach Bar and Restaurant, while Jimmy Cliff bawled out 'Reggae Nights' through the muffled speakers. That night, De Burs Promotions were presenting 'Crown Prince of Reggae' Dennis Brown in concert. This elderly dreadlocked jammer resembled a cross between Mangosuthu Buthelezi and the Maharishi Mahesh Yogi. Brown was to be backed by Lloyd Parks and the We The People Band, while Gummy Dee was the MC. Tickets went from J$350.

We moved on to Rick's Café, home of the Caribbean's most spectacular sunset, according to the billboards. Here Red Stripe cost three tokens, and, to be fair, the venue matches La Med in Camps Bay or Cape Maclear in Malawi for vivid sunsets. Rick's Café also has a 15-metre rock that falls away to the sea below. The brave dive like swallows into the surf. One large, in fact, tremendously huge and hefty, Spanish lady leapt in to the biggest cheer of the afternoon. An American was fearless enough to dive instead of leap, but her back flipped forward at the bottom of her arc and she hit the water with a crack.

'There be another meaning for Red Stripe now,' cackled the Rastaman next to me.

America is geographically close to Jamaica and its citizens appear to make up the bulk of the tourists on the island. These Yank visitors favour tropical shirts in designer vomit hues. And whereas other foreigners point out the indigenous sights on vacation ('See the Eiffel Tower. Ah, the Taj Mahal!'), Statesiders feel happiest when pointing out bastions of Americanism: 'Hey man, there's another Burger King.' Americans are, in the main, famously oblivious to other cultures. All over Jamaica are huge billboards advertising American home-from-home comforts and offering security blankets like the AT&T phone company, which implores visitors to 'call the States collect'.

A jet flip from Miami to Montego Bay takes just an hour and a half, and you can get a return ticket for under $200 on certain American carriers. But then you'll have to deal with the flight attendants. Is it just me, or are the hostesses on privatised US airlines the worst in the world? Often in their middle years, these crabby matrons find themselves no longer in a position to snare a pilot or some other desirable mate, and they are thus doomed to stalk the skies slamming down Bloody Marys in front of cowering passengers, or throwing dagger glares your way when you order another Coors Light.

Frankly I had a much better time aboard the Air Jamaica Express flight to Kingston from Mo' Bay. This flimsy looking 16-seater plane was decked out in the bright hues of the national carrier. Air Jamaica must be the only commercial airline that can rival SAA's Ndizani jumbo when it comes to colour schemes. AJ's livery is a cocktail of lemon, guava and turquoise and the airline promises it is 'Soaring to new heights'.

I had travelled to Kingston, against the impassioned advice of Montego Bay taxi drivers, to catch some sport. Jamaica were playing cricket against India at Sabina Park. Sachin Tendulkar's team had travelled to the Caribbean straight from their drubbing at the hands of the South Africans and were widely expected to be mere cannon-fodder for the West Indians. As it turned out, the Indians only lost the rain-marred five Test series 1–0, and in that match they were chasing less than 150 for victory.

Sabina Park can hardly be compared with some of the smarter cricketing venues in the world, but it must be brimful of atmosphere when the terraces are filled. Unfortunately, the day I turned up, it was obvious that the four-day game in the Caribbean suffers a similar lack of support to the South African version. I was surrounded by a mere smattering of fans, many of them schoolkids in their khaki uniforms. Disco music blared throughout the day's play from the Red Stripe Mound opposite the executive box-studded main stand. Vendors sold vials of coconut water, Red Stripe and Ting in buckets of iced water, and the Blue Mountains formed a beautiful backdrop to the ground.

In the Jamaican team that day was a lithe and lanky fast bowler called Franklyn Rose, who had just been drafted into the West Indian team for the first Test against India. His inclusion had come as something of a relief to the cricket administrators on the island. Whereas in the Seventies and Eighties, high-class Jamaican (and West Indian) fast bowlers were as common as sunscreen on a Negril beach, latterly the conveyor belt of classy quicks has stuttered to a halt. One of the reasons put forward is the advent of cable television in the Caribbean. Not that islanders have become couch potatoes watching American soaps during daylight hours. Rather, TV has beamed NBA basketball into their homes, and the money-making opportunities that a career in hoops offers have many youngsters considering this alternative to the traditional sporting avenue of cricket.

It might be simplistic to say that cricket was one of the only ways to island prosperity, in the manner that boxers punched their way out of poverty-stricken ghettos, but there's no denying that cricket has brought material wealth to generations of West Indians. Yet the money that can be made from one NBA season probably exceeds what a cricketer can make in a decade-long county and Test cricket career. There's no financial contest. West Indians also have an ideal physical build for basketball. Think of Curtley Ambrose, Ian Bishop and Courtney Walsh. All are towering, athletic and well co-ordinated. Had they been born in the States, there's every chance that this trio would now be multi-millionaire prima donnas whingeing about the bonus clause in their mega-bucks Miami Heat or New York Knicks contract.

For the continuing success of cricket on the islands, the likes of Franklyn Rose will need to carry the torch for the next generation of Caribbean fast bowlers.

Another sport that had forced cricket on to the back-burner the week I was in Jamaica was soccer. The day after watching India at Sabina Park, I found myself at the National Stadium for the most important World Cup qualifier in Jamaica's history. The Reggae Boyz had exceeded all expectations by winning through to the final stages of the Concacaf World Cup qualifying group. In the process they had beaten the highly fancied Mexican side 2–1 in Mexico. Jamaica has never been renowned for its footballing skills, though the Caribbean has produced players of the calibre of Dwight Yorke, the Trinidadian striker who plays for Aston Villa in the English Premiership and is a boyhood pal of Brian Lara.

When Brazilian Rene Simões became technical director of the Jamaican national team in 1994, he revitalised soccer on the island and earned Jamaica FIFA's Best Mover Award for 1995. The World Cup qualifier had been hyped in the media all week, and that Friday night before the game, Jamaica's sports minister had implored the fans, who have been known to question a refereeing decision in less than courteous terms, to behave themselves at the big match.

'I expect the fans to treat the stadium as they would treat the furniture at home,' she told national television in tones reminiscent of a high-school head librarian.

There had been much conjecture about the timing of the match. Kick-off was at noon, sweltering by any standards, stifling in Jamaica in February. The move had been made to give the Jamaicans an advantage, as the Statesiders were coming from their frigid midwinter. But one newspaper pointed out that the Americans had been training under the Florida sun for the past week, and the move could backfire.

Nevertheless, the stadium was packed and humming with anticipation an hour before kick-off. The bleachers of the bowl-like structure offered no protection from the blistering sun and were alive with Rasta-coloured banners and replicas of the Jamaican flag. I sat in the cheap seats, a move I regretted later as I stared at the mirror that night and saw a scorched apple-red face gazing back. Although liquor was officially banned, Red Stripes and little sachets of Appleton's Rum were as common as confetti at a wedding.

The game began at a ferocious pace, and the Boyz had two great chances in the opening 15 minutes. The score-sheet remained blank, however, and in the second half the pace understandably wilted. The Jamaicans plugged away and enjoyed the majority of the possession, but they couldn't penetrate the American defence. For the last quarter of an hour, the Americans hardly ventured out of their penalty area, but they clung on for the goalless draw and the precious point.

The Jamaican World Cup campaign would later deteriorate. Their next game was away to Mexico and it was decided that the team would travel two weeks ahead of the game to acclimatise. A friendly match was arranged against a local first-division team. The game was a mere 15 minutes old when one of the Jamaican players took exception to a tackle and launched a Cantona-style kick at his Mexican opponent. Both teams then indulged in a pitch-wide free-for-all that forced the referee to abandon the game.

To compound their misery, the Jamaicans were then whipped 6–0 by Mexico in the qualifier. During the first half, one of the Jamaicans refused to follow his coach's instructions and instead shed his jersey and stalked from the field. He was banned for three years. The rest of the side squabbled about money, miffed that they were receiving considerably less than one or two star players. A chance at World Cup glory fizzled out amid petty acrimony.

While in Kingston that weekend, I went to the Bob Marley Museum at 56 Hope Road. Marley's former home has become a shrine to the icon of reggae and is a popular pilgrimage for the schoolchildren of Kingston. In the yard is a colourful cement statue of Marley – guitar in hand, football at feet – and the walls are decked with murals containing slogans like 'Liberate Marijuana'.

Jamaica Gold? That sums up Marley's record sales, not just what he smoked. Inside, the museum is packed with examples of Marley's fascination with Africa. As well as the obligatory nods to Ethiopia's Emperor

Haile Selassie, there is a Zimbabwe corner on the first floor of the museum. Marley wrote a song for that country's independence and played a concert in honour of the occasion at Harare in April 1980. You can also see a replica of Marley's original record shack in Greenwich Town – 'Wail 'n Soul' – as well as the bicycle he used to ride around town selling records, and the hammock he used to lie in and smoke and dream and conjure songs.

Outside the house is a well-kept flower bed in which tender shoots of marijuana bud, and there is a beehive on the roof, which in Jamaica is a sign of prosperity. In one of the outbuildings behind the house, one can still discern bullet-marks in the walls, testimony to a shooting in 1976 when Marley was gunned down for political reasons. Marley survived, but a bullet lodged in his arm, and doctors said if they removed it, he'd never be able to play the guitar again. So Bob carried that bullet around in him until he died of brain cancer in 1981.

Outside the Marley museum, I took a photo of a resthouse and its sign: 'No Drugs, No Pimping, No Prostituting'. A Rasta walked by muttering to his mate about me taking his photo. I assured him I had only snapped the building, not him. 'Okay. One love, mon,' he said, giving me the Jamaican handshake. 'Tanks for de respect, mon.'

Rastafarianism may be a majority religion on the island, but the dreadlocked followers of Haile Selassie would appear to have some competition from one of Jamaica's three television stations. Trinity Broadcasting Network is a charismatic preaching channel that fills the airwaves on a 24-hour basis, dispensing plastic-wrapped pep-talks for the masses. Late one night, fortified by rum, I watched and listened for a fascinating half-hour as one Laverne Tripp, a southern Baptist preacher who looked as trustworthy as Robin Williams in *Cadillac Man*, struck the fear of God, literally, into his audience. Laverne Tripp had hair slicked back into a ponytail, was dressed in a shiny suit and a loud tie, and had a wife at his side who wore strident make-up, big blonde curls and showed evidence of surgical enhancement.

Laverne Tripp started making big promises and I took notes. 'Begone, foul spirits of the devil,' he decreed. 'If you wanna be free of nicotine, alcohol, drugs, lust, perversion, anger or greed, just reach out and touch your TV screen now.'

I followed his instructions to the letter, feeling a bit like that little girl in *Poltergeist*, and was disappointed to receive a mere static shock. Tripp was undeterred and continued in foam-mouthed fury for another quarter of an hour before finally signing off by reminding his viewers, 'And remember to send in your donations. After all, they make this programme possible. I would not dare to ask you how much to give. I ask only that you measure the value of this ministry to you.'

I might not have received divine providence through my television set, but I will admit that I was struck by a revelation as I lay in my Kingston hotel room that night. A vision danced before me clear as gin. An entire industry has sprung up targeting the dim and the desperate and there's precious little tact when it comes to prising loose the money.

But maybe ample doses of Laverne Tripp are a daily requirement for making life in Kingston more palatable.

There was an almost tangible level of tension in the sprawling capital city. Little of the laid-back atmosphere of Montego Bay survived here, and the taxi driver from the regional Tinson Pen Aerodrome flatly refused to drive the direct route through Trench Town to my hotel. The begging was also more aggressive and unrelenting in Kingston, as were the insistent invitations to buy ganja and peruse the souvenir stalls. Still, I went for a few beers at a local tavern most nights, and felt no more spooked than if I'd been in downtown Rosebank.

One morning *The Gleaner* reported that a local politician and owner of the Skateland Roller Disco Entertainment Centre in Halfway Tree Road had been shot dead at a tavern just a block away from where I'd sat downing Reggae Spiced Rum. Police counted 19 bullet wounds.

The newspaper's cartoon that day featured a politician in confrontation with a housewife. 'I have proposed a BILL here for a body to monitor the police force,' said the politician. 'How about a bill to monitor the GUNMAN dem?' said the housewife, hands on hips, holding a newspaper with a headline reading, 'Triple murder – five-month-old baby shot'.

I'd been away from home for about two weeks, and had been feeling the first longings for the familiarity of my own bed. Hats off to Kingston and its maze of crime for making sure I felt right at home.

I think the Jamaican capital and Johannesburg should negotiate twinning rights directly.

Pacific Ocean
AUSTRALIA
Perth
Sydney
Canberra
Melbourne

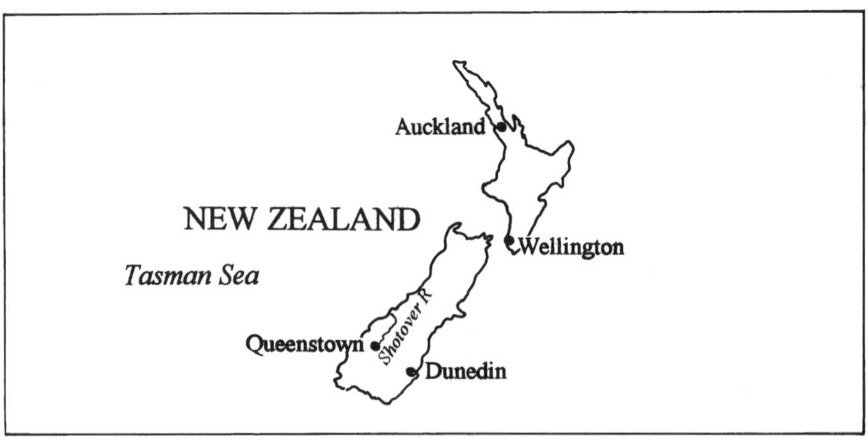
Auckland
NEW ZEALAND
Wellington
Tasman Sea
Shotover R.
Queenstown
Dunedin

CHAPTER THREE

The Year of Living Dangerously

SPORTS WRITING IS sometimes regarded rather condescendingly by so-called hard-news journalists. For instance, some of those scribes who spend their days in parliament. One of the reasons, I suspect, is that they believe being near important people like the president must therefore make them important too. Even though their function is largely just to jot down MPs' musings in Pitman's shorthand, like a corporate suit's personal assistant, these types tend to look down their noses at people who occupy their time chasing ball games.

Having worked in both news and sports reporting, however, I've yet to come across any evidence that rehashing party political press releases is any more taxing, or rewarding, than coaxing a logical sentence from an international outside right. Whether reporters fawn over cabinet ministers or hang around practice fields, there seem to be certain traits that are common to journalists in any area. Such as jumbo-sized egos, Olympic-qualifying standard whingeing, and a tendency to dress like extras in the 'Bring out your dead' scene from Monty Python's *Holy Grail*.

Personally, I feel that some of those hard-news journalists should think twice before scorning us trifling sports writers. After all, according to any number of public opinion polls, it's the news reporters, not the sports hacks, who are fighting relegation alongside the likes of estate agents and used-car dealers in the Trustworthy Occupations championship.

I worked in the news department of *The Star* for nearly four years. A typical working day at this Johannesburg newspaper in the early Nineties was nothing if not varied. A morning might be spent chasing reactions to someone's bright idea to hold a charity rhino braai. An afternoon could see you on the scene of a murder, trying to piece together the bloody sequence of events from bewildered witnesses. Then it might be off to chart the latest demo march's progress through the city streets.

Some of the stories I covered were bizarre. Once a woman phoned claiming she'd seen uniformed firemen from a northern suburbs fire station 'savagely kicking and beating a black man dressed in a blue overall'. This had happened on the pavement outside the station late one night. The woman had been driving home from the movies, and swore she was '150 per cent' certain that a brutal beating was taking place. She circled the block and on returning to the scene saw the firemen now jumping on the body. 'I've never seen such force of violence used against a human being. Two firemen were kicking him in the head and another two were beating him with long batons,' she said.

The Star ran the story, and almost immediately the paper, the woman and I were made to look rather foolish. A barrage of callers phoned to say they'd witnessed the assault too, but the 'victim' was nothing more than a fireman's rescue-drill dummy. It was all a joke. The firemen had been letting off a little steam. The scary notion that some firefighters' idea of a good time is to mutilate humanesque dummies is another story entirely.

The first story I covered as a news journalist was for the *Sowetan*. This was while I was still on a six-month cadet training course that *The Star* runs for newly recruited reporters. *The Star* had an exchange scheme with the *Sowetan* at the time, and some of us cub reporters worked in that newspaper's Industria offices. The *Sowetan* may provide 'the soul truth, daily' for the country's largest township, but it knows better than to keep its offices within those sprawling, crime-soaked streets.

It was a crisp April Sunday, the first weekend of autumn back in 1991. The phone rang at 9 am. I had just arrived for work and was in a Sunday kind of mood. The voice on the line was calm and measured. The caller said he was phoning to notify the newspaper that something was happening in Kagiso. He said there seemed to be a bit of trouble at Swanieville squatter camp. Hut burnings or something. He wasn't sure.

So photographer Robert Magwaza and I reluctantly set aside our coffees and toasted mince and headed for the West Rand. I was a green cub reporter whose exposure to township life had been limited to a handful of games at the Soweto Cricket Club.

I'm fairly certain, however, that nothing could have prepared me for what we saw that morning in Swanieville. From the approach road to the squatter camp, curling plumes of black smoke hinted at mayhem. As we entered the camp, we saw the extent of the 'trouble' the telephone caller had spoken of.

The first corpse was a man lying stiff on his back, hands sawn through and flapping loosely by his sides. Another body was covered by a red blanket. Two bare feet stuck out the bottom. A hand jutted from the blanket. It was stiffly raised, frozen in that position from trying to ward off blows.

We drove down the camp's dirt road. Most of the corrugated-iron, makeshift huts had been reduced to smouldering ashes or were still ablaze – orange tongues of flame licking at the deep blue sky. Intense waves of heat passed through the car as we drove by. Owners were trying to salvage possessions – a sofa, a chair or two, bulging plastic bags.

There was no sense of panic in Swanieville, no milling crowds, no gaping onlookers. The storm had passed and people were carrying on with their lives. Someone ate a packet of chips while walking indifferently past a body. A woman breastfed her baby not 10 metres from a horribly charred corpse. This body too had its rigid arms raised in the air.

Two shell-shocked survivors were the local chemist and his wife. They'd been woken by gunshots and screaming at about 5.30 am. The chemist had looked through his door and seen an armed and massive impi, wearing red headbands, moving down the street. The Swanieville chemist grabbed his family and together they hid in a back room of the store. When the impi smashed the windows of their shop, the chemist's wife dived into the deep freeze. The impi stormed the store, yelling they wanted to see the 'dog who sleeps here'. The chemist said he'd nearly passed out with terror. He and his daughter were just metres away, cowering under shelves.

The chemist and his family were lucky. They remained undetected, and the impi moved on.

Twenty-seven people were killed – hacked, shot, torched – in that predawn raid on the Swanieville squatter camp. The perpetrators were the inmates of a nearby hostel. Most survivors said the impi had been accompanied by police. A *Sowetan* reader had opened the following day's edition of the newspaper, read the Swanieville story and then recognised the photo of a dead body in denims and red sweatshirt as her brother. He was the single parent of five children under the age of twelve. The reader was these youngsters' only living relative. All five children had been missing since the attack. There was desperation in the sister's voice: 'It is cold out there and there are many terrible things happening. I don't know where they went, or even if they are alive, I don't know where to start looking.'

That baptism of death in the killing fields of Swanieville was my first ever by-line in a newspaper. Elsewhere in the world, I'm led to believe, reporting careers begin more gently. Cub reporters might be sent to cover the mayoress's tea party. But graphic scenes of death have been everyday experiences for most South African journalists. As the 1994 elections approached, *The Star*'s newsdesk issued bulletproof vests to reporters and photographers who found themselves increasingly in the line of fire.

Some of the stories I had to cover were especially nasty. Once, a frantic call to the newsdesk saw picman Jacoob Rykliff and I haring to the scene of a shooting on the old Vereeniging road, south of Johannesburg.

At around 7.30 on that late summer morning, a cream-coloured Volkswagen Passat had pulled up at the Eikenhof four-way stop. The vehicle was on a routine journey, taking three children to school. Inside were two adults, their 14-year-old son, and two other schoolgoers in the lift club, a 13-year-old girl and another teenage boy. As the Passat prepared to pull away from the intersection, the driver noticed a metallic green BMW 5 series vehicle approaching at speed. The BMW stopped close behind, an occupant stuck his head out of the window and raked the Passat with continuous rounds of AK-47 fire. The BMW then made a U-turn and disappeared back up the highway.

Despite being struck three times in the back, the Passat's driver managed somehow to maintain control of his vehicle and steer it to a service station a kilometre down the road. A pump attendant there said the car fishtailed into the garage at high speed. He saw that the right rear wheel was ripped and flat, and all the windows apart from the windscreen had been blasted out by the gunfire. The driver, in a blood-caked trance, managed to stagger from his car and phone for an ambulance.

According to the attendant, the wife in the passenger seat was already dead by the time her husband phoned for help. He said their teenage son was still alive at that stage. The boy had been sitting in the rear seat on the driver's side. When the car halted, the teenager had slumped from the rear door. He died on the garage forecourt before ambulancemen could reach him. The fallen boy's grey school trousers protruded from the red blanket used to cover him. The sleeve of his white school shirt was also visible. It was soaked dark red with drying blood. The teenage girl had a savage wound in her head, and was airlifted to the Johannesburg Hospital in a critical condition. She died later that day. The other boy was unharmed.

In the back of the bullet-scarred station-wagon lay three schoolbags and a girl's brown school shoe. Size three. One of the satchels had sprung open. It was filled with brown-papered schoolbooks, a towel and a red juice bottle. A pair of broken, blood-stained spectacles lay on the floor behind the driver's seat.

Police concluded there was no motive for the shooting. Though no doubt someone would later try to pin a vague, half-baked political motive on to a cowardly act of child murder.

Grey school trousers, red-soaked school shirt, broken, blood-stained children's spectacles.

The worst of images.

They remain with me to this day.

News journalism fast lost its sheen. How do you explain to the mother of a boy who's just been killed in a car accident that her feelings would make a good newspaper story?

In early 1994, I joined *SA Sports Illustrated* magazine. I didn't have to think about the offer too long. The most recent news story I'd covered at *The Star* had been a politicians' tour aimed at adding impetus to a pre-election peace initiative. ANC heavyweights Cyril Ramaphosa and Joe Slovo had decided they would travel to volatile Katlehong and stroll among the Inkatha-dominated hostels to show they could venture anywhere with confidence. The tour proved to be the polar opposite of a peace mission.

The politicians were walking down a street in the Dikgole section of the township. A fairly large entourage of press, supporters and other hangers-on were in tow as the ANC duo acknowledged cheers opposite the Mazibuko hostel. At that moment, a sound exactly like firecrackers echoed from the direction of the hostel. Hardened people in the group, however, recognised the sound as the unmistakeable crackle of AK-47 fire. Bullets zinged and whined in the air. One pinged back off a signboard and scuffed the earth near my feet. Reporters and onlookers dived to the ground while ANC bodyguards and members of the shadowy township self-defence units returned fire, then frantically encircled Slovo and Ramaphosa, who were whisked through gardens, across backyards and up driveways back to the safety of their cars. It was probably the first time Cyril Ramaphosa has been anything other than the epitome of composure. He was breathless as a Sky TV mike was shoved in his face for instant comment. Slovo was pale and panting. The politicos survived unscathed, but three people died in the attack. One was a five-year-old child bicycling innocently by. Another was Abdul Shariff, a freelance photographer working for Associated Press. He was shot in the chest, and died after being rushed to Natalspruit Hospital. Hardened lensmen who went to the hospital wept after identifying their colleague.

The world of sport proved a welcome respite from the potentially deadly world of South African news journalism. I was also quickly introduced to the scope for travel that is such a bonus for today's sports writers. The first trip I took for the magazine was a whistle-stop tour of New Zealand and Australia ahead of the 1994 rugby Test series against the All Blacks.

That fleeting trip Down Under was also my first ever introduction to the South African rugby supporter abroad. Immediate impressions were that these supporters' trips feature their own competitive nuances. Medals are probably awarded in these three categories: Most Lagers Swallowed in One Sitting; Least Sleep in a Seven-day Period; Most Staggeringly Charmless Chat-up Line.

In order to qualify, the fans would hit King's Cross in Sydney, for example, at noon and disappear into pubs like the Bourbon and Beefsteak till close on sun-up. Most of these supporters were built like your average Springbok rugby fan, that is to say around 6 feet 4, with stomachs like they'd smuggled a motorcycle helmet under their replica Springbok jerseys, moustaches resembling squirrel tails, and voice volumes that would have had town criers applying for desk jobs. Many behaved as if their wives kept them at home in iron manacles, tossing them raw joints of beef every third day and hiding the keys both to the liquor cabinet and the *Hustler* magazine racks.

Needless to say, on the chatting-up-sophisticated-Sydneysiders-while-slurring-drunkenly-in-a-green-and-gold-polyester-windbreaker score, the fans seemed to be achieving less success than an Allan Boesak prosecution team. Some fans sought solace by holing up nightly in the red light districts, armed with adventurous hormones, aching heads and gold Mastercards – a winning combination indeed, particularly from a bordello owner's point of view.

One day we took a lunchtime boat cruise from Circular Quay, with the famous harbour bridge to our left and the Opera House to our right. We were soaking up the culture, drinking deeply of the spotless surroundings, wallowing like muddied warthogs in the sheer joy of spending this particular morning of our lives in this splendid Australian city.

The sun shone powerfully and encouraged listless musings. Foster's lagers were consumed while the billowing white sails belonging to the ship used in the movie *The Mutiny* drifted past. All was serene. That is, until a stout fellow with a beard you could hide a wasp nest in snapped a cassette into his ghetto-blaster. And, for the next two hours, we sailed among the waterfront attractions of Sydney to the accompaniment of Leon Schuster braying, 'Hier kom die Bokke'. On a scale of inappropriateness, it was like ordering a quarterpounder and fries at a restaurant such as Maxim's.

Which, knowing some of those guys, was not beyond the realms of probability.

Luckily, I had work to do and thus had a ready-made excuse for escaping the beer-soaked existence of my travelling mates when necessary. One of the interviews set up was a chat with walkabout Wallaby winger David Campese, the man whom his own coach once described as occasionally having a faulty connection between his brain and his mouth.

Campese's sports store nestles in the leafy north Sydney suburb of St Ives, known locally as St Africa because of the number of South Africans who have settled there. The store, on the second floor of a neat shopping mall, is hard to miss: the name 'Campo's' is lit in blazing neon yellow. The in-store television was showing a 1989 British Lions–Australian Wallabies Test. Campese had not yet arrived, so I watched the action for a while. The first incident I saw was Campese trying to run the ball clear from his own tryline, fluffing a pass, and the Lions pouncing on the loose ball to score the match-and-series-winning try. The incident said a lot about the way the world's leading Test try-scorer approached the game.

At that moment, the tracksuited Wallaby wandered into his store. He saw me watching the video, and chuckled when he saw the slow-mo of his most memorable howler.

'That's how it goes, mate. You know, like, who gives a pooh? Sometimes things work. Sometimes not.'

No regrets, no ducking, no diving, no punches pulled. That's the Campo method. He might be regarded as arrogant in South Africa, but he made no bones about the fact that he saw South Africans as massively conceited on their return to international rugby in 1992. Not that Campo holds any grudges towards South Africans. He's your archetypal Aussie sportsman who's not afraid to speak his mind. He talks in the way he plays rugby, unpredictably and with lots of flair.

'I like to play the way I see it. If I see something, I'll call for the ball. It's that simple. I mean, I don't want to stay out on the wing and just watch the forwards take it away, thinking, "Oh hell, this is boring, I'm not getting the ball."'

The interview took place before the era of professionalism, and Campese, widely perceived as the game's first millionaire, was adamant that South African players were the best paid in the world.

'The way you guys in South Africa look after your players compared to the way we look after the players. Gee! England are always complaining about Australians getting money and the like, but who gives a pooh? I suggested years ago, why don't they just take 5 per cent of the gate takings of a Test match and put it in a fund? Then just divide it out at the end of the year or something. If you've played 70 Tests for your country, then they can say, "Look, we really appreciate it, here's $500 000 for all the years you've given to us." But I wouldn't change a thing. That's life. Why make more money? Does it make you happy? I was brought up in a town of 24 000 people in Canberra. I'm not a private school person, I went to a public school, and we never had a lot of money. My dad always told me if you want to buy something, pay cash. And those sorts of things you cherish. The biggest thing in rugby is that it's a false life, not a real life. And if I take three knocks in a row, that could be that. Thanks for coming. I've given for Australia since 1982, I mean that's my life. So how can people say, "Oh, he's rich. What a great life!"? I still train five days a week. I finish work here at 4.30 pm, and I'm training till nine at night. I'm rarely here at the shop, so I've got to put more effort and time into that. When I finish rugby all these people will say, "Thanks very much, we don't need you any more because you're not playing." So after that I'll probably go and buy a $10-car or something.'

Sure, Campo.

Much as it pains me to say it, given the natural competitive tension between South Africans, Australians and New Zealanders, most of the Aussie and Kiwi sportsmen I've spoken to over the years have tended to buck the stereotype of being mouthy, ego-soaked, sheep-shagging louts.

There's a well-known story about former Test cricketer David Boon. He's said to have consumed something like 64 tinnies of lager on the plane trip from Australia to England, thus setting a new world record for in-flight bingeing. Australian cricket teams, apparently, set much store by such records. The impression such tales leave is that David Boon is a coarse, loud-mouthed ocker with corks dangling from his bush hat.

In reality, he's a man studious behind spectacles and so softly spoken one has to strain to hear him. I once asked Boon to provide a lowdown on the Australian cricket players for a magazine article. I'd expected to interview him and write it myself. But the chunky number three insisted on doing it himself, and later phoned me to say the piece was done and dusted and waiting at his hotel reception. I picked up the envelope and found a neatly handwritten thousand-word story inside.

Former Australian flyhalf Michael Lynagh remains the most genuine sportsman I've ever interviewed. No matter that he'd doubtless heard all the questions before; he considered his answers, took his time, and seemed sincerely interested in being asked to spare an hour of his time.

If there is a generalisation to be made about sports writing, in my experience it's the bigger the star, the better the interview. Most sporting superstars realise that media coverage is an important part of maintaining their public profile. The problems come with those players who *think* they're stars.

An exception to the dream Antipodean interviewee was Allan Border, the original 'Captain Grumpy'. The former Aussie cricket captain makes England's Mike Atherton look like a *cum laude* graduate of a Dale Carnegie charm school. I once asked Border to do an interview for *SA Sports Illustrated* while the Australians were playing a relaxing match against Boland in tranquil Stellenbosch. It was a good time to approach him as he wasn't even playing in the low-key match. I asked if he could spare a few minutes. I said I was from the biggest sports magazine in the country.

To which he replied, 'Well, whoopee do, mate, that means f... all to me.'

It doesn't take long to work out why New Zealand is known as the Land of the Long White Cloud. Wake up early enough, peer beyond your hotel curtains, and there a band of white mist hovers eerily, an endless plume of cigar smoke wafting above the horizon. It's as if some biker god in leathers and chains is blowing smoke rings from on high.

Auckland also deserves its nickname of the City of Sails. Wherever the eye roves in the city's network of waterways, yachts dot the scene, jam the Waitemata harbour and bottleneck the Hauraki Gulf. Auckland is said to have more boats per head of population than any other city on the planet. When these boats return to the harbours and pack away their sails, the masts resemble a field of white crosses in a war cemetery. Sailing is so ingrained in Aucklanders, there's even a yacht anchored in the middle of downtown to commemorate some noteworthy seafaring victory. This vessel stands near the Loaded Hog pub. The first time I visited this tavern, there was a burly Kiwi bouncer guarding the door. On hearing a South African accent, he unleashed a torrent of Afrikaans abuse, *vloekwoorde* that would have made even an Auckland sailor blush. But there was no malice intended. The bouncer had just ended an eight-month working holiday in South Africa, and his new friends there had wasted no time introducing him to the more colourful aspects of the language.

Dunedin is the southernmost major town in New Zealand, after Invercargill. It lies nearly 46 degrees south and only 20 degrees north of the Antarctica coastline. In winter, the beaches of Dunedin, a university town, are lapped by the uninviting slate-grey South Pacific Ocean.

The Springboks played the first Test of the 1994 series at Dunedin's Carisbrook Stadium, which is surely the world's most forlorn rugby Test ground. Behind one goal, the stadium is exposed to the elements and affords a perfect view to those on the railway line behind and in the houses perched on the adjacent hillside. In Dunedin's case, these elements are a raw, snarling ocean wind and sub-zero temperatures. In the 1983 test at Carisbrook between the All Blacks and the British Lions, the home team wore thermal gear and mittens and bone-chilling hail fell throughout the game. The stands are bleak wooden structures. The journalists are treated to facilities you might see in some period sports movie of the Forties – like hard, utilitarian wooden work benches.

The concept of comfortable grandstands has not yet filtered down to New Zealand's South Island. In fact, virtually all New Zealand's rugby stadiums are spartan places, highly inappropriate for such a rugby-mad nation. The closest to a South African-style superstadium is Eden Park in Auckland. Even this venue has its oddities, such as the rock-hard cricket square in the middle. Not exactly the place to be trapped at the bottom of a ruck. South Africans remember Eden Park best for the infamous, controversy-racked 1981 series. During the Test match in Auckland, a light aircraft buzzed the ground, and Kiwi prop Gary Knight was felled by one of the flour bombs that the pilot, apparently fuelled by anti-apartheid fervour, kept dropping from his plane.

One night, accompanied by a couple of Springbok followers, I wandered into a pub in the middle of Dunedin. Here we found a set-up that could have come straight from an Oliver Stone Vietnam movie. On the stage was an elaborate reed structure that was obviously supposed to be some type of hut. Around this dwelling stood a number of men in olive and green camouflage gear, their faces smeared with war paint. Just as I thought we'd stumbled on to a Moody Killers In Army Gear benefit dinner, the MC bade the entire room welcome to Dunedin's Annual Duck-calling Competition. For the next three hours we stood transfixed, pausing only to order more Speight's beer. The reed hut was in fact meant to be a duck hide. Each competitor would be called up individually and then disappear into the hut. The contenders had small flute-like instruments on which they would warble elaborate and complicated tunes. These tunes were rated by the enthusiastic, packed audience. The more vivid the applause from the floor, the higher the ratings. After the eighth duck-calling competitor had been applauded off the stage, it became a little clearer why some New Zealanders have such an intense desire to invent death-defying pastimes like jet boating and bungee jumping. Anything to avoid another session of duck-calling.

On the whole, New Zealanders would seem to inhabit a moist, green, sleepy country, which is, I suppose, reason enough for so many South Africans to consider it a choice escape from the crime-riddled land of their birth. In Aotearoa, as the Maoris call New Zealand, front-page newspaper headlines are apt to shriek 'Schoolkids Fail Breathalyser Test' or 'Milk Coupons Pilfered – Four Held'. It is virtually unprecedented for a policeman to be murdered in New Zealand. In Gauteng, cop deaths are so common, the papers often bury the story on page four.

South Africans would also identify with New Zealand's obsession with rugby. Whereas in most parts of the world, open grassy spaces are dotted with soccer posts, in New Zealand, rugby goals dominate the rural landscapes. There's also the rugged beauty, for this is a land of lakes and mountains, geysers and fjords.

However, New Zealand's surface serenity fails to hint at the latent madness bubbling beneath the skin of some of its citizens. When it comes to getting their kicks, Kiwis aren't easily satisfied. My other theory on why they apparently need to devise terrifying, adrenaline-pumping ways of seeking pleasure is as a reaction to the tranquillity of their land. So it's no surprise to discover that New Zealanders have turned bungee jumping and jet boating into profitable ventures that are now popular throughout the world.

Queenstown is a spectacularly photogenic winter sports resort that could grace the box of any jigsaw puzzle. Situated a couple of hundred kilometres north-west of Dunedin, in the heart of New Zealand's South Island, the town has grown and prospered around a deep blue lake and snow-dappled mountains, one of which, Coronet Peak, is New Zealand's premier ski resort. With wide-open pistes, well-groomed slopes and plunging valleys, there's terrain to suit all abilities. There's never a shortage of snow either, as the resort tops up Mother Nature's best efforts with loads of fresh, machine-made powder.

Queenstown is proud of its reputation for hardy, blood-curdling outdoor activities, and the resort is home to the 'Awesome Foursome', an aptly-named excursion that provides a day's worth of uncut thrills.

This day begins with a jet boating trip on the death-grey Shotover River. Jet boating has consistently been voted New Zealand's top outdoor activity. The jet boats are flat-bottomed vessels capable of violent turns of speed. Our pilot welcomed aboard his apprehensive cargo with a knowing grin, then powered his boat full throttle down river, shearing mere inches away from rocks that jut from towering cliffs. The blurring rush of speed distorts facial features. The pilot showed a penchant for gunning his craft directly at the solid walls of granite. Just as metal-grinding impact appeared unavoidable, he flicked his wrist slightly. The boat obeyed and veered sharply away from the rock face, leaving a boatful of bug-eyed tourists whimpering in a blend of terror and delight. The jet boating *pièce de résistance* is the high-speed, 360-degree 'Hamilton Turn', in which the pilot again powers the boat at top speed down a flat stretch of water, then suddenly wrenches the steering violently. The boat arches clear of the water like a hooked fish, pirouettes gamely in the air, then lands back on its belly with a flop.

After a short trip in an overland vehicle, we came to the launch site for the second leg of the Foursome, white-water canoeing. It was around 5 degrees centigrade and we were required to strip and don full wetsuits, crash helmets and life jackets. Then we stepped aboard a helicopter, which whisked us to our starting point. An optional extra, the third leg of the Awesome Foursome, was a bungee jump out of the helicopter. When this was suggested, we all started whistling and looking the other way.

The white-water near Queenstown may not rival the Zambezi River for sheer volume and power, but the Shotover River and its mazy canyons proved trickier than its African counterpart. More to the point, the water was infinitely more frigid.

Bungee jumping was the final stop on the itinerary. Queenstown is the world capital of bungee – that quintessential sport for those feeling the need to manufacture their thrills. In this resort, wherever there's a bridge, there's someone nervously teetered on the edge, ankles tethered to a rubber rope. But you certainly wouldn't catch me doing it. The Gruesome Twosome was enough for me.

After a day of such boisterous activity, tiredness creeps up like a cat burglar and mugs you while you're not looking. But in Queenstown there's so much to do at night that it's not permissible to retire early. Lively *après*-Awesome Foursome activities include revelry at the Red Rock pub, while more sedate nocturnal offerings include the cosy Swiss Iglu, a Swiss chalet-type pub or reasonable facsimile thereof, where piping hot cheese fondues can be washed down with steel-cold schnapps.

On the morning of May 2, I woke up in my room at the Queenstown Holiday Inn and flicked on Sky News. Motor racing was being screened. In my vague semi-conscious state, I realised there was something amiss. There was no action, only a barrage of slow motion replays. A crumpled blue and white car was perched at the side of the track. Nearby, a scrum of medical workers were bent over someone in white fireproofs. They had tense looks on their faces.

I moved closer to the TV. In San Marino, the tiny republic forming an enclave in Italy, the time was 2.17 pm. Ayrton Senna's Williams Renault car had just failed to negotiate the Tamburello corner, the flat-out left-hand curve, just after the pits, at the Imola track that hosts the San Marino Grand Prix. His machine had hit a concrete wall at 260 kilometres per hour. As the television cameras homed in, it appeared that Senna's head was moving a little. A good sign. The emergency medical team were on the scene within seconds. Formula One's specialist surgeon Syd Watkins directed a frantic team of doctors. The cameras, realising the magnitude of the impact, finally withdrew their all-seeing lenses, and the world had a bird's-eye view of a knot of doctors working to save the life of the world's best racing driver.

But things were looking bleak. A steel suspension arm from the snapped-off right front wheel of the Williams had pierced the Brazilian's yellow helmet. Senna was airlifted to hospital but within hours was pronounced clinically dead.

At the previous year's South African Grand Prix, I'd been fortunate enough to meet Ayrton Senna. He was just wandering through the media area above the pits in shorts and a McLaren polo-shirt. He was relaxed and stopped to joke with James Hunt, the former champion and commentator who was also to die shortly afterwards. When Hunt moved on, I managed to chat with the legendary Brazilian for a few minutes. He seemed content shooting the breeze with a local journalist.

The South African Grand Prix was the first race of the 1993 season, and Senna had arrived late. He said he could have done with another two or three months without driving. When asked how he maintained motivation each new season, Senna said, 'I just try and do the best I can. If I can keep up my performance level, the results will come as a consequence. I've had a good long break, I'm in good health and it's time to go again. Hopefully, I can get to the level I like to be at as quickly as the last two years.'

Regarding the McLaren team's decision to use the previous season's cars, Senna hinted at disappointment.

'We all would like the best cars and best equipment available at all times. I think perhaps sometimes in the past I'd express my feelings stronger than today. But that counts in my favour now. I've won three championships and worked with the same team for the last four years. If it's not possible to have the new car, then it's not possible. We'll have to wait. The championship is about 16 races. You need reliability as well as a quick car.'

Even in such a brief chat, it was obvious that Ayrton Senna was not only a superb racing driver but also a deep-thinking, fiercely driven human being.

Now he was dead. I remembered our brief meeting as I lay in the dark of the Queenstown hotel room. The first smudges of dawn were beginning to reveal the beautiful outline of the far-off mountain and the deep blue Lake Wakatipu at its lower slopes. When someone dies doing the thing he loved most, and was so masterful at, it shakes the rest of us mere mortals.

Sports journalism. News journalism. It didn't seem to matter which type of reporting I was doing, the early months of 1994 were tragically laced with death.

CANADA
UNITED STATES OF AMERICA
New York
Washington DC
Atlanta
Miami
North Atlantic Ocean
MEXICO
North Pacific Ocean
Caribbean Sea

CHAPTER FOUR

Super Bowl? Try Hyperbole

THE SAN FRANCISCO 49ers' dressing room, way down in the bowels of the Joe Robbie Stadium, is in disarray. The orange-and-turquoise-walled chambers are littered with abandoned red-and-gold football helmets, spent Gatorade bottles and discarded shoulder pads. Champagne is being fizzed, popped and sprayed down the backs of unsuspecting players. Some revelling athletes pour this sticky liquid into their sweaty helmets and swig heartily. Bear hugs are exchanged and palms slapped in a orgy of high-fives. Exultant phrases include 'Goddamn awesome, man'.

Don't ever make the mistake of thinking American football players are only hefty because of their padding. These gridiron gladiators are hardly coddled wimps only worthy of looking Kobus Wiese in the Adam's apple. They are of World Wrestling Federation dimensions.

I can vouch for this personally because most of the 49ers who are taking turns hoisting the gleaming silver Vince Lombardi trophy are wearing no clothes. Three triumphant San Franciscans are conducting interviews with female reporters in a jostling throng to my left. Not one of these players wears a stitch. They stand, hands on hips, while the journalists thrust mikes under their mouths, or else they carry on towelling themselves in a far from self-conscious manner. There is scant awkwardness, few inhibitions. At a temporary television studio rigged up in the corner of the dressing room, each 49er is being summoned to tell America his personal angle on the Super Bowl triumph. Some players also strut to the camera naked, causing the cameraman to take care with his framing in case he beams disturbing images into Middle America's living rooms.

I feel a nudge in my back while leaning forward to hear Jerry Rice critiquing his game-clinching touchdowns. San Francisco left-tackle Frank Pollack, 6 feet 5 inches and 285 pounds, elbows me out of the way, camcorder clamped to his left eye. He's videoing the chaotic victory scenes and issuing instructions that no one is heeding. 'Jerry, we gotta capture the moment, come on, man,' he chunters.

Rice is a wide receiver, the equivalent of a rugby wing. He has hands safe as velcro and the speed of a cheetah. At the moment, he's in tears. He scored three touchdowns tonight, and together with quarterback Steve Young (think of the flyhalf) has ensured that the 49ers are the first team ever to win five Super Bowl titles. Apparently Rice was in tears before the game. During the game too. In the locker room, his tears mingle with the black 'war paint' daubed beneath his eyes, like smudged mascara on a *Priscilla, Queen of the Desert* cast member.

Ken Norton Jnr., son of the Seventies boxer with the sledgehammer punch, is possibly the most elated of the entire 49ers squad. He has just become the first footballer to win three consecutive Super Bowls. Norton Jnr. played linebacker for the winning Dallas Cowboys the previous two years. Earlier in the season, he signed a five-year, $8-million contract with the 49ers. This was a somewhat different salary from the $565 000 minimum wage he received with Dallas. When asked why he had joined the 49ers, Norton had said, unsurprisingly, 'Like 10 or 15 years from now, you have your kids asking, "Well, why can't you afford to send me to college, Dad?", and I would have had to say, "Well, I decided to play for the Cowboys instead of San Francisco."'

Each player's locker space has an individual name-tag and ample room for him to hang his smart threads. Deion Sanders, the 49ers cornerback, is known as the snappiest dresser on the San Francisco roster. An unsullied silk suit and a complicated leather jacket hang creaseless in his locker. His much-written-about jewellery is not to be seen, however. Sanders emerges from the shower cubicles and wedges his way past the masses. He unsheaths a blow-drier and begins working on his hair. Dressing will take time.

By appearing in tonight's Super Bowl, Sanders has become the only athlete to have won a Super Bowl ring and played in baseball's World Series. He turned out for the losing Atlanta Braves baseball team in 1992. When he still played football for the Atlanta Falcons, he once appeared for both the Falcons and the Braves on the same day, arriving at the baseball diamond by helicopter. Sanders must have enjoyed that. He is fond of the spotlight. In the lead-up to the Super Bowl, newspapers reported daily on the Sanders fashion and jewellery choices, as well as his modes of transport. He usually arrives at games in limousines, but here in Miami he chose to tool around town in a $240 000 black Lamborghini, which he said was 'a present from me to me'.

The San Francisco 49ers' beaming owner, Eddie de Bartolo, walks into the locker room. He's a short man. He wears a smart suit and tie, and has a humble manner. De Bartolo bought 90 per cent of the 49ers back in 1977, and was only 31 when he took over the franchise. The players drench him in bubbly and hoist him up on to their shoulders in seconds, bouncing him like a fire survivor on a safety blanket.

Just as you don't need to know all the 'Dark Side of the Moon' lyrics to appreciate Pink Floyd, nor do you need to be steeped in American football to enjoy a Super Bowl. I'm a case in point. I've been to two gridiron games in my life. Both rank among my greatest sporting memories. But don't ask me to start quoting rushing records or the percentage of passes completed. The nuances and the statistics are irrelevant. The gilt-edged occasion more than suffices. Many Americans would lop off their own arms to go to a Super Bowl. Come the end of January each year tickets to the big game are as elusive as honest politicians. Luckily, NFL officials happily endorse the press applications of foreign journalists. They are only too keen for us aliens to publicise their funny game.

The Joe Robbie Stadium in Miami was the venue for the 1995 Super Bowl between the San Francisco 49ers and the underdog San Diego Chargers. There could hardly have been a better venue for the all-Californian final. The beach and the art deco district of South Beach allowed the players to think they were in Santa Monica, weaving between bikinied rollerbladers and tanned retirees exercising their poodles.

Most of the more serious Super Bowl action took place over the MacArthur Parkway in downtown Miami. For instance, adjacent to the Joe Robbie Stadium was a football theme park called the NFL Experience, which celebrated the seventy-fifth anniversary of the National Football League. It was like Disney World for football freaks. Here the fan became the star – people young and old were queuing to throw footballs at sensor-driven targets, kick footballs through uprights, or take a hand-off and leap into the end zone over a line of inflatable players. The NFL Experience covered 182 000 square metres, the equivalent of 15 football fields. There were autograph signing appearances from the football stars; a broadcast booth was available for anyone wanting to announce their own favourite NFL moment; there were cinematic presentations of the greatest moments and players in NFL history and a guide to the landmarks of the game through time.

American sports stars take their community work seriously. One booth at the NFL Experience was devoted to a scheme known as FACT – short for Football and Academics a Championship Team. This scheme featured football trading cards on which anti-drug, pro-education messages were printed for fourth-grade schoolchildren. Stellar names like Dan Marino of the Miami Dolphins and Emmitt Smith of the Dallas Cowboys made presentations one afternoon on the benefits of staying in school and steering clear of gangs and narcotics. Smith, who is one of the NFL's best-paid players, had just graduated from college, having been determined to carry on studying through correspondence to please both himself and his mother. This was no small feat of discipline for someone who earns more in a day than most people make in a year. Particularly in an environment that encourages lavish, feet-up lifestyles. Smith relayed his story to the gathered press and to the kids. Schools across the country had been challenged to come up with a song that best suited the FACT sentiments. The winning school was from Washington and they performed their rap number with the exuberant confidence that characterises Americans.

Anyone who doubts the power that athletes have as role models for children just had to look in the awe-struck eyes of those eight-year-olds in Miami when Emmitt Smith told them 'staying in school is cool'. In latter-day South Africa, there's surely scope for our top sportsmen to contribute in similar ways. After the FACT speeches, I asked Dan Marino for a message for the kids of South Africa. He looked at me with an air that suggested he didn't have a clue where South Africa was, let alone why one of its citizens had been allowed into the Super Bowl. To his credit, though, he then launched into something along the lines of 'The message is the same to kids everywhere in the world, even up and coming countries like Africa.'

Marino is the veteran Miami Dolphins quarterback who is still spiralling footballs toward the end zone in the hope of one day reaching a Super Bowl. He also owns a nightclub in Miami's Coconut Grove district. This area was aswim with revelry during Super Bowl week, as was the entire length of South Beach's Ocean Drive. One place that might have considered offering me and the friend I was with the pub equivalent of frequent flyer miles was the Howl at the Moon Saloon. This Coconut Grove bar featured two hugely talented pianists duelling with each other under the strobe lights. One would play a few bars from a song and the other would then have to respond and embroider on the ditty. It was like watching an ivory-tinkling version of the mandolin scene from *Deliverance*, and made for many a raucous evening of slurred singalongs.

Partying is serious business during Super Bowl week. These seven days are not for the lily-livered. Most of the big game sponsors host a massive bash, and the media is, of course, more than welcome. Evenings are spent swanning from one open bar to the next in the courtesy shuttle buses. On the Friday before the game, there was also a glittery lunch in honour of the international press. Buses picked us up from our hotels around noon and whisked us down to the harbour, where we boarded the *Caribbean Princess* ocean liner. This multi-storeyed vessel was as spangled as Broadway by night and housed mirror-walled casinos and vast dining saloons. It tootled round the bay decanting vast loads of food on to our plates, while Japanese mis-greeted Germans, the British ignored the French, and Italians hollered at the waiters for more Parmesan on the pasta.

The American Football Super Bowl is, simply, the ultimate sporting spectacle. It's like watching a combination of soccer's World Cup Final and the Oscars on Guy Fawkes night. The game might not have packed the emotional punch of watching one's country in a rugby Test match or a one-day cricket international, but for me this made it better. I could drink in the spectacle from a neutral stance, and not fret about whether the ref was biased.

At the 75 000-capacity Joe Robbie Stadium four hours before kick-off, Super Bowl tickets with a face value of $200 were changing hands for anything up to $1 200. Hundreds of fans paraded desperate signs for tickets. One Brad K. Bergoine used the occasion to punt for a job. His sign read: 'Wanted. Marketing position with a winning team. Honk if you want a CV.' His gamble paid off. He told me he'd been offered two positions on the spot. South African school-leavers, take note.

More orthodox forms of gambling are big business during Super Bowl week. A $4-billion flutter to be exact. One Las Vegas punter put $2,4 million on San Francisco to win, more than double the previous record bet for an American sports event. At 8–1 odds he was to get his money back, plus $300 000.

Such frivolous treatment of cash wouldn't have pleased at least one man in the Joe Robbie Stadium parking lot. An earnest, bearded fellow in thick glasses wore a 'Repent or Burn' sandwich board and bellowed megaphone messages at the gathering crowds such as, 'Super Bowl is an insignificant diversion. A small fry. Turn to God for truth and salvation.' One hawker had a stall nearby selling T-shirts with retaliatory slogans; for example, 'Christ is coming ... look busy'.

The stadium car park was a sea of boisterous tailgate parties. These manic pre-game festivals of beer make the celebrations at King's Park after a Natal rugby game look funereal. One Winnebago full of Chargers fans had made a leisurely, boozy, 48-hour voyage from San Diego. It showed. Window salesman Dave Myers and a car full of his closest friends had journeyed down from Orlando and paid to tailgate in the parking lot. They had no tickets for the game and didn't plan to buy any. They came instead to soak up the atmosphere and then head off elsewhere to watch the game on TV. 'We want to get the Super Bowl experience. We want to see the Chargers fans with the lightning bolts on their heads and their painted faces. You don't need tickets to tailgate. This is our way of being part of it,' explained Myers.

Chargers fans who didn't make the trip to Miami also had a chance to be part of the special Super Bowl atmosphere. San Diego's Jack Murphy Stadium had opened its gates on the big day, and 58 000 fans turned up to party and watch the game on a giant video screen. That same morning, Uruguay's national soccer team had arrived in San Diego for an exhibition match against Mexico. The match promoter bussed the team from the airport to their practice ground next to the Murphy Stadium. He kidded the non-plussed South Americans that 58 000 people had turned up to watch them train.

The 2 847 accredited Super Bowl journalists were housed in the stadium's massive press enclosure. We each received a commemorative seat cover filled with various giveaway gizmos – CD-ROM NFL games, a miniature radio with earplugs to tune into the game, a dinner box including sandwiches, fruit and juices, and a promotional Breathe Right nasal strip, which was said to widen the nasal passages and thus allow more oxygen intake for athletes. In a year or so these gimmicks were to become popular with sportsmen such as Francois Pienaar and Liverpool's Robbie Fowler. Quite how these things were to aid us reporters, I'm still trying to figure out.

On the leaf-green Astroturf way down below, things began to happen. As kick-off neared, I tried to make a note of the visual feast before me that America's best choreographers had prepared for our entertainment. There were fireworks and there was smoke. There were men 3,5 metres tall with bones hanging on their chests. There was a carnival-style flamingo on stilts. A yacht made of humans moved across the field. Some 300 little girls arranged themselves in the shape of Florida, after which they scattered in all directions, assuming the shape of the San Diego Chargers offence. There were Ninja warriors. There were monks in brown robes. There were green laser beams criss-crossing the still Miami night. Three blimps, fifteen banner-towing small planes, five hot air balloons and twenty-two helicopters clogged the airspace above the Joe

Robbie Stadium. And a quartet of fighter planes passed overhead at the split second that anthem-singer Kathie-Lee Gifford reached the uppermost note of 'The Star-spangled Banner', their thundering unison almost drowning out the stadium announcer's roar of 'Are you ready for some football?'.

During the game, the cute giveaway radio in the press pack came in handy for the gentleman behind me. He was a generously girthed fellow, cut roughly from the same mould as the late John Candy. He had a mate with him called Stevie. It appeared that the Candyesque figure was a sports talk show host from Kansas or Missouri or North Dakota or some other rural outpost. He listened to the game on his little freebie radio and kept up a running commentary on the match for the full four-and-a-half hours.

'There goes Jerry, Stevie,' he bellowed from the kick-off, as the 49ers wide receiver took a Steve Young pass and scythed down the middle of the field to score.

'Raymond from Hoochawalla's gonna love that one, Stevie,' roared the stout gent, as Rice scored again midway through the first quarter. He was obviously missing his listeners.

Interval entertainment at the first Super Bowl back in 1968 came courtesy of the University of Arizona marching band. You might say the half-time shows are a little more involved these days. In 1993, Michael Jackson virtually delivered an entire concert, complete with the usual rhinestone gloves, smoke and lasers. In Miami, Disney produced a 15-minute action adventure entitled *Indiana Jones Adventure: Temple of the Forbidden Eye*.

Jaded Super Bowl veterans complained that the half-time show, and even the new TV commercials, were better than the game itself. In fact, most observers agreed the contest was one of the dullest in history, a mismatch between one of the greatest attacking sides of all time and a team that had sneaked its way into America's sporting showcase. Nevertheless, Super Bowl XXIX had a special significance for San Francisco's Steve Young. For years he'd lived in the shadow of legendary 49er quarterback Joe Montana. By throwing six touchdown passes, a Super Bowl record, and being voted the game's Most Valuable Player, Young went a long way towards exorcising the Montana ghost. A record 75 points were scored in the game, which ended 49–26 to San Francisco. Young had even managed to get in for a late touchdown himself to seal the Chargers' fate.

'They're history now, Stevie,' yodelled the Candy lookalike. 'I can't wait to hear from Old Ted next week.'

The day after Super Bowl, I rented a van and nosed north toward Atlanta with a friend who was in the States on business. Driving in America requires fleetness of mind, especially for those of us accustomed to using the left-hand side of the road, since instinct impels you to look the wrong way at intersections. As a pedestrian it's even more risky. I've lost track of the times I've stepped into American roads after looking vainly for traffic, only to be almost sideswiped by a blindside Mack truck, whose driver then treats you to a receding blast from his mournful horn.

Atlanta is home to the baseball Braves, the footballing Falcons and the basketball Hawks. We went to the local Omni basketball stadium twice over the next few days to see two of the most diverse personalities in American sport.

In the first match, the Hawks took on the Golden State Warriors. Again, the marketing hype that permeates American sport was in evidence. A massive red and fluffy radio-controlled Hawk buzzed the crowds in the stadium, dropping free meal vouchers from McDonald's to the clamouring kids. During the breaks, Dwight Anheusser and his frisbee-catching golden retrievers enthralled the crowd.

Sport and business strut hand-in-hand in the USA. Not for nothing are American sports teams called franchises. Athletic ability is merely the foundation on which to build elaborate marketing plans and tinselled promotion schemes. The Golden State Warriors team featured a player who had himself become highly marketable in the best All-American tradition, although the manner in which he had reached the money-soaked National Basketball Association was far from conventional.

Manute Bol was born in Sudan. He is a member of the Dinka tribe. He is 7 feet 6 and ¾ inches tall and his legs account for nearly 5 feet of his body length. Bol is the tallest player in the history of the NBA. He can stand beneath a basketball goal and grab both sides of the backboard at the same time. He is literally head, shoulders and half a torso above the opposition.

Bol's journey from nomadic tribesman to chicken-endorsing basketball superstar is an inspiration to anyone harbouring sporting ambitions in supposedly obscure nations. In his brilliant book *Africa: Dispatches from a Fragile Continent*, *Washington Post* journalist Blaine Harden tells the tale of how Bol was unearthed, if such a word can apply to a being of such towering physical stature.

One of Bol's cousins played on the Sudanese national basketball team. This athlete had grown up with Manute and reckoned anyone that tall surely had a future in hoops. He thus brought Bol from the parched desert wastelands to Khartoum, the Sudanese capital. This transition was fraught with obstacles. Many of the people in Khartoum received Bol like a circus act. He didn't like being stared at, and he used his fists and his feet to shoo away the onlookers. But Bol's height had its advantages too. He was allowed to eat at his cousin's friend's restaurant for free because he attracted customers who gawked at him during their meals.

During early basketball sessions with his cousin, Bol proved hopeless. The first time he tried to dunk the ball in the basket, he ripped a tooth out on the net. His grip on the ball was shaky. That's because three fingers on his right hand are clawed – a disability inherited from his Dinka family. He also couldn't shoot, couldn't jump, couldn't push. But Bol had an acute sense of timing when it came to blocking the ball.

He persevered at this strange game. His freak height was sufficient to stimulate interest among American coaches. In 1983 he won a scholarship, sight unseen, to New Jersey. Bol couldn't read and write, however, the minimum requirements for earning and retaining a scholarship. His short stays at a number of colleges proved academically fruitless. Yet in 1985 Bol was drafted by the Washington Bullets in the professional NBA. Some people in the game sniggered. According to Harden, one coach predicted Bol would break like a grasshopper, 'an arm here, a leg there'. As it turned out, the African ended up the top blocker in the League, with the second highest total in history. His role in the team was simple. To get in the way of the opposition's more talented players. Bol's all-round skills were virtually negligible, but he had the canny knack of making crucial interceptions. Soon Manute Bol became known as the 'Sudan of Swat'.

With on-court success came the endorsements. Bol was chosen to represent a fried chicken company. A life-sized poster stood tall and proud in a thousand stores nationwide. The Manute Bol Chicken Pack was dreamed up by the marketing gurus. It contained 'nothing but legs', and proved a big winner.

Bol was traded to the Golden State Warriors in 1988 and the following season again led the NBA in the number of shots blocked. That evening I was in Atlanta, Bol showed his extraordinary capacity to read the play and make timely interventions. Until he lost his balance and fell awkwardly. He met the floor almost in slow motion, like a giraffe spreading its legs at a water hole. It was the end of the game for Sudan's most famous export.

Two evenings later the Hawks hosted the San Antonio Spurs and I had another chance to view a singular NBA character. Though Dennis Rodman was still a relatively traditional basketball player in those days.

This was before he moved to the Chicago Bulls and began to head-butt referees, dress in women's clothing, hang out in gay bars and dye his hair in shades of radioactive green or lipstick pink. Before he kneed a cameraman in the groin, and was thus suspended from the league. Before he announced Madonna among his pile of sexual conquests. (The Rodman verdict on the Evita gal's bedroom prowess: 'She's no acrobat, but then she ain't no dead fish either.')

Born and raised in a tough part of Dallas, Rodman's father, the aptly named Philander, was absent from young Dennis's life. Rodman drifted from school to the streets and eventually landed up working as a janitor at Dallas–Fort Worth airport. Until he was arrested for stealing watches.

He was always good at shooting hoops, however, and in 1986 joined the Detroit Pistons, whom he helped to back-to-back NBA championships in 1989 and 1990. Rodman began displaying his eccentricities while still with this club. He started missing practices, seeing shrinks and telling anyone who cared to listen how much he wanted to leave the club. He also added a dozen tattoos to his frame, repeatedly took off his shoes in mid-game and shaved slogans into his increasingly multi-coloured scalp.

Rodman was once found by police in a nightclub parking lot. It was 5 am, and the player was dozing in his truck with a loaded deer rifle under the front seat. This incident formed the opening paragraph of Rodman's autobiography, *Bad as I Wanna Be*, the cover of which featured Rodman naked astride a Harley-Davidson. He began: 'On an April night in 1993, I sat in the cab of my pick-up truck with a rifle in my lap, deciding whether to kill myself.'

Rodman might be famous for his wild mood swings, but he is also known for his generosity. In Detroit he would sometimes drive through the streets of the toughest neighbourhoods, doling out money to vagrants. Sometimes he'd take them home to clean, feed and send them off in good spirits. Once he struck up a conversation with a homeless man, and then emptied his pockets to him, handing over more than $1 000. 'So many people need so much, I don't need possessions,' he reasoned.

Similar sentiments were expressed when Rodman was found after he went missing from the Pistons for a month. The frantic Pistons' player–director was only just short of issuing a picture of him on milk cartons when the player was discovered in Las Vegas. In a matter of days shooting craps, he'd lost $35 000. The reason? 'I hate money. I went to Las Vegas to lose. So I could feel normal.'

Rodman was a picture of normality that night in Atlanta. The only thing that distinguished him from his peers was his outstanding rebounding ability (the rebounder tries to intercept opponents' passes, guard the hoop and generally throw his weight around). Rodman tops the rebounding league almost every season, and his skill in this department was why he was bought to partner Michael Jordan and company at the Chicago Bulls.

After the match, Rodman announced his end-of-season activities that year. He would be hosting a TV show called *Bad to the Bone* in which he was to tour the world's tattoo parlours and red-light districts.

And South African rugby coaches get in a dither trying to harness James Small?

Domestic jet travel in the United States is tolerable for one reason and one reason only. Telephones. Most American carriers offer phones that spring forth from the seat in front of you. There's nothing that makes you feel more in touch with the cutting edge of technology than being connected while cruising at 10 000 metres. Even better is when the person you're calling asks where you are.

'Well, right now I'd say we're over-flying Washington. Yep, I can see the Potomac River down there, and there's the Lincoln Memorial. Hello, looks like they're hoovering the carpets in the White House.'

The call I made *en route* from Atlanta was to the press officer of the New York Rangers, the Big Apple's premier ice hockey team. I was in New York for a day or so to wind up the Super Bowl sojourn, and a discarded newspaper on the Delta Airlines flight had confirmed that the Rangers were up against the Tampa Bay Lightning that evening. The game was to be held at one of sport's true Meccas: Madison Square Garden. As the Delta flight hit an air pocket and bucked like a rodeo rider, the press officer said no problem, tickets would be waiting at the gate that night.

The Garden is, of course, the venue that has seen some of the world's greatest boxing bouts. The press room is a fine oak-panelled sanctuary with walls adorned with posters billing some of the fights of the century. Muhammad Ali's feature prominently. The venue is also home to basketball's New York Knicks. The ice hockey and basketball seasons run almost concurrently. One night the floor will be thick-groomed ice, the next it will be buffed and polished pine for the squeaking size-12 sneakers of some of the world's best-paid prima donnas.

The game between the Rangers and the Lightning failed to attract a full house. The Rangers were defending Stanley Cup champions, but had started the new season shakily. A new potential messiah, the aptly named Mark Messier, had failed to be the inspirational signing the city had hoped for, and the Rangers were languishing around the middle of their division. Around me in the bleachers I heard the curt comments of a typically feisty New York crowd. Like sports fans in many big cities, the Rangers faithful were proving fickle when the times got tough. Just as Gauteng Lions rugby fans desert a non-winning team, the Rangers played to derisive cheers. The cracks got more vicious when the Lightning took a 2–0 lead. Rangers eventually hauled back the two goals but had to settle for a draw. For a home game it wasn't good enough. The crowd filtered into the cold and misty New York avenues muttering darkly.

Samuel Pepys once spoke of being tired of life should one ever tire of London. In the twilight years of the twentieth century, this adage has surely transferred across the Atlantic to apply to New York City. No city in the world stimulates, excites and inspires like New York. Stand in one of the great north–south avenues that plough through the cigar-shaped island of Manhattan and look up. The sight is vertigo-inspiring. Skyscrapers appear to topple as the wintry sunrays fight down through the concrete canyons to reach the bustling, breathing streets below.

I first visited the city in the late Eighties when these streets were dangerous and filthy, panhandlers loomed from dark corners demanding dollars and one needed alert 360-degree vision on the subways. By 1995, things had changed. New York had cleaned up its act. The graffiti had been whitewashed from the subway stations. Police blitzes on high-crime areas like Times Square had succeeded to the extent that, even after a late-night Broadway show, the threatening atmosphere that many people associate with New York was absent. A newspaper survey showed that the city no longer figured among the 25 murder capitals of the United States. New Yorkers, often portrayed as prickly and self-obsessed, were putting on a smile for the world.

Nowhere was the sprucing more evident than in the famous yellow taxi cabs. A whole bunch of strict regulations now welcomed taxi passengers. Drivers, whether they hailed from Lagos, Lahore or Las Vegas, must be able to speak English. On my first time in New York, it had been easier to find someone who could pinpoint South Africa on a map than it had been to find a cabbie who spoke the native language. I remember once asking a cab driver to take me to Central Park. He didn't know where or what this odd place was. Another driver once took a couple of us to Bleecker Street in Greenwich Village late, late one night. He congratulated us on being South African. This was a time when congratulations for being a white South African were rare and worthy of suspicion. 'You guys know what to do with those f…ing blacks down there,' said the cabbie. 'That's what they should be doing here, man. I tell you, one of them tries to get in my cab…' He patted his jacket pocket, which concealed an ominous bulge. We hastily melted into crowds of Bleecker Street revellers and dope peddlers, and later decided to walk the 15 blocks home.

These days, New York taxis are less likely to have a homicidal bigot behind the wheel. These vehicles are also fast and cheap. While the subway may be even more economical, taxis provide a series of New York vistas that are unavailable on other modes of transport. You can hurtle 60 city blocks in a few minutes late at night, criss-crossing the vibrant, distinctly separate communities that make up Manhattan. Try doing that in the cramped, twisted streets of London or Paris. It's also impossible to get lost in the grid of New York's streets. And what's more, taxi travel lets you see those Manhattan manholes belching steam just like in the movies.

On my last morning in the city, as a light, feathery coat of snow began covering the coloured neon of Times Square, I took a cab to the corner of Twelfth Avenue and West Thirty-first Street. Sometimes you need a fresh perspective to fully appreciate a city's charms. And there's no better way of taking an alternative look at the maze of New York than by enjoying a helicopter flip over this city of skyscrapers. Such a trip is particularly useful for first-time visitors. When the chopper starts spiralling skywards, the imposing concrete and glass edifices that tower above while you tramp the avenues begin to look like blocks of Lego, and the city's vast layout swiftly sheds any menace.

Liberty Helicopter Tours is one of a handful of companies offering unforgettable sky-views of New York, and they'd agreed to give me a flip in exchange for an article. It was a superb swop. The chopper ride was fully narrated and the six-seater Eurocopter jet helicopter was snugly air conditioned, a must for frigid February mornings.

As the chopper rose above the Hudson River and bore south, the first discernible sight was the twin towers of the World Trade Center. The pilot pointed out the financial district and the world's largest stock exchange. To survive among the pinstriped Gordon Gekko-types of Wall Street, they have a saying round these parts: 'You gotta fake it till you make it.' The tour included all the city boroughs, the Chrysler building, Times Square, New York harbour, the East River, the Yankee Stadium and the city's much sung-about bridges. Then, a squirt of jet power and suddenly the spiked headdress of Lady Liberty loomed so close I could almost blow her torch out. Heading uptown, we made eye contact with the Empire State Building's 30-storey-high antenna. The sharp point of its radio mast looked capable of piercing the chopper's bulbous dome and sending us reeling into the snow-coated, dinky-toy traffic below. I thought of James and the Giant Peach.

My most abiding memory of the flip was of hovering over Central Park, the city's 51-block retreat among the concrete. The thickening carpet of snow had turned the city oasis into a winter wonderland. Benches looked like elaborate ice sculptures. Treetops resembled lace doilies. Some city dwellers had strapped on skis and were gliding easily through the park, leaving thin trails in the snow behind them. Soft early morning light glinted from the park's iced-over reservoirs.

It felt good to be alive. Privileged to be eavesdropping on the world's greatest city from this seat among the gods.

Like Frank Sinatra advised, start spreading the news…

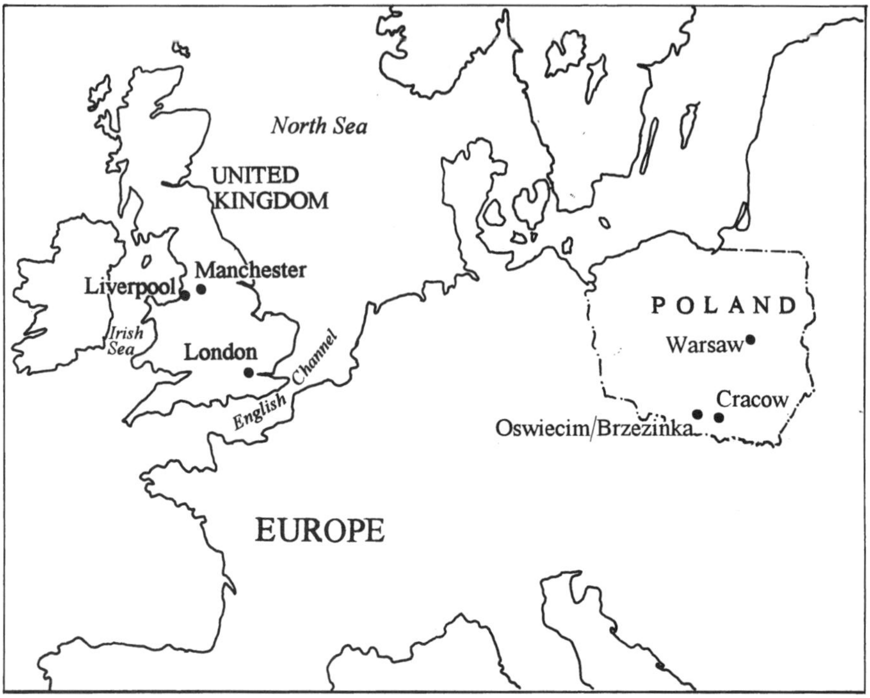
North Sea
UNITED KINGDOM
Manchester
Liverpool
Irish Sea
London
English Channel
POLAND
Warsaw
Cracow
Oswiecim/Brzezinka
EUROPE

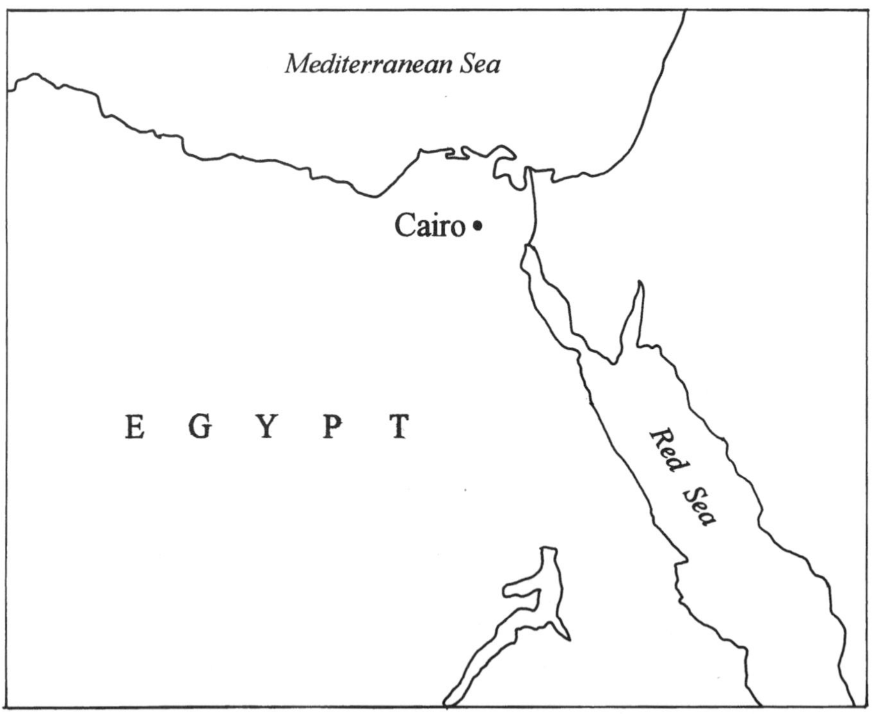
Mediterranean Sea
Cairo
E G Y P T
Red Sea

CHAPTER FIVE

Desperately Seeking Barbie

THE 1996 FA CUP FINAL promised to be a sumptuous affair at which English football buffs could feast like hogs at a trough. Arguably the finest two teams in the land had survived the minefield of the early rounds and would meet in the climax of what many regard as the greatest knockout tournament in the world.

In the red corner, Manchester United, reigning League champions and FA Cup holders. Brimming with abrasive skill in the form of Eric Cantona; youthful vigour via David Beckham and the Neville brothers; and feistiness from Peter Schmeichel, whose greatest weapon after his talent for shot-stopping is his ability to bully his defence into line by yelling abuse at them.

In the, well, in the red corner too, but, for the purposes of this tie, in the green-and-white-squares corner, Liverpool. John Barnes silky in midfield; Steve McManaman weaving deft patterns down the flanks; Robbie Fowler a wired, explosive predator in front of the goal. The last time these two giants of the English game had met in the Final was back in 1977, when United won 2–1. A footballing banquet worthy of the gods lay in store 19 years later.

To get to England I'd taken the scenic route. EgyptAir was offering bargain flights from Johannesburg to Heathrow via Cairo. How cut-price? The stewardesses lined up at the door of the aircraft offering passengers either a dinky bottle of red wine or a box of chocolates. We had to make a choice.

The otherwise liquorless flight touched down in Cairo at 6 am and, as our connection to London only left later that afternoon, we were taken on a swift tour of the Egyptian capital. We were whisked off through a sprawl of awakening suburbs to the doors of the opulent Hilton Hotel, through its carpeted hallways to the back of the building where the Nile awaited us. A trip down the waterway that is the lifeblood of this city beckoned.

Our guide wandered over to a boat tethered to the shore and aimed a kick at a pile of rags. The lump metamorphosed into a slumbering boatman, who rubbed the sleep from his eyes and reluctantly fired up the outboard motor. The Nile was huge, grouchy and brooding, like André Markgraaff jotting notes on the touchline. Discarded petrol containers and coloured plastic bags dotted the water. We puttered past a sign saying 'The Nile, a Clean River in a Clean City'. Dozing our way down river, we finally managed to shake off the effects of the flight just as the boat returned us to the Hilton. From there we piled into a minibus for a tour of the pyramids, another bonus thrown in free for flying EgyptAir. These towering relics are a short drive from the city centre and loom suddenly beyond the palm trees and the high-rise buildings – vivid history squatting cheek by jowl with urban disorder.

The pyramids are home to a hardened bunch of hagglers whose life's work is to extract Egyptian pounds from tourists in any manner possible by offering camel rides, mini metal pyramids, matchstick Nile feluccas, blown-glass camels and any manner of sordid souvenir. One extravagantly robed gent wanted to photograph me aboard a camel. He was as persistent as athlete's foot and said I could get on the braying, spit-speckled beast for free. I eventually agreed, and nimbly side-stepped his pricy offer of snapping the moment with his Instamatic by saying he could use my camera instead. When I disembarked, he rubbed his thumb and forefinger together.

'I thought you said it was free,' I said.

'The camel is for free. The cost for me clicking your camera is ten pounds.'

Back at the airport in time to catch our connection to London, I was in the middle of buying a newspaper at the kiosk when the entire concourse suddenly dropped to its knees for ten minutes. I had no choice but to wait, palm outstretched for change, while the noon Islamic prayers were completed.

Arriving in darkened, bone-chilling London around happy hour, the city was awash with brawny, tattooed football fans hoovering beer ahead of the following day's big match. I met up at the hotel bar with a friend and travel agent who was organising a Cup Final sortie for a group of 40 clients. I'll call him Jethro.

Drama was hovering. Many sports tour operators exist perilously, often through no fault of their own. Many of the tickets to top sports events are sold through only a few favoured travel agencies. This means that the rest of the operators can only come across tickets in one of two ways – they can repurchase tickets from authorised dealers, or they can take their chances on the black market.

Jethro was well versed and streetwise in the hazardous business of cadging tickets off touts, though this time he'd managed to acquire 20 of his required allotment of tickets through official channels. So far so good. He'd also received written confirmation from a tout with whom he'd done deals before that once Jethro arrived in London, the other 20 tickets would be awaiting him. The settled rate had been £200 per ticket, and this sum had been agreed in writing by fax.

That afternoon, the tout had contacted Jethro and confirmed that the tickets were indeed safely nestled in his blazer pocket. There was just one thing. The asking price was now £400. When Jethro spluttered into the mouthpiece that they had agreed on £200 per ticket, the tout retorted with a succinct 'Take it or leave it, guvnor'.

Such are the vagaries of dealing with the black market. I glanced around at our South African-accented drinking companions. A father with his teenage son sat opposite me. The boy was decked out in Liverpool beanie hat, Liverpool scarf, Liverpool replica shirt and Liverpool tracksuit. He clutched a copy of *Shoot* magazine, which trumpeted a giant-sized poster of Liverpool's Jamie Redknapp as its centre spread. This was clearly a once in a lifetime chance for father and son to watch their long-distance heroes at the home of football. At the bar several other South Africans animatedly discussed the upcoming game. Each and every client had paid a minor fortune for the trip. And now it appeared there'd be less than the necessary number of tickets.

Jethro hastily agreed to meet and negotiate with the tout at Waterloo train station, where the black marketeer was disembarking from Bolton. We arrived there before the appointed hour. The train was on time, and plenty of loud, intoxicated football fans spilled on to the platform. But no tout. We waited more than two hours for the last train from the northwest. Still no ticket-bearer.

Trudging back to the hotel, we bumped into some of the South Africans from the tour group revving it up at a pub in Leicester Square. Jethro had told them the match tickets would be handed out that evening. Most wanted to take possession of their precious passes there and then. When they were asked to wait until the next day, there were voluble rumblings of discontent.

It wasn't until 10.30 the following morning that the tout eventually made contact. By this time the desperate edge to Jethro's voice was impossible to disguise. And the tout, of course, had raised his asking price again. This time to £500. There was no option but to take the tickets and worry about the economic battering later. Money and tickets changed hands amid acrimony.

We took a coach to the stadium, winding our way regally through London's north-western suburbs. As we neared the ground, the trickle of soccer fans thickened into a snake of colourfully dressed supporters. Lunch had been arranged for our group at the Greyhound Pub, which was within staggering distance of the famous twin towers of Wembley. Steaming heaps of pie, chips and baked beans were washed down with plentiful flagons of lager. Outside the pub, fans from the two teams steadily congregated. Each abused the other heartily. The United fans were in particularly good voice, having clinched the League title the week before. They reserved their loudest insults for Kevin Keegan, manager of the Newcastle team that United had pipped to the championship. English football may contain more than a sprinkling of hooligans, but many fans are deft linguists who skilfully adapt famous song lyrics into witty, abusive soccer chants. The United faithful had taken the tune of the old 'Daydream Believer' song and put the following words to it:

> Cheer up, Kevin Keegan,
> Oh what can it mean
> For a sad Geordie bastard
> And a shite football team?

Outside Wembley, ticket touts were scarce. This was hardly surprising. The morning newspapers had warned that a batch of forged tickets was in circulation. Anyone holding counterfeits would be denied entry to the ground, whatever the source of these tickets. We strolled up the famous Wembley Way, the concrete promenade that leads to the stadium. Police mounted on horseback separated the Liverpool and United fans at this point, and the supporters were then ushered from this thoroughfare to their seats at partitioned areas of the ground. This slice of sports apartheid was a wise precaution. The relationship between these two groups of fans can be as acrimonious, and occasionally as violent, as an Itchy and Scratchy cartoon.

Neither I nor Jethro had a ticket for the game. I had a vague notion of being able to use my South African journalist credentials to get a press pass for the Final and had written away weeks before the game applying for accreditation. But when I phoned Wembley on arrival in London, they were having none of it. Unlike, for example, the American Super Bowl officials, who actively encourage foreigners to come and publicise their game, the FA Cup Final is a massive, self-marketing event that evidently needs no help from obscure South African magazine editors. I used the tried and trusted journalistic method of emotional blackmail, pleading that I'd raided the savings from an impending liver transplant fund to fly all the way over from Johannesburg to see my team perform before succumbing to the scalpel. Though normally, if Liverpool and Manchester United were playing in my front garden, I'd draw the curtains. There's only one United, and that happens to be Leeds. But the Wembley voice remained as polite and firm and imperturbable as only a British voice of authority can be. The media allocation had been filled. I'd be getting no press pass.

So there we were outside the legendary Wembley stadium, on a bracing, blue-sky FA Cup Final day, and with no means of access. It was like being present at the Last Supper and then being told, sorry, you'll have to make do with McDonald's. With just half an hour to kick off, we'd run out of ideas for scrounging a ticket or two. Jethro spotted a knot of fans dressed in South African rugby jerseys. He wandered over to say hello. In the group was the son of Bafana Bafana coach Clive Barker. He and a bunch of mates had used a dollop of South African ingenuity to ensure they got in to see the match. They'd volunteered to be stewards at football matches back at the start of the season. There was method in their plotting. The reward for standing in the sleet overseeing games in front of a gallery of a few hundred was possible access to the FA Cup Final, where they'd have to usher people to their seats but could then watch the game from the terraces. The group had made their mark in an early season game between Watford and Gillingham. A rowdy fan had invaded the pitch, and one of Barker's mates had pinned him with a rugby tackle of Henry Honiball dimensions. This effort had cemented the South Africans as a core part of the Wembley security operation.

Ten minutes to kick-off. Hardly a soul was left outside the ground. The pub television seemed the likeliest venue from where we'd watch the big game. Finally, in one last circuit of the stadium, we happened upon a shifty tout who unsheathed a single ticket from inside his jacket like a chancer trying to flog stolen watches in the Smal Street Mall. The dog-eared ticket he was offering for £100 was in two pieces. But the halves matched. Jethro, magnanimous fellow that he is, had seen a number of Cup Finals before, so it was decided I'd go in and watch the game while he'd try to ferret another ticket from somewhere. If not, he'd head back to the pub to nurse a sorry beer in front of the telly. I grabbed the ticket and sprinted for the turnstiles. I had a momentary seizure when I remembered the counterfeit scare, but the ticket was valid and I reached my seat just as the teams kicked off.

All my life I've wanted to be among the throngs at Wembley when the crowd launches into its stirring, pre-game rendition of 'Abide With Me'. This hymn has been sung at every FA Cup Final since 1923. When it was replaced in the late Forties by a demonstration from the Coventry Ladies Keep-Fit team, such was the public outcry that it was swiftly restored the following year, and has remained an integral part of the Cup Final pomp and ceremony ever since. I was thus gutted to enter Wembley just as the last soaring notes of 'Abide With Me' fluttered away from the stadium like peace doves released at an Olympic Games opening ceremony.

Wembley is due to undergo a major multi-million-pound facelift over the next year or two, and, in all honesty, renovation is sorely needed. Although the ground is something of a relic as far as stadia worldwide go, the roar that greets the teams at a Cup Final is truly special. The enclosed nature of the ground ensures that this clamour echoes and flows around the terraces like an aural Mexican wave. And, say what you like about their other habits, British soccer supporters know how to back their teams. Being at an FA Cup Final is like being at a rock concert, only the audience does all the singing.

Unfortunately, the game failed to match the acoustics. In truth it was a drab, tense contest with little or no sign of the standard of football that the teams were capable of producing. So often greatly anticipated finals fizzle out into easily forgettable affairs, with the pressure of the occasion squeezing the life out of any semblance of carefree play.

Incredibly, both seats next to me were empty. At half-time a rotund Israeli plonked himself down on the seat to my left. He was scoffing a greasy burger and gobs of mustard dripped down his chin. He sat fiddling with his cell phone, mused through the programme, and then 15 minutes before the end, stood up and left. The seat to my right remained vacant throughout. The Israeli missed the only goal of the game. Eric Cantona, anonymous until the eighty-sixth minute, volleyed home from the edge of the box through a forest of Liverpool players. It was enough to seal an unprecedented double 'Double' for United: FA Cup and League Championships in successive years. Cantona's reward? Being spat on by Liverpool supporters as he walked up to collect the trophy from the Duchess of Kent. Perhaps because of this lady's gracious presence, 'Le King' managed to restrain himself from kungfu-ing the culprit this time.

After the final whistle, we gathered at the Greyhound again. Jethro was in an upbeat mood. He'd safely secured tickets for all members of his group, and none of the tickets had turned out to be forgeries. Another band of South Africans had been less fortunate. At least 15 members of a different touring party had been saddled with counterfeits. All had gained entry to the ground. All had been turned away as they tried to take up their seats. Grown men had wept.

Jethro had another story to tell. He'd wandered back to the Greyhound to watch the match on television. There he discovered a tout with one spare ticket. The game had begun and the tout was keen to offload at any price. He offered it to Jethro for £75. Jethro duly handed over a motley wad of rands, dollars and pounds and jogged the 400 metres back to Wembley. The match was a mere ten minutes old. He passed through the turnstiles and went in search of his seat. Before he could safely sit down, a yellow-vested steward took the ticket and checked it against the list of forgeries. Sure enough, Jethro's ticket was among the tainted. Jethro was taken to the cops and grilled as to the source of this corrupted ticket. Given his experiences at the hands of touts over the past two days, he was only too happy to provide details. The 1996 FA Cup Final was destined not to welcome Jethro Batty.

I had a few days to spare after the Final, and, not particularly wanting to cool my heels further in freezing London, I decided to ring a friend I'd recently met in Johannesburg. Izabela Tomaszewska was a Polish travel agent who'd come to the annual Africa Travel Market at Kyalami two months previously. I'd shown her the sights of Gauteng, such as they are, and she'd performed a particularly memorable early morning dance on the tables at the Long Island Iced Tea Bar in Illovo. When I bleated over the phone that London in May was far too freezing for a South African to endure another five days, she suggested I take the two-hour Lot Airlines flight to Warsaw and spend some time in central Europe.

It became clear that Poland was to be no ordinary travel destination the minute we left Okecie Airport. Izabela had come to meet my plane, and somehow I'd managed to wedge myself and my luggage into her toy-like Fiat 125. She flicked on the stereo and we found ourselves speeding toward downtown Warsaw accompanied by Rolf Harris's version of 'Stairway to Heaven'. And this in the land that gave the world Chopin.

Perhaps the DJ was playing a joke. After all, the Poles' sense of humour, like their capacity for alcohol, is legendary. Given their turbulent history (the flat countryside makes an ideal battlefield, and Poland's neighbours have rarely been slow on the uptake), a sense of humour has been vital for survival. *Contemnir procellas* – 'to defy the storms' – is Warsaw's motto. No wonder. Almost 90 per cent of the city was destroyed during World War II and at least three quarters of the population lost their lives.

There are as many Polish jokes as there are brands of Polish vodka, which is saying something. And the locals' keen eye for amusement appears to have sharpened since the demise of communism. The new stock exchange building, for instance, used to be the Communist Party headquarters. The best Polish joke I encountered during my stay was, however, the hotel prices in central Warsaw. There's a severe shortage of international standard accommodation in town, and those Western chains that have muscled in recently charge rates matched only by Olympic Games host cities.

For example, the Marriott Hotel, opposite the railway station, had rooms starting at $300 and topping $1 000. There was no gushing help from their staff either. Their sniffy logic was: if you're a Westerner, you've obviously got bucks to blow, so don't waste your time and ours pondering the exchange rate. Luckily, Izabela had sorted me out with a room at the formerly state-run Hotel Metropol. The Poles take the phrase 'single room' seriously. The bed was the size of a cupboard door, the balcony was an industrial-sized flowerbox and you couldn't have drowned a labrador in the bath. From the knee-high veranda railing, I could see the trams and dinky Fiats jostling along the wide boulevards of central Warsaw, and to my left squatted the brooding wedding cake structure of the Palace of Culture. This best-known symbol of Warsaw was built during the Stalin era as a stronghold of communism. But its new identity is now as a bustling business centre. In the streets around the palace, rows of informal, bustling stalls – like Bruma Fleamarket but with babushka dolls instead of baggies and beads – completed an atmosphere of burgeoning enterprise.

Poland is like a moulting butterfly: midway between shedding the drab pupa husk of its past and trying out those spectacular, yet unsteady new wings of freedom. Socialism died swiftly in these parts. One minute locals were swopping grim jokes in meat queues, the next they were trekking Stalin's statue to the outskirts of town and planting a Burger King sign atop the Palace of Culture. Well, not just Burger King – and not quite atop the Palace. But the tender buds of capitalism sprouting throughout Warsaw all bear bright neon foliage: Pizza Hut, Reebok, Taco Bell, Adidas, Nike. You can't stroll more than a few blocks without one of these unmistakable icons of Western culture looming in the sky.

I needed to convince myself I was not in just another Western European capital, and a look at some of the apartment blocks the following day gave weight to preconceived notions about ex-Iron Curtain countries. Utilitarian apartment blocks – huge, faceless slabs of grey concrete – blotted out the sun. Washing hung on dingy lines. These human ant-nests truly do their best to adhere to the stereotype of nightmarish Eastern bloc architecture. The sole nod to aesthetics was exteriors smeared with mud-coloured concrete. The first company beating a path to post-communist Poland should have been Plascon.

By contrast, Warsaw's old town square – Rynek Starego Miasta – is bordered by proud, attractive buildings in colourful pastels, reminiscent of Sandton's Village Walk shopping centre. The old town was razed by the Germans during World War II. And I mean razed. In typically thorough Teutonic fashion, the capital was systematically demolished block by block. An edifice or two remained, but generally speaking nothing of consequence in Warsaw is older than Felicia Mabuza-Suttle. After the war, the elders simply dusted down the plans and rebuilt their city from scratch. The old town's narrow cluster of cobbled streets still empties out into the beautiful square, which is home to a number of enticing pavement cafés. One might be in Paris, an impression strengthened by a visit to the Old Town overlook, which, if perhaps not quite the same as standing on Pont Neuf and gazing wistfully down the Seine, docs offer a grand sunset view of the Vistula River.

Preparations for a night on the town in Warsaw involve nothing more complex than a pair of feet. Most worthwhile spots are within walking distance of the city centre, though the streetcar system is easy to use and covers the entire city. There's also a subway that will get you within a block of any Warsaw destination. It's dirt cheap, with a monthly pass costing the same as a two-day London Underground ticket.

On my first evening in Warsaw we found ourselves in the Beer Cave pub, a new, pseudo-Western outdoor venue behind a downtown shopping mall. Here the patrons were being rocked gently by a straggle-haired, three-piece group, which churned out heavily accented covers of Seventies rock songs. It was a balmy spring dusk, perfect for contemplating the sounds of Eric Clapton, even if Old Slow Hand was coming at us in thick East European tones: 'Oh my darleenk, choo look wunnerfool tewnight.'

Warsaw was sublimely mild after the chill of London. I was dressed in shorts and a Bafana Bafana replica soccer shirt. After draining my Zywiec lager, we rose to leave, only to be distracted by a voice coming from a nearby table.

'Hey, South Africa!'

I turned to see the only black face I was to encounter during my visit to Poland. I expected to be greeting Dumile from Diepkloof, on a mission from some job as an ambassadorial clerk in Moscow, but instead shook hands and sat down next to Brian Scott from Georgetown, Guyana. Brian had watched the South African soccer team rampage through the recent African Cup of Nations, and, being a West Indian, was eager to catch up on the latest cricket news. Reluctantly, I broke the news that the Windies had blasted South Africa out of the World Cup. Scott was also a journalist. He'd studied in Georgetown and done a postgraduate course in Poland, where he'd met and married a local girl and was now a household name in the local radio world. He was at the Beer Cave to discuss a proposal to become a TV talk show host. But after my arrival he all but ignored his potential boss, and the pair of us sank Zywiec lagers and chatted cricket long into the night. The TV exec sat nodding vacantly at the pair of us, and making small talk with Izabela, who after a while suggested she entertain the bemused man by replicating her Long Island table dance. In the interests of prolonging Brian Scott's journalistic career, I advised that she remain exactly where she sat.

Cricket in Poland? As unlikely as catching some biting British comedy in Warsaw? Perhaps, yet later that night, we bumbled into a reasonable facsimile of an Olde Englishe pub near Jerozolimskie Avenue, Warsaw's main drag. The barman loitered around polishing beer mugs and cackling at the TV. Poland is a hardy bastion of Catholicism, but Monty Python's *Life of Brian*, of all things, was on the tube. The English soundtrack had been muted, but the demented voices of John Cleese, Michael Palin et al were still audible. The dubbing featured a lone, monotonous Polish voice trying frantically to keep pace with the verbal gymnastics of the Pythons. I eyed the barman, convinced he wouldn't possibly appreciate the peculiar nuances of the British humour. But he sniggered in all the right places, and practically split his sides during the 'Release Roger' scene. So much for notions of sterile, stodgy life in former communist cities.

Anyone will tell you that to visit Poland without seeing Cracow is like flying cut-rate to Cairo with only a mini flagon of red wine for company and then skipping out the pyramids. So one morning, I blundered around Warsaw Central Station trying to find someone who could aim me in the direction of the appropriate platform. I'd spent about 20 minutes trying to figure out the difference between arrivals – *przyjazdy* – and departures – *odjazdy* – before I eventually got on the correct PKP *expresowy* train to Cracow.

Cracow is a beautiful town nestling near the Carpathian Mountains, 250 kilometres south of Warsaw and not far from the borders of the Czech Republic and Slovakia. The university here is one of the oldest in Europe, dating from 1364, and the historic Wawel Castle on a bend of the Vistula River is an imposing landmark that was used as the Nazi headquarters in Poland during World War II. Cracow is also the town where Oskar Schindler started the enamelware business that blossomed into a war-time haven for Jews. Schindler would later be immortalised by the Jewish community, and *Schindler's List*, the movie of Thomas Keneally's brilliant book *Schindler's Ark*, would finally bring a directing Oscar to Steven Spielberg.

I found lodgings at a private house. Some locals in this town have cottoned on to the fact that not every Westerner in Poland is there to party on his or her bottomless company expense account. I was cornered at the train station by a scruffy chap with week-old stains on his shirt collar, who offered me an *en suite* room at his house for something like R3 a night. He spoke good English and, when I showed signs of indecision, presented me with a tattered, yet glowing letter of reference from a pair of Australian backpackers. They were right, and I spent three excellent nights in Cracow.

Just 60 kilometres west of Cracow lie Oswiecim and Brzezinka. These Polish towns might be anonymous to most Westerners, but they are exceedingly well known by their German names, Auschwitz and Birkenau – the war-time concentration camps that have been preserved as chilling reminders of the depths which men plumbed during those years.

During a tour of Auschwitz layer upon layer of unalloyed evil steadily accumulate and overwhelm the visitor. It seeps from the stark black wrought-iron gates and the plain brick barracks and permeates every corner of every room. Even our guide, a feisty Pole who wouldn't let me tape-record her narrative, faltered during some of the more graphic descriptions of how the Nazi war machine turned death into a bureaucratic industry; how there was eager competition for contracts to build crematoria and supply tons of the deadly Zyklon B gas; how the camp's *Lagerführer* and his underlings sat around tables dreaming up ever more efficient ways of murder and corpse disposal.

My first glimpse of the concentration camp was through a film of grey spring drizzle. They say the birds don't sing at Auschwitz. Instead, the only sounds that day were of boisterous schoolchildren chasing around the gravel of the bus-choked car park.

I had bought my R75 ticket for the Auschwitz trip from Cracow Tours at the Hotel Cracovia, the establishment where Schindler used to wine and dine SS head honchos. About 15 others had turned up for the ghoulish outing. The tour began with a grainy 20-minute black-and-white movie taken by the liberating Soviet army on January 27, 1945. The film revealed devastation on a haunting scale: skeletal bodies being trucked into mass, open graves; Nazi doctors experimenting on dull-eyed twins and handicapped Jews.

From the hi-tech theatre, our group filed outside, past the former SS garages and workshops on the left, then via the SS guard house and office of the camp supervisor just outside the electrified fence, and through the wrought-iron gates bearing the cynical inscription *Arbeid macht Frei* – 'work makes you free'.

Block 11, the so-called Block of Death, is the only original building left of the 28 double-storey blocks that made up Auschwitz 1. Many of the now-renovated blocks are devoted to telling the horrors of the Holocaust through displays and photos. Inside these blocks hang huge monochrome photographs of Jews being trucked from all over Europe to Auschwitz. There are also glass display cases featuring suitcases, clothing, shoes, artificial limbs and crutches taken from victims. Behind one such display case in Block 4 are empty cans of Zyklon B. These small, bluish gravel pellets were produced by the firm Degesch, whose profits from the sale of the death-inducing gas between 1941 and 1944 totalled DM300 000. Six kilogrammes were needed to kill around 1 500 people, and 20 000 kilogrammes of Zyklon B were used in Auschwitz between 1942 and 1943. The hair of most victims, which was shorn off to be made into jacket lining for German submarine officers, showed traces of the gas.

We moved on down the sandy camp road. On the left were blocks devoted to 'Material Evidence of Crimes', including fading records of thousands of prisoners. To the right, the collective gallows and the camp kitchen, where musicians strummed a bizarre, up-tempo beat to which inmates worked at a jog-trot.

The first room on the left in the Block of Death was where sessions of the Gestapo court were held. The most frequent sentence was execution at the Wall of Death, where candles and a floral memorial still remain. Beyond was the Auschwitz crematorium – a plain brick bunker with a chimney jutting into the sky. Trees surround the bunker and on entering the thick wooden door you find yourself in a blank, bare, claustrophobic place. In the corners, candles burn.

In Birkenau, 3 kilometres away, the sights are still more chilling. Thirty times bigger than Auschwitz, it has been left untouched since the war.

No glossy guidebooks or glass-case displays. Just stark, windswept bleakness. Entry to Birkenau is through a squat brick building with a raised watchtower, which gives a wide-angle view of the entire 172-hectare complex. Directly in front of the tower are the railway platforms where most of the Jews deported from Hungary arrived. At the end of the unloading ramp are the remains of two crematoria and gas chambers, blown up by the retreating SS in an attempt to conceal their activities. In the far north-eastern corner of Birkenau, behind the international Monument to the Victims of Fascism, lies a pond that to this day remains clogged and grey with the ashes of thousands of victims.

There's a little souvenir shop just outside the Block of Death in Auschwitz 1. It sells postcards, books and videos. I found it a touch bizarre, but the reason for its existence is simple, said the saleswoman. No one must forget. Like the plaque at the entrance to Auschwitz says, 'The one who does not remember history is bound to live through it again.'

A few stiff drinks are needed after a visit to Auschwitz, and the gloriously spacious town square of Cracow is home to a number of buzzing little eateries. Each evening I would wander to the Hotel Saski just off Slawkowska Street and buy the previous day's English newspapers, then retire to the Café Rudolfi for an update on the soccer results, a couple of Zywiec lagers and some roast chicken.

One night I met a bloke from New Zealand. He was trying to sell scuba diving gear to the Poles, but was having difficulty. We downed a few lagers, and then tried some local vodka. He had Black Death. I sampled Bison Brand, which comes in a bottle with a long blade of bison grass in it and has a kick like a Cantona volley. On the advice of the waitress, we later retreated to a nearby disco, a smoky underground cavern with velvet upholstery and darkened niches to which couples could retreat for privacy. But mostly the patrons sat quietly in small groups nursing drinks. The younger generation of Poles have readily embraced Western fashion. Many were diehard members of the Levi's, silver-lipstick and black-heels brigade. The girls tended to own chiselled cheekbones, porcelain skins and silk scarves knotted at the throat. The older generation, by contrast, conformed more readily to the disparaging stereotype of an Eastern European citizen – suety, ill-kempt and wearing clothes that looked like mal-tailored versions of dolls' outfits.

Speaking of which, my sortie to Poland was to prove highly successful in more than one sphere. My ten-year-old niece Katie has something of a Barbie doll fetish, and my overseas schedules are often dominated by trying to juggle interview times with raids on local toy stores. I've lost count of the hours I've spent prowling the aisles of Hamley's in London, casing the halls of FAO Schwartz in New York or bickering with toy vendors at exotic locations in a desperate bid to extract a handsome deal for the latest brand of Barbie.

I'd received strict written instructions before leaving for London, because there was a complication this time around. The doll required was not a Barbie but, in fact, Shelley, who I believe is Barbie's baby sister. Shelley comes in a variety of confusing domestic forms – Shelley in the Pram, Shelley in the Cot and many more besides. The challenge of this journey was to return safely with Shelley in the Bathroom. I'd planned the assault with military precision, calculating I had exactly 75 minutes to race from Heathrow to Hamley's and back on my return from Warsaw. Recalling an interview I'd once done with a sports psychologist, I'd already replayed the mission several times in my mind, like an ace forward visualising a Cup-winning penalty strike.

However, in much the same way as a horse junkie can't avoid the high street betting shop, I found myself automatically entering the first toy store I saw in Cracow. Beaming down from the first shelf I cast my eyes upon was the very item I coveted, at a mere snip of the London price. I gathered up the precious commodity, handed over the necessary batch of zlotych and left the store light of heart. I believed I even leapt and clicked my heels together. Shelley in the Bathroom in the luggage.

My last trip was to another Cracow landmark, the Wieliczka salt mine. This might sound like a fiendish outpost where anti-government plotters were sent to live out the rest of their sorry lives amid back-breaking hard labour, but it is, in fact, a working salt mine and one of the most fascinating places I've ever visited. Wieliczka has been painstakingly carved out over the past eight centuries, and, though it still produces salt, it's as a Unesco World Heritage site that it now earns its keep.

An entire little settlement has been hollowed out underground, mostly by three miners who began hacking at solid walls of salt in 1896. They were still pausing to down tools and wipe the sweat from their brows 67 years later. By this time, they'd fashioned, among other things, a phenomenal complete subterranean chapel from one block of salt, with functioning chandeliers, staircases, ornate carvings and a minutely detailed sculpture of the Last Supper, all forged from the granite-like salt.

To be frank, this mine trip is not to be recommended for those of a claustrophobic disposition. Ten people are wedged shoulder to shoulder in two lifts stacked one on top of the other. You then plummet into jet-black nothingness for about 60 metres. You cannot see your finger in front of your face. The only sounds are of your own heartbeat and the distant dripping of salt and the smell is a mixture of mustiness and damp. If you are in the top lift, the contraption comes to a dead-stop 3 metres above the ground, so that the lift below can empty first. The sensation of being stuck in this black-shrouded elevator for a minute or so is not one I'd care to repeat.

We waited for the Wieliczka lifts to transport us up in the pitch darkness back to the surface. The lingering to return to the surface proved lengthy as closing time was nearing and every tourist was leaving at the same time. A choir visiting Cracow from Bosnia took advantage of the lull. They burst into song, and their voices filled the cavernous underground, bouncing off the walls, careening back through corridors, ricocheting and echoing back and forth through the mine.

The birds don't sing over Auschwitz, but that evening at Wieliczka there were joyous sounds in the air. I reflected on the previous fortnight. I'd visited the pyramids at Giza. I'd witnessed the FA Cup Final at Wembley. I'd seen a chapel carved from salt. And I had Shelley in the Bathroom snuggled safely among the socks in my luggage.

The Zywiec lagers tasted especially satisfying that night.

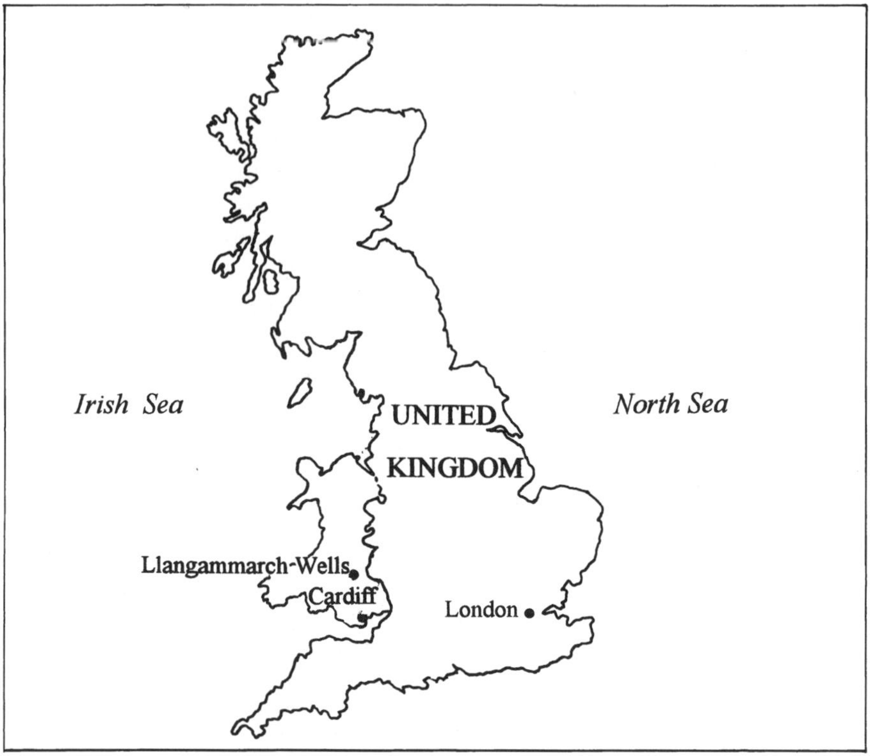
Irish Sea
North Sea
UNITED
KINGDOM
Llangammarch-Wells
Cardiff
London

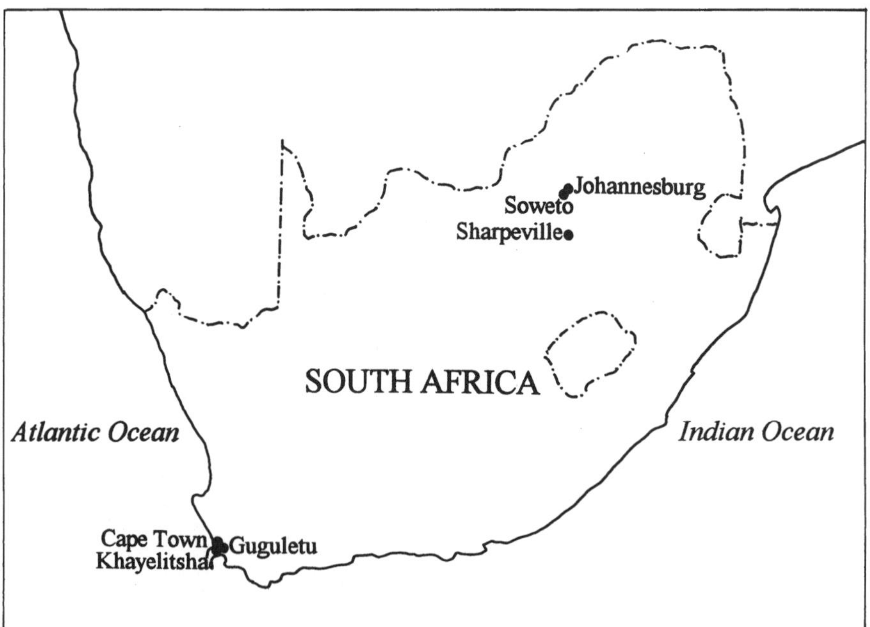
Johannesburg
Soweto
Sharpeville
SOUTH AFRICA
Atlantic Ocean
Indian Ocean
Cape Town
Guguletu
Khayelitsha

CHAPTER SIX

Champions Past, Present and Future

WALES IS AN emerald-green nation the size of the Kruger Park, and, as the 1999 rugby World Cup in that country approaches, its marketers are hell-bent on proving there's more to the tiny principality than leeks, choirs, ex-coalmines and former flyhalves.

And there is. Unpronounceable place names for a start. Welsh schoolchildren surely snap up all the medals in global spelling competitions. After all, unless little Gareths and Gwendas want to roam the streets and valleys searching for home like Dylan Thomas after a bender, they have to wrap their primary-school minds and tongues around such town names as Llanhraeder ym Mochnant, Machynlleth, Eglwyswrw, Trawsfynydd and Maesycrugiau.

Then there's that railway station up north – Llanfairpwllgwyngyllgogerychwyrndrobwllllantysiliogogogoch. Try saying that after a few pints of Brain's bitter. Try saying it sober. Never roll down the car window to ask for directions in Wales unless you have phonetic translations of all towns in an 80-kilometre radius.

Talking of beer, Wales has lots of it. Brain's is the local tipple in Cardiff. There's also Welsh whisky, concocted at a distillery that exports crates of the stuff to the United States. In fact, they've been making the stuff in the valleys since AD 365, and the Scots are said to be in a snit, maintaining that Welsh whisky brewers fast forward the hallowed process a bit. The Welsh say the Scots don't like the competition.

That's the thing about the British Isles. Each little nation hates the other as much as Soweto township dwellers resent hostel inmates. Despising thy neighbour is an all-consuming hobby. I attended the farewell concert to the legendary Cardiff Arms Park, which is being rebuilt for the World Cup. One item featured a tribute to the Five Nations rugby teams, and the announcer could barely mouth the words 'And now let's welcome England' before he was drowned out by a chorus of throaty boos from the terraces.

England and Wales are not on speaking terms. Slagging-each-other-off terms definitely. Bopping-Pom-boy-on-the-head-with-a-Brain's-bitter-bottle terms maybe, but speaking terms no. This could have something to do with recent rugby results, but might also be because Wales supplies England with subsidised water from the valleys, while the Welsh must pay the full rate for their own crystal-clear, ready-to-flog-to-Evian aqua. (By the way, is there any significance in the fact that 'Evian' spelt backwards reads 'naive'?)

But maybe the Welsh have a bit more than the English to be proud about anyway. They certainly might have, to judge from the spectacular country hotels in the baize-coloured countryside where I stayed during the Springbok tour of Wales in late 1994. How Green Was My Valley? Very green indeed.

One such lodge was the Lake Country House in a tiny village called Llangammarch Wells. Each room here was named after an animal in the area. In my Otter Room was a four-poster bed, sherry decanter on the sideboard and a deep sunken bath. Downstairs was a snug lounge with a roaring fire and library. And a dining room with a lengthy wine list and cuisine to commit murder for. Once, after a long, liquid dinner, the host sidled up saying, 'Oh, did I tell you folks that that Welsh wine with which you washed down your rack of Welsh lamb is 14 per cent alcohol? Madam, could you please refrain from standing on your head in the floral centrepiece?'

The service in such places was of a calibre designed to shame South Africans, who know that back in their own country, waiters and shop assistants tend to respond at the speed of a shifting glacier. At breakfast one morning, I tried to sneak from my seat for a glass of juice and was nearly frogmarched back to my chair. 'I'll get whatever it is you need, sir,' cooed the doe-eyed waitress.

The sports on offer at the Lake Country House included 'country gentlemen's pursuits' like fishing, shooting, riding and golf. As well as 'feeding carrots to Dobbin the pony' and 'throwing breadcrusts at the swans' in the three-acre lake from which the hotel derives its name. It was like gate-crashing the set of an *Alice in Wonderland* remake. Such was the tranquillity of the place, the soothing hues of early morning light on the dew-soaked croquet lawn, it reduced us violence-hardened South

Africans to talk of early retirement to the valleys. The only disturbing moment of our stay was the look in the owner's eyes when we told him the car-jacking stats in Jo'burg.

Some people don't like the Welsh capital city of Cardiff, accusing it of being grey, mildewed and slightly rough at the edges. You could have fooled me. It's a great city for wandering around conducting pithy investigative journalism into the ways and means of all things local. Of course such reporting has to be done in the pubs, and Cardiff is one five-star pub crawl. The city centre is compact and walkable. Enticing taverns lace the length of main thoroughfares like St Mary Street. Places like the Rat and Carrot, Newt and Cucumber, and Philharmonic pack in the youngsters. Then there's the outdoor café life down by Mill Lane, just opposite the Marriott Hotel. The proprietors of eateries in this area have finally cottoned on to the fact that not every visitor to the British Isles enjoys pubs in which you need to strap on a coalminer's helmet to see the person sitting next to you. Where the decor isn't smoke-riddled velvet upholstery and pork-scratching-encrusted carpets. Where you don't place your tepid pint of bitter on stained beer mats atop fake oak tables. Don't get me wrong. I'm as fond of dark, fume-filled British free houses as the next man. Only sometimes it's nice to see what they've actually put on that plate in front of you. On second thoughts, maybe not. In Cardiff, I probably stumbled on the reason why those pubs are so dimly lit after all. Whoa! What's that thing wriggling in my rarebit?

Pubs close at 11 pm in Wales, as they do elsewhere in Britain. But that doesn't stop the serious. Kiwi's Bar off Mill Lane pumps until late. Never have I experienced such a sheer volume of semi-sober bodies as midst those twin floors of throbbing humanity. Nightclubs like Zeus near the Park Hotel in Queen Street cater for the late night party-till-you-puke set. Only woe betide anyone who shows up in jeans (though I can report that they are open to slurred bribery in a South African accent).

There's clearly a plot to get tourists to Wales and it's a simple one. Kill them with kindness. Or carbohydrates. And fine wine. Or buckets of Brain's bitter. And countryside so eye-catching it should have an age restriction. Wales is possibly Europe's best-kept tourist secret. When can I go back? Because someone told me they even play rugby there too.

I'm joking about the latter, of course. Welsh rugby might be plumbing the depths right now, but they have a proud list of legends who have worn the famous scarlet jersey. The nation's glory days were in the Seventies, when excessively talented backline players seemed to drop off some production line deep in the valleys. The kingpins of the great Welsh teams of the era included Barry John, Phil Bennett, Gerald Davies,

Gareth Edwards, J.J. Williams and J.P.R. Williams. And even though there appears to be a gremlin or two in the production line these days, rugby remains as deeply ingrained in the Welsh national psyche as it is in New Zealanders and most white South Africans.

Although the Springbok rugby team reached its peak at the 1995 World Cup, the seeds for the team's famous march to victory were sown seven months earlier in the mud and cold of Wales and Scotland. Coach Kitch Christie was at the helm for what he termed his 'ambulance job' on South African rugby. Christie had been brought in to take over from Ian McIntosh, who had been dumped, prematurely some thought, after the Boks lost the 1994 series 2–0 in New Zealand. The British tour united Christie and his Transvaal captain and work colleague, Francois Pienaar. Christie liked to call Pienaar 'Cappie'.

Cappie was under a little pressure in Britain. It was ironic that while South Africa basked in the novel glow of national unity, its rugby fraternity should remain divided over the choice of its captain. Even though, beyond the borders of the new nation, the choice of Jacobus Francois Pienaar as South Africa's leader was so obvious. The blond flanker was hailed in hard-bitten Australia as the best-ever touring captain during the 2–1 series defeat of 1993. That nation's coach at the time, Bob Dwyer, named Pienaar the fastest, most destructive flank in world rugby. Throughout the England tour of South Africa the following year, glowing references to the 27-year-old 'emancipated Afrikaner' were as common in British newspapers as references to Princess Di's clothing bills.

Yet the unhappy reality was that the powers that be in South Africa were far from unanimous over the choice of Pienaar as captain. There were some who said he was not good enough, not fast enough, not tough enough. Some said he wore the wrong clothes, drove flash cars. They said Pienaar was a better diplomat than a player. And that hurt.

We were chatting in the captain's room in Cardiff's Marriott Hotel. It was the eve of the Test against Wales at the Arms Park, and the visiting captain was tugging on a stick of biltong from a healthy stash he kept in his room.

'All I can say is that I know that I'm first picked as a player, then as a captain. No one should be picked because he is a good captain, especially in a team game. It stings when people say that I'm a good diplomat but not a good player. I can't understand it. I have a feeling there are camps who want me out but it is difficult to understand their motives. I think that people need a scapegoat and they see me as one. But what is more important to me is how the players feel about me, if they respect me. When you're captaining a side, there are two options. You can either play for yourself, or for your team and *then* for yourself. I always choose the latter role, as I put the team's interests first. My personal play is not affected because if a team plays well, naturally the captain also then plays well. If a captain is not there to instil confidence and help others in their game, why pick a captain at all? Nobody likes a loser, the fans only follow winners. It happens all over the world – just in South Africa we are more passionate.'

Was the anti-Pienaar sentiment in part due to that 'enlightened Afrikaner' tag?

'Maybe it is, maybe it isn't. Rugby has changed a lot over the years, and so have the players. I have an open approach to the game and the spectators. It's amazing what can happen when you reach out your hand to help. We may not have known the words to "Nkosi Sikelel' iAfrika" when we played that first Test under the new flag against England in 1994, but that was one of our tasks in New Zealand. By the end of the tour, the whole squad could sing it.'

Such talk was probably construed as revolutionary in some quarters. At the very least, it was a clue to Pienaar's mixed popularity in some parts. This open, friendly, decent ambassador for all that was good in the fledgling South Africa was an obvious target for the hard-headed brigade who still swirled the old South African flag from the bleachers.

Perhaps some locals still liked their rugby players strong and silent. Perhaps they still do. Hulking, semi-literate, cauliflower-eared caricatures who wrestle cattle on the family farm to stay fit. That's how occasional sectors of the overseas press enjoy stereotyping the Springboks, even though these days nothing could be further from the truth. Pienaar was the first of a different breed, and some people didn't like that.

What else did they say was wrong with the skipper?

They said he was always injured. That made him blink in that Cardiff hotel room. For just an instant there was a trace of anger in his voice.

'Some people say that I am injury-prone, yet last season I played 42 games, and there were only two – the Currie Cup Final where I was concussed, and the second Test against Argentina where I injured my ankle – that I didn't finish. How can you call that injury-prone?'

Pienaar was never one to ditch his uncompromising style of play for the sake of avoiding injury and clinging to the captaincy. An ankle ligament flared in the first Springbok trials of 1994, but instead of being given time to recover, he was forced to show his fitness for Transvaal. The World Cup was less than 12 months down the track. With the need for uniformity and consistency in team selection paramount, the selectors should have told him, 'You're part of our plans, you will lead the team, now go and rest that ankle for the big event.'

But Pienaar wouldn't be drawn down that line of thinking. He had a job to do. He wanted to captain his country to victory in the Arms Park the next day, and lead his nation in a satisfactory World Cup campaign the following winter.

'We should be looking for solutions to our problems, and not try to hide from them. We need to have a vision, and a goal. We need to ask ourselves, "Do we want to win the World Cup next year, or do we want to win every Test between now and then?"'

The Welsh might well have beaten the Springboks that following day. It was only when Chester Williams dived over in the corner for the match-clinching try that a 20–12 victory was secured. That try was the second best moment of the day. The highlight, of course, was hearing 65 000 Welshmen singing 'Land of Our Fathers' in the cathedral of Welsh rugby. The higher notes swirled and dipped around the stadium in the most glorious manner.

Almost an hour after the game, when the crowd had filtered home or into the Flyhalf and Firkin pub just opposite the stadium, I walked from the press box down to the underground car park exit. There I saw a blond man in a green blazer. He was crowded by a scrum of young signature-seekers. Francois Pienaar, alone and smiling, again doing his country proud.

I next saw him a month before the World Cup began. We wanted to paint his face in the colours of the South African flag for the cover of the World Cup edition of *SA Sports Illustrated*. When we reached the offices of SA Heating and Cooling in Midrand, where Pienaar worked alongside Kitch Christie, a British TV crew was setting up cameras in Pienaar's office. They were filming a day in the life of the Bok captain and thought it would be nice to take a few shots of South African rugby's most famous face being painted. So there the skipper sat. Because time was against us, I interviewed Pienaar during the painting process. Undaunted, Pienaar showed he had the ability to deliver coherent answers while being photographed, painted and filmed. Captaining a top sports team these days is a task only for the multi-talented.

The session also showed that Pienaar was hardly the money-grabber many critics have portrayed him as. The only fee he wanted from the 90-minute session was a copy of the photos. The British TV crew said the then England captain, Will Carling, wouldn't have got out of bed for less than £10 000 for a similar project.

The World Cup was, of course, a massive month in the lives of most South Africans. And even if the much-heralded 'One Team One Country' slogan sounds a bit hollow these days, there's no doubt the Springboks' triumphant march to the Webb Ellis trophy fleetingly united the nation. This much was obvious during the victory parade through the streets of Johannesburg on the Tuesday after the Final. The roads were clogged with well-wishers of every hue, age and job description. Some might have used the occasion to skive off work for a few hours, sure, but most lined the streets to give vent to a novel feeling of national pride.

The world's eyes were focusing on the cream of South Africa's athletes during the World Cup. These players had been cocooned in fine hotels, practised on lush playing fields, had any and every obstacle to their triumph smoothed away.

Far from the television cameras and the glory, I wanted to probe the other side of sport in South Africa. To visit some of the country's townships to see what was happening there while those wearing green and gold were bringing honour to the nation. I would concentrate on lesser known sports. The big three – rugby, cricket and soccer – all had much-trumpeted development programmes that were enjoying varying degrees of success. But what about those living in obscurity who harboured dreams of being Formula One racing drivers, professional golfers or world champion athletes? There must be plenty of youngsters with such ambitions tucked away far from the headlines. How do they set about achieving their dreams?

So photographer Tertius Pickard and I spent a week in Soweto, Sharpeville, Guguletu and Khayelitsha, searching for enticing sports stories buried deep within. We met some interesting characters.

The heat and dust of Soweto clings to your clothes, and in front of many roadside dwellings, dogs, goats and the occasional pig nose idly at piles of rubbish. When the heaped litter becomes unbearably ripe, it is set alight and plumes of smoke billow. Two years earlier, such smoke signals were black and acrid, from tyres being torched at makeshift roadblocks manned by the comrades of community self-defence units. During the World Cup month, the tension in the sprawling township that more than a million people call home had largely dissipated, just as that hazy cloak of a Sowetan dawn is burned away by early sunrays.

In Chiawelo, in the western corner of the township, chattering children in black-and-white uniforms headed off for school past a gutted double-decker bus that was used as a fruit and vegetable store. Not far from this bus was Gazankulu Primary, a school known for its sporting prowess. The school invariably cleans up in local athletics meets. It's also famous as boxer Dingaan Thobela's alma mater. But Gazankulu's most distinguishing feature is its squash court.

Squash was one of the first sports to make in-roads into Soweto. The kids had been bussed to élite northern Johannesburg clubs like the Wanderers and Parkview from about 1987. In 1992, when transport costs proved prohibitive, the idea of building a squash court in Soweto was first mooted. With the help of local building contractors, the court became a reality.

The Gazankulu Primary facility is no ordinary squash court. It serves two functions. In the morning it is a classroom for toddlers. Pre-schoolers receive two meals a day there and learn songs like 'If You're Happy and You Know It, Clap Your Hands'. In the afternoon, the blankets are folded away and the court is used for its intended purpose. The outside back wall of the court has also been plastered and court lines drawn in the adjoining playground so that, in effect, one court has become two.

In 1995, the two best-known players who used the court were Jonathan and James Letlake, 16-year-old twins from nearby Vuwani School. When someone first mentioned squash to Jonathan, he assumed they were talking about orange juice. That was in 1987. But the twins learned the game swiftly, and were both now playing for the Transvaal Under-19 B team. Strictly on merit. When asked why he loved the game, Jonathan gave a reason that sounded a little practised, like a verbal titbit for the benefit of a wide-eyed foreign journalist. 'I play squash because it keeps me off the streets. If I was not playing squash, maybe I'd be a skelm, maybe running around stealing cars.'

Like the Gazankulu squash court, Theo Mthembu's compact sweatbox of a gym has been used for a variety of functions. It was once a nursery by day, a dance studio in the afternoon and then a gym in the evening. These days, in the early afternoons, the only hint that this Dube landmark is a boxing venue comes courtesy of British boxer Chris Eubank's foppish pose in a 'Night of the Giants' poster on the otherwise stark wall of the gym.

But at about four every afternoon, a pack of eager juniors drift in to limber up on the chipboard floor. There is no dressing room or shower in Theo Mthembu's gym, though there are coat hooks so that the boxers can hang up their jackets. These hooks have been the most extensive additions to the gym over the past decade. Some boxers train in dress shoes and work trousers. George Ngwenya coaches the youngsters, a couple of whom look barely old enough to tie their own shoelaces. If, indeed, they had shoelaces. 'Bra' George is in his sixties and is taut and wiry. He joins in the squats, leg-raises and Russian jumps, and thinks nothing of swatting a young boxer on the ear when the tempo wilts. George played softball, did body building and boxed before turning to coaching. That was after he was stabbed in the arm and mouth one night and lost his punching power.

During our visit, the climate inside the Dube gym became humid and heavy with the sweat of athletes when the seniors arrived for training at 5.30 pm. By the time Baby Jake Matlala, the 4-foot 10-inch WBO flyweight champion, turned up, the small windows were fogged with the fighters' body heat. Matlala has spent the bulk of his 32 years training in these spartan surroundings. When he became world champion he finally moved out of Soweto, but he saw no reason to change his regular workout venue.

Theo Mthembu sauntered in from his house up the road in time to impart half a century's worth of wisdom to Matlala and the other seniors.

'Baby Jake is a hero to these guys,' said Mthembu. 'If the gym is good enough for him, it's good enough for them. Though it would be nice to have a bigger, better place with air conditioning or showers. But there's no money. We have to be realistic.'

Mthembu was apparently a mean boxer in his day. Like Marlon Brando in *On the Waterfront*, he could also have been a contender. Mthembu was in line for a trip to the 1948 Olympics in Helsinki, but politics ended that dream. He joked that only one car was safe from the hijackers of Soweto – the Toyota Cressida that the tiny world champ drove. 'Baby Jake Matlala' was painted on the side. 'Everyone in the township has so much respect for Matlala, they wouldn't dream of taking his vehicle,' explained Mthembu.

Philip Kekana had never owned a vehicle, although he'd always been fascinated by anything mechanical. The first car he drove was his brother's hearse. At the age of 16. Kekana had no licence, but still undertook lengthy trips from Soweto to Natal and the Northern Province with only corpses for company. Once he was stopped by police. Kekana sat nervously in the driver's seat, trying frantically to thumb-suck a suitable story. But the cops didn't even ask the skinny youth for his licence. Instead they prised open the casket in the back to ensure no guns or grenades were stowed within.

When we met him Kekana was driving what some might still call a coffin on wheels – a modified Ford Laser in Stannic Group N races. His first race had been at Kyalami three months earlier, and he'd finished near the back.

'I was nervous. At the start, they came past like they were chasing me with a tank. I was glad to see the chequered flag, just to know that I'd finished the race. I've got to learn to go quicker on the bends. Even some of the Class E guys were overtaking me.'

Kekana was the first black driver to give racing a whirl, with enormous help from Sasol. Motor racing, after all, is beyond the reach of most people, never mind the colour of their skin. Kekana still was making his living as an advanced driving instructor in Zone 1, Diepkloof, and was also a part-time taxi driver. Whereas some cynics might be inclined to suggest that any Sowetan taxi driver worth his salt would automatically be a contender for Kyalami, Kekana's unorthodox leisure pursuit was met with anxiety back home.

'My girlfriend didn't like the sport. She was worried, but she's started to support me now. At home they tell me I'm going to get killed racing these cars. But it's not like robbing a bank or stealing a car. That way, I would know I'm going to die. On the track, I have my skills, there are marshals and the car is protected.'

'Cheeky' Mabuto is the swimming coach at Emthenjeni swimming pool in Section 2 of Guguletu, one of two pools in the Cape township. In 1993, six youngsters approached Cheeky and asked her to coach them. She had long coached swimming and water polo, as well as soccer. In fact, name the game, and she probably teaches it. Cheeky is one of township sport's many unheralded Jill-of-all-trades.

'The men are lazy. All they want to do is sit on the couch and *suip* beer,' said Hassiem Bester, Western Province Swimming Association development director, as one reason why female coaches tend to outnumber males in townships.

It was a freezing June morning in the township, but a bunch of kids were happily splashing in the shallows. One was Colin Zonde, a burly 16-year-old who had taken to swimming after being invited to watch a Hungary v. Western Province water polo game in 1994.

'He could swim okay,' remembered Cheeky, 'but I had to teach him the right strokes.'

The result was that Zonde was now playing water polo for Western Province and was picked for the South African Under-16 squad to tour Europe later in 1995.

Like many sports development stories, the learning process at Emthenjeni swimming pool had turned full circle. Zonde and his mates take it upon themselves to coach younger swimmers in the township. They've even formed a team. They wear the name of their club, Guguletu Gunners, on their blue Speedos.

Sharpeville's place in this country's turbulent history was cemented on March 21, 1960. Unarmed township dwellers marched on the local police station to protest at pass laws. Skittish police panicked and fired live rounds into the retreating crowd. Sixty-nine people died.

Today, Sharpeville's central sporting magnet is the George Thabe Stadium, its threadbare soccer field surrounded by a worn grass athletics track and bleak steel bleachers. The track is home to Lekoa Athletic Club. Formed in 1980 with about 30 members, the club began life to keep coach Nelson Ncala fit for boxing. The club has since groomed some of the most talented cross-country and middle-distance track athletes in the country. At the time of our visit, the most recent prodigy to step from the treadmill had been John Moripede, who ended eleventh in the World Junior Cross-Country Championships in Durham, England, earlier that year. The Transvaal team included 30 Lekoa athletes at the 1995 SA Junior Championships.

Ncala was still in charge of the club he had founded. With stopwatch in hand and thin riempie at the ready, he didn't blind his athletes with science.

'I believe in short distances. I like to work with small kids and they must not go too far too quick. They must stick with track and cross-country. The problem is that some of these bigger clubs poach our youngsters when they get really good and then they change our methods. If the runner gets a pain in the stomach then the coaches at these places say, "Okay, stop." We say, "Push on, push on", till that thing vanishes.'

A group of 35 youngsters were out training that day. Many were barefoot, some wore school shoes without laces, others wore scuffed and split dress shoes. The squad began by circling the kilometre-long footpath outside the stadium. The course was strewn with ruts and sharp rocks.

'I want to have world class athletes. We have them here in the townships. There are many, but they must be nursed,' said Ncala. 'If we can keep our youngsters in track and cross-country, we will match the Kenyans. But most of them take to the roads too early.'

Lekoa athletes have run with and against white kids since the formation of the club. Once, a Lekoa tyke of about nine beat an older white boy in a cross-country race in Vanderbijlpark. The white boy's father was angry and claimed the Lekoa athlete had taken a short cut. Officials maintained the win was fair. The beaten boy's father ranted on, and the race was re-run – with an even more resounding win for the Lekoa kid.

Soweto Country Club is the only golfing venue in Soweto. It has a handful of Indian members, a couple of whites, but the vast majority are, of course, black. Veteran local tour professional John Mashego often tees off at Soweto. He started the game relatively late in life. Mashego's first love was soccer, but at the age of 27 he was ready for a change.

'I tried all sports – tennis was no good as I was getting old. So I went bowling with the old guys for three months, but it was really boring. Then my brother just told me to play golf.' Mashego bought a two-iron, a five-iron and a sand-wedge. The putter would come later. For the time being, he had to use the wedge on the greens. In 1978, the Soweto Country Club was a dog's breakfast of a course. But Mashego, being an enterprising, entertaining character, wasn't deterred.

'I used to sneak in at about four o'clock each day when the members had finished playing. Here at Soweto and also in Killarney. In about 12 months I could beat my brother. From then on I didn't look back. I never played with a double figure handicap. I started with 4. Soon I was playing off plus 2. Somebody told me to turn professional, so all in all in 15 months I was ready to turn pro.'

Mashego was now in his forties, one of a handful of black golfers on the local tour. Top-class black golfers are as rare as Highveld rain in winter. Anywhere in the world. When Tiger Woods boomed 330-yard drives down the Augusta fairways on his US Masters debut in April 1995, he was only the fourth black man to play in that prestigious tournament. South Africa has had two celebrated black players: Papwa Sewgolum, with his cross-handed grip that took him to three Dutch Open titles in the Sixties, and Vincent Tshabalala, who won in France the following decade.

Mashego has had his moments on tour. He's led a couple of events going into the last day without ever landing a big one. He's been there, done it, and, of course, suffered the racial slurs to prove it.

'Once I went to a tournament in Newcastle, about eight years ago. They booked us in a flat, but we were kicked out by some Afrikaans students. They called us names of course. My fellow players who are close to me, they can call me anything, they can call me names. I call them names also. The thing is I know I am black. I don't need anyone to call me black.'

Mashego was eager to impart his years of experience to black up-and-coming golfers like Mawonga Nomwa, the 24-year-old Pimville kid who learned the game as a caddy at Soweto CC and finished twenty-ninth in the SA Masters in 1995. While we spoke, a child of about six was hacking around on the tees using a bent piece of fencing, and he was propelling the ball about 15 yards.

'I hear people talking about development. I don't know, maybe I don't know what development is, but I see nothing at all. We need to teach the kids, give them equipment. Our youngsters here have nothing. They have no shoes, no clubs, they must steal clubs from us, they must steal golf balls from us. I don't want things to happen when I am dead. I want to see it right now.'

Whatever your colour, life's tough on the local winter tour. Even the winners seldom capture headlines. Mashego reckoned he needed to finish in the top five every week to break even. A trip to Newcastle would cost him over R1 000, a tournament in Port Elizabeth more than R3 000.

'I've got two kids to feed. I have a girlfriend, who I want to marry. But I can't get married with this golf – it takes all my money. I'm married to golf.' Mashego fired up his Jetta for the 400-kilometre drive to his next tournament, which was due to start two days before the rugby World Cup Final. He had been following the rugby.

'South Africa will win easily. They will be too strong. This event means far more to South Africa than to New Zealand. For New Zealand it's just another game. For South Africa it's a chance to send a present to the whole of this country.'

Francois Pienaar and his Springbok rugby players duly brought joy to South Africa. And, ultimately, our little scratch at the surface of the townships' vibrant sporting life showed nothing we didn't know all along. It confirmed that the biggest problems facing sporting advancement in such areas are the twin f-words – finance and facilities. Acceptable sporting venues would be a great start. Like Kevin Costner said in *Field of Dreams*, 'If you build it, they will come.' Our little sortie also showed there's a burning desire to compete and a great deal of goodwill to nurture the talent. It showed that anyone, given the chance, can drive a racing car, hit a cross-court boast, serve an ace or swing a mean seven-iron.

That just as surely as white men can jump, so can black men swim.

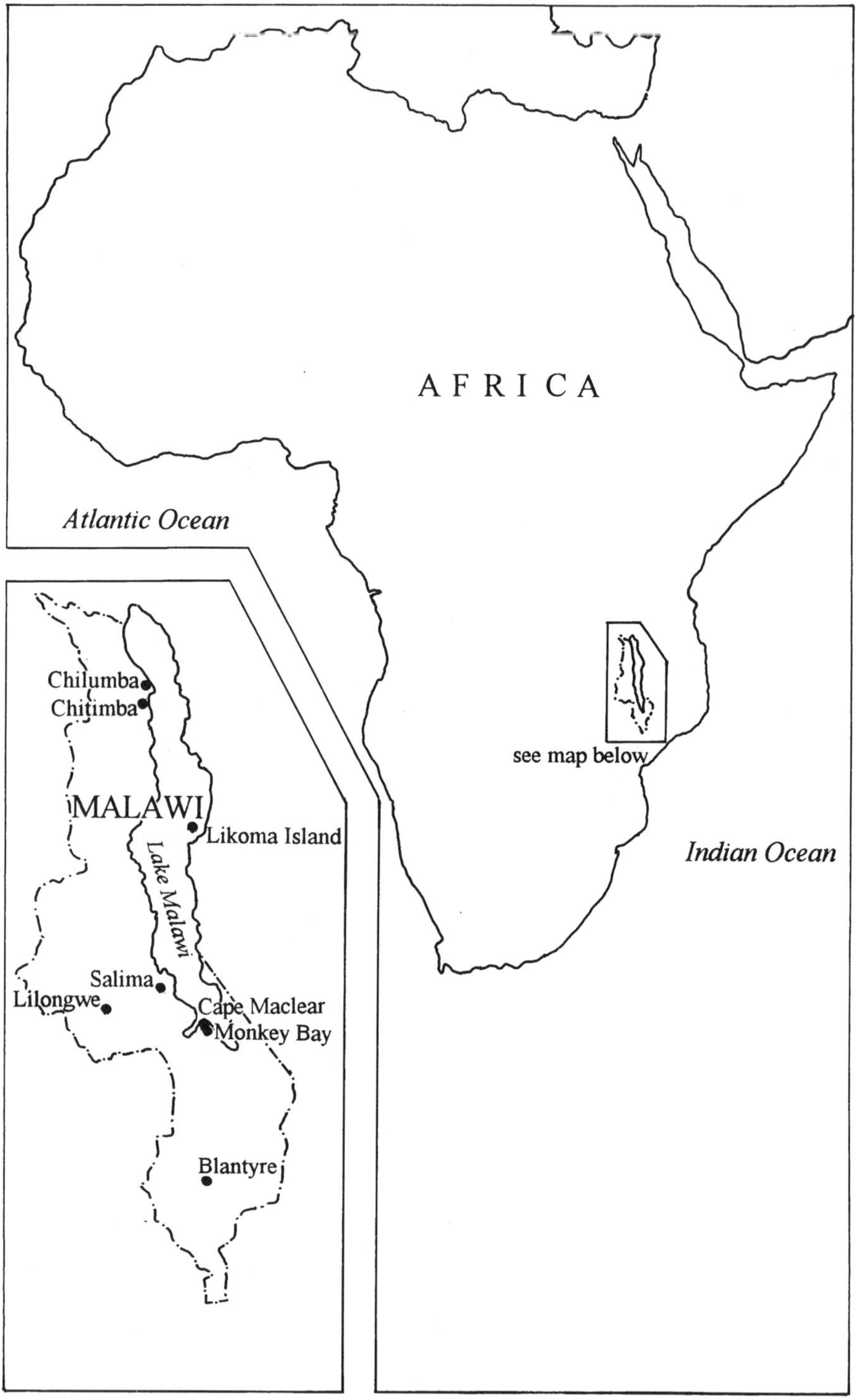
AFRICA
Atlantic Ocean
Indian Ocean
see map below
Chilumba
Chitimba
MALAWI
Likoma Island
Lake Malawi
Salima
Lilongwe
Cape Maclear
Monkey Bay
Blantyre

CHAPTER SEVEN

'What About Blacelet?'

MALAWI, THAT THIN, central sliver of our vast continent that markets itself as the Warm Heart of Africa, has long been a magnet for straggly backpackers, budget travellers, global adventurers and even burnt-out sports journalists.

Thanks to Malawi's benign attitude towards Pretoria during the apartheid era, South Africans have long savoured the white beaches, tranquil waters and generally slothful existence that Lake Malawi, in particular, inspires.

For more than a decade, most of these travellers have headed for Cape Maclear when visiting the lake. This speck on the southern lakeshore merits no more than the most cursory of acknowledgement on maps. But it has a dramatic physical setting, beneath a bowl of green hills that stretches down to flat maize fields, a village of thatch-roofed mud huts and the beaches of the balmy lake beyond. The village is fairly isolated. The nearest town is Monkey Bay, a 20-kilometre journey over tortuous, winding roads that are close to impassable during the rains. There is no electricity in Cape Maclear. Until recently, there was but one telephone, a party line at the Mr Stevens Guesthouse, which behaved as eccentrically as the owners of this ramshackle collection of budget lodgings.

The complete absence of mod-cons has for me always been the principal attraction of Cape Maclear. For more than a decade, it's been the destination of choice once my batteries dip into the red zone and abrupt regeneration is required. At first, back in 1985, there were only two places you could stay in Cape Maclear. There was Golden Sands, the camp ground near Otter Point, where snorkelling in the clear blue depths brought one face to face with the greatest variety of tropical fish anywhere in the world.

The other lodge was, is and always will be Mr Stevens. Though the name is misleading. There are actually three veteran and identical Mr Stevens: three brothers – Ernest, George and Dumaurier – local villagers who in a moment of inspiration around 15 years back hatched the idea of providing cheap food and lodging for the sweaty travellers who kept turning up on their patch of pristine lakeshore. In the early years, the brothers made as much money from milking the route to Monkey Bay as they did from housing foreigners, or *mzungus*. The only means of access to Cape Maclear was on the back of their mortally decaying bakkie, which would commute to Monkey Bay daily to stock up with indispensable items for the continued wellbeing of life in Cape Maclear – Green and Brown Carlsberg beers.

Outside the guesthouse each morning, this bakkie would begin filling up with passengers as soon as the first brushstrokes of dawn began streaking the canvas of the night sky. The human load was generally an assorted bunch – mothers with tiny, wide-eyed infants clamped to their bosoms, old men wielding grease-sodden bicycle parts, fishermen burdened with dried, rancid-smelling *chambo* to sell in town, and hungover backpackers desperate to catch the bus from Monkey Bay to Blantyre down south or Lilongwe up north.

The Mr Stevens who was driving – I never did work out which one – would, meanwhile, enjoy a languid breakfast, stretch, burp, scratch his armpits, add up the Greens sales from the night before, bark at the kids who hung on the verges intent on prising a kwacha or two from the *mzungus*, and finally amble forth to fire up the bakkie at around 8.30 am. At this point, the engine would usually wheeze gamely for a few seconds, threatening ignition, then abruptly expire. Or it would be discovered that the rear wheel, buckling under the ballast of 40-plus passengers, was suddenly as flat as a supermodel's chest. Or that the driver could only engage reverse gear. The trip would thus be abandoned with a 'such is Africa' shrug from whichever Mr Stevens was at the wheel.

The locals would accept these frequent mechanical seizures as an inevitable consequence of gambling with life in the twentieth-century fast lane, and return to whatever it was they had been doing. After all, tomorrow would be here in 24 hours' time. The bulk of us foreigners, however, would frantically ransack our brains for a viable transport alternative, and colourfully curse the continent in general and Mr Stevens Guesthouse, Cape Maclear, Malawi, in particular.

Nevertheless, Mr Stevens got lucky. The humble dwelling made it to the pages of the Lonely Planet *Africa on a Shoestring* guide, the bible of anyone 'doing' the continent on the cheap. In the late Eighties, throngs of international tramps beat a path to Cape Maclear, and Mr Stevens raked in the kwachas.

Incidentally, that *Africa on a Shoestring* is to me more of a nuisance than anything. Not only is it hopelessly out of date the minute it's set to print, but also every whitey intent on 'having an experience, like shoo wah' in Africa swears by it. The result is you get the same motley assortment of retrenched diner chefs from Dagenham, disillusioned barmaids from Bondi Beach and Jesus-sandalled teachers on sabbatical from Christchurch all taking identical routes through Africa and pitching up at exactly the same destinations. Most people at Mr Stevens in the late Eighties would have bumped into each other at some stage of their African odyssey. Usually at Lonely Planet-recommended guesthouses in places like Marrakesh, Accra, Lagos, Bangui or Kinshasa. They would then compare notes at each location, while carping about the quality of the dope and the state of the roads, like competitors crossing off checkpoints on some continent-wide pedestrian rally.

After the frenzy of the 1995 rugby World Cup, I was in need of a lengthy intermission from the pressures of deadlines. So once the celebrations had ceased, I took an Air Malawi flight to Lilongwe, persuaded a private-vehicle owner to take me the 240 kilometres from the capital to Cape Maclear for K200 plus a sackful of T-shirts, a soccer ball and that day's copy of *The Nation*, and found myself deposited outside Mr Stevens just as dusk was turning the sky a variety of pleasing hues.

Unfortunately, even though I'd last visited Mr Stevens just two years previously, I was ill prepared for the changes those years had obviously done to my roughing-it psyche.

Mr Stevens is fine when you are young and eager and care not whether you've bathed this week, or that it's taken three hours for your *chambo* and chips dinner to arrive, or that you've been eating *chambo* and chips for the past 12 nights. For me it was the wasteland of cigarette stompies on which I pitched my beach towel the following morning that finally convinced me I'd outgrown the backpacking phase. I checked out and headed elsewhere.

A number of competitors to Mr Stevens have sprung up in recent years. Places like Top Quiet, The Gap and Bazzary Billion's Ritz Hotel with its slick marketing campaign plastered on a whitewashed hut wall – 'Home of the famous lemon and banana pancake'. This humble mud structure had photos of London's swanky Ritz Hotel on the wall. There the similarities ended.

There was also Chembe Lodge. I'd heard about this addition to the Cape Maclear accommodation scene via the villagers' grapevine. Chembe Lodge falls somewhere in between Mr Stevens-like disorder and the upmarket resorts of Club Makakola and Nkopola Lodge, which are replicas of any ordinary three-star South African beach resort, and are popular with respectable middle-class South Africans, who honeymoon there and then boast to their friends about their soul-cleansing experiences in the 'real Africa'.

Chembe Lodge takes its name from the local village of which it, and Mr Stevens, is part. It's the brainchild of a man with a multi-national pedigree. Oliver Reprich was born in Canada of German parents, is a South African resident and now lives in the room marked 'office' at the lodge. The vision is to attract those still drawn to the primitive, unspoilt beauty of the lake, yet who aim a rung or two higher on the comfort ladder than they did during their backpacking days. In other words, someone like me.

Accommodation at Chembe is in luxury tents anchored beneath quaint grass roofs and offering splendid views of the lake. Another drawcard (besides three hours of electricity daily) is the huge thatched dining and pub area. That very pub is where I am now writing these words, and as a locale for inspiring ill-disciplined writers it has few equals. It's my second visit here, and as I type, barman Max, who is decked out in his snappy blue Chembe Lodge T-shirt, takes care of me. Every hour he refills my glass with Quench water from a plastic bottle. This water bears an impressive stamp of approval from the Malawian Bureau of Standards. I'll take their word for it, despite apparent evidence of six-legged life within.

My routine here at Chembe is simple. I wake at around 7 am and stagger through to the dining area for an omelette and toast. Then I wander up to the shower at the back of the lodge where I luxuriate under the only hot water in Cape Maclear, courtesy of a fire-heated drum behind the ablution block. At 8.30 I go and prop up the bar. Not to order vast amounts of Greens or Malawi Gin and tonics, but to snap open the laptop in the hope of pounding out a fresh batch of words for this book.

Even though Lake Malawi is a stunning site for keyboard-pounding, it's sometimes difficult to get things done. Most writers will tell you that the hardest thing about writing is… writing. That dreaded moment when you have to face those 26 letters on the keyboard and hammer away. At these moments I find myself distracted by most things. For instance, though the reading matter here at Chembe is limited, I've still devoured all the back copies of *Out There* magazine. As well as old editions of *The Nation*. In today's paper, for example, I was drawn to an article criticising

President Bakili for putting his face on Malawian currency. When he ousted veteran Kamuzu Banda (or, to give him his entire distinguished title, His Excellency the Ngwazi Doctor Hastings Kamuzu Banda President for Life), Bakili said it was time to remove the cult of personality from Malawian politics. No way would his mug adorn the banknotes. Now, two years later, there he is, smiling smugly from the K50 bills. To be fair, at least that journalist had the freedom to reprimand the new president. Banda was famously hostile towards any form of perceived criticism. When I first visited Malawi I was told a story about an expatriate farmer who had named one of his pigs Kamuzu. One night he'd let slip this nugget of information after one Carlsberg too many. The next week the police paid him a visit, and within a month he was deported.

While I psych myself up for a morning staring at the laptop, Max is taking stock, adding up the Green empties and Squadron rum tots, and the beep of his calculator is the sole unnatural sound I hear. The milk-white beach is just a 90-degree head-turn to my left. The hills stretch away to the horizon and the lake is mirror-still today. The most excitement I've had since arriving here was when a ladybird fell between the Enter and Shift keys of my computer and I spent five minutes extracting it. The only other disturbance is the rustle of the breeze, which curls its way under the thatch and ruffles my hair in a far from displeasing manner.

The dining area at Chembe is open-plan. There are no walls, merely a high thatch roof that becomes a nightly playground for the bats, which resemble stricken fighter planes spiralling to their doom as they tear about the eaves. It appears they must surely smash headfirst into something, until their radar senses an obstacle and they veer clear of the danger. The dining room is also home to animal skulls. A tuskless hippo head stands sentry at one entrance. A vast set of crocodile jaws, a gift from one of the villagers, guards the other. Crocodiles are virtually sacred in these parts, their gall bladders regarded as potent muti.

In fact it's so powerful I've been thinking of using it, like garlic to a vampire, to ward off the persistent kids around here.

Each time I make my way back to my tent, the local children, who hang beyond the fringes of the lodge, call out to me. 'What about canoe?' they ask. They want to take me in a dugout canoe round to a nearby island. For a small fee, they'll bring along fish and a few Greens, and we'll munch under the noon sun and then go snorkelling.

'What about washing?' they ask, if I'm not up to messing about in boats. The local kids perform a fine laundry service at the lake – within three hours if the sun's fierce – and they charge rates well below those of Holiday Inn Garden Courts.

'What about blacelet?' they continue, if the first two requests have been declined. The people in this country, like their neighbours in Kenya and Tanzania, have trouble with 'l' and 'r' when speaking English, so that 'bracelet' comes out as 'blacelet' and 'Malawi' sometimes becomes 'Marawi'.

I bought two bracelets fashioned from phone wire the day I arrived, even though these kids insist that everyone I know back in South Africa will surely want at least three each. But I will not budge. Another reason for my not supporting these fledgling entrepreneurs is that Chembe Lodge has the only telephone in town, apart from the hit-and-miss party line at Mr Stevens. Guess where the kids get the phone wire?

Actually the kids aren't that bad. I just sent one to the village 2 kilometres away to fetch *The Nation*. He came back empty-handed and insisted he couldn't then keep the kwachas I'd given him for his troubles. They're a peaceful, friendly, conservative lot here in Malawi. A smile is the first thing you'll be greeted with, followed by *muli bwanji* – 'hello' in Chichewa.

There is a sense of timelessness about Cape Maclear. The lake, the village, even the people seem unaltered whenever I return. But some things have changed since I first visited these parts. In 1985 the children wanted a kwacha for the washing, no matter how vast or mud-streaked the load. These days they negotiate in dollars. Cape Maclear has also become an embryonic water-sports mecca, with ventures offering scuba diving, kayak safaris and sailing jaunts. Since the demise of apartheid, a number of entrepreneurial South Africans have opened businesses here, seduced by the sprit of the lake, the charm of the amiable people and the quality of the ganja. The latter is, I think, the prime motivating factor behind most spontaneous decisions to relocate to these shores. But paradise has its downside too. Not least wading through a bureaucratic quagmire for permission to start up businesses. Most of these ventures are half-baked fantasies that go belly-up after a few months.

While I have no inclination to open a scuba school here, I like to think I was one of the first *mzungus* to introduce snorkels and other such water toys to this place. Maxwell, an eight-year-old who hung around Mr Stevens a few years back, was very keen on such white man's playthings, especially when I explained you could breathe through a snorkel even when underwater. Before I could explain that the tip of the snorkel had to remain above the surface in order for this miracle to occur, Maxwell had strapped the device about his head, plunged down to about 2 metres and taken a huge breath. He shot spluttering to the surface like a cruise missile.

Ten years later Maxwell was to pilot the rubber duck that took me from Cape Maclear to the port of Salima. This trip of about 30 kilometres across the lake in fact equates to a 100-kilometre shortcut back to Lilongwe, as it cuts out the terrible roads of the southern lakeshore. The day was blustery and the lake lapped menacingly at our flimsy vessel as we motored away from shore. Soon no land could be seen, only tall, wet, messy waves. The swells were getting heavier and the wind churned the water dangerously. Lake Malawi is known as the Calendar Lake as it's 365 miles long and 52 miles wide. When storms whip it up, 4-metre swells are common, and it's no different from being stuck plumb in the middle of the Atlantic Ocean. That day, to compound a sense of impending peril, the engine of the rubber duck kept cutting out, leaving us bobbing on the lake like an abandoned cork, waiting for a swell that for some reason would kick-start the engine once again. I was convinced that Maxwell, my luggage and I were doomed to a liquid grave, and my confidence was hardly enhanced by knowing my life was in the hands of a boy who, a decade earlier, had failed his snorkel test.

We somehow survived the trip, and each time I come back to Malawi I have a Green with Maxwell and we reminisce about our shared trauma, like veterans recalling Vietnam.

Of course, Maxwell is a lot older now. He's a pretty cool dude these days, wearing his hair in dreadlocks and sporting two earrings in his left ear. In fact, he's just wandered into the pub here at Chembe – Rasta chain round his neck, denim jacket and cut-off shorts. The earrings were a gift from an Australian backpacker. One or two of the local dudes here do a roaring trade in soothing every imaginable need of addled, love-lorn overlanders. Innocence was lost in Cape Maclear the day the first Lonely Planet-clutching pioneers tramped through the village. These days, Maxwell is a fully paid-up member of the Cape Maclear Rent-a-Rastas.

Maxwell is here swopping conquest tales with Allison, assistant manager of Chembe Lodge. Allison is another story. A one-man backpacker magnet. While I'm trying to write, he's reading to Maxwell the contents of a much-folded letter. The letter is addressed 'Allison, Cape Maclear, Malawi'. And reads, 'Dear Allison, I'm sorry to hear you have a girlfriend. I was going to come to Cape Maclear today, but I have to be at work. I'll come later in the week. Love, Jill.' Jill's from the States and is currently beavering away to improve the lot of the Malawians in that do-good ole American way. Allison has a box full of similar letters. He goes nightly to The Gap, a boisterous pub-restaurant-lodge run by some South Africans up the beach. Here Allison can take his pick of Norwegian, Dutch and Israeli travellers, all eager to broaden their African experience in every way possible.

There goes the phone. It's obviously working today. Some days it isn't.

'Thank you for calling Chembe Lodge,' says Max the barman. It's long-distance – for Maxwell. His ex-girlfriend from Australia is on the line. Maxwell spends ten minutes updating her on the Cape Maclear scene. He comes over all sheepish when it becomes clear to us eavesdroppers that he has to tell the Australian girl he loves her. I'm sitting here just to his left, pretending to be writing stories. Allison comes up behind him, tickling his back. The chef Kelvin coos Chichewa love verse in Maxwell's ear. Maxwell rolls his eyes and then starts making squishy kissing noises into the receiver. Eventually he hangs up. The girlfriend has been on the line from Adelaide for 20 minutes and has promised to come back to Malawi in June.

'Here to keep you warm in the winter,' observes Kelvin.

'Yeah,' ponders Maxwell, 'but that means I'll have three girlfriends here at that time. That could mean problems.'

The local kids might be prepared to admit defeat as far as canoeing, laundry and bracelets go, but they won't take no for an answer when it comes to the time-honoured Malawian tradition of swopping addresses. Malawi is the undisputed global home of Pen-pals Unlimited, though it might be given a run for its money in this regard by Togo. Each child you stumble across on your lakeshore travels will have a surprisingly fine ability to read and write English and will diligently take down your name and address so they can 'correspond' with you. And they're as good as their word. Too good in fact. After every trip to Malawi, I receive a torrent of mail asking for stationery, exercise books, money to start businesses, Walkmans and the like. Not that the pen-pals are all children. On an early trip to Malawi a few of us took the ferry that chugs up and down the length of Lake Malawi each week. On board we had our photo taken with the chief purser of the ship. Two months later I received a letter bearing a wildly colourful Malawian stamp. It read:

> Dear Peter
>
> With much pleasure to air the views on this space. Well, I am one of the pursers on MV *Ilala*, and we met there on your way from Monkey Bay to Chilumba and Chilumba to Chitimba. On this trip

you were five in number, including ladies. We had a nice stay all of us on board. This time I think you do have a clear picture of me. But I have been awaiting one from you, all in vain. Looking forward to hearing from you.

Yours truly,

Arthur G.M. Mtambo

I rushed guilt-ridden to the photo shop and swiftly dispatched a print.

I remember the trip well. We had first-class berths on the good ship *Ilala*, which meant we didn't have to sleep on the lower deck surrounded by goats, fetid drying *kampango* (lake catfish) and chickens, but on the empty upper deck instead. The ferries are the buses of the lake and provide the sole access to the outside world for remote lakeside villages. The *Ilala* and its sister ship, the *Mtendere,* ply the waters and make frequent stops at settlements along the way, anchoring about 100 metres from shore. Then dugout canoes from the villages will engage in a mini aquatic grand prix, paddling furiously to be first to the ferry in a bid to sell their take-aways – mangoes, bananas, little *usipa* fish.

At these stop-offs, we would climb to the top of the ferry, the equivalent of a three-storey building, and jump off into the sparkling blue depths. Our fellow passengers crammed down below would applaud and holler and only just stop short of grading our leaps like Olympic high-diving judges. We'd then re-board through third class, taking care not to drip water on sleeping children, trip over tethered goats or stand on the cockerels.

One of the best stops that the ferry makes is at Likoma Island. This small oasis is roughly halfway up the lake, near the Mozambican coast. While the ferry drops off supplies here, you can hire a dugout to take you to the island. A short walk brings you to the doors of a magnificent cathedral, St Peter's, whose sudden presence is as awe-inspiring as it is incongruous. The cool stone walls radiate an alluring silence, and tall, stained-glass windows complete the sensation of being somewhere in Europe, rather than on a remote African island. The Anglican cathedral is a stirring feat of architecture, and was painstakingly built between 1903 and 1905 by Scottish missionaries, each weighty stone being lugged across the lake.

Another prolific Malawian letter-writer was Geoffrey Kapichira. middle-aged villager from Cape Maclear. He was much more to the in his eternally polite letters. For example, I received this co dence in early 1993:

Hello Peter,

In the first place I wish you my most respectful regards. Then how are you feeling over there. Back to me here, things are cool both physical and healthy-wise. Well the idea behind jotting this letter is with an intention of reminding you of what you are sending me. I mean the CASSETTE RECORDER. And on top of this please try to send me compacts of music by Lionel Richie, Bunny Wailer, Peter Tosh, Black Uhuru, Run DMC, Lucky Dube, Bob Marley and L.L. Cool J. That's if possible. Would you mind if I ask you about my personal clothes, like a wind breaker, sweat shirts, trousers and a pair of shoes size 7, as well as a sleeping bag? Otherwise let's only pray for life and guidance from God. Lastly I have no more words to proceed and I am just wishing you well in your everyday undertakings.

Best Wishes.
I remain,

Geoffrey Kapichira

PS. Please, please don't forget to pay the custom charges.

These letters continued in varying degrees of desperation over the years. Although these promises were a figment of Geoffrey's imagination, each time I returned to Cape Maclear I ensured I went to say hello and give him a few T-shirts, jeans and so on. After the World Cup in 1995, I again arrived with a bundle of clothing for Geoffrey and his relatives. I knew where he lived in the village because he'd once invited me and a Canadian girl, who was teaching English at Chembe, for dinner and to meet his grandmother. Geoffrey had cooked us eggs and rice in his mud hut.

In 1995, when I knocked on the bamboo door of his home, Geoffrey's grandmother answered. She remembered me, and we exchanged pleasantries as best we could, seeing as neither spoke the other's language. It was left to one of Geoffrey's young nephews to translate the news that my old Lake Malawi correspondent had passed away. He'd died of malaria the week before I arrived. Malaria is a big killer in Malawi. With the dire lack of medical care available, the children are particularly vulnerable. During the rainy season there's a funeral, featuring a heartbreakingly tiny coffin, every other day.

I sometimes have company while I'm trying to write here at Chembe Lodge. Saulo is now 14, and I've known him since he was about 10 when he offered his services as laundryman, the traditional first rung on the ladder to economic empowerment for the children of Cape Maclear. I once bought a leather soccer ball for Saolo and his mates. We used to organise games – Villagers v. *Mzungus* – on the bumpy expanse of ground beyond the village maize fields. I'd normally turn out for the whiteys but sometimes guested as an honorary villager seeing as I'd visited Cape Maclear so often. One time I played for the villagers against a bunch of skinhead international tramps from the UK. We were 4–0 up when the backpackers started trying to hack at the locals and fling racial insults. A young girl watching the game was hit in the face when a backpacker kicked the ball venomously at a villager, who ducked out of harm's way. The girl lost an eye.

Saulo has made a habit of coming around to the lodge after school most afternoons. He sits next to me, leafing through the pile of books by my computer. He knows I'm trying to write so he just sits here, and our conversations are limited to around ten words an hour.

'How was school, Saulo?'

'OK.'

'What did you learn today?'

'Maths. And social studies.'

Then there'll be silence for an hour.

'What else, Saulo?'

'Nothing much.'

More silence.

At the moment, Saulo seems really keen on learning about this laptop, and I could do with a break from all this, so just excuse me while I go through the basics with him.

SAULO PHIRI. STANDARD 6. HALLO FROM CAPE MACLEAR.

There you go, see how quick the kids cotton on round here. He wrote that himself. Even if I did have to help him out with the space bar.

Yesterday I told the writing to *voetsek* in all 11 official Rainbow Nation languages and took a trip on *Hello Afrika*, the catamaran belonging to Chembe Lodge. It's one of life's finer pleasures to stretch out on the net-like tarpaulin on this sleek craft while the water churns beneath. There's even a stereo system aboard with muffled speakers, so you can blast the fishermen from their canoes with U2's 'Achtung Baby' at full volume. All hark to the calls of Africa: the majestic roar of the lion, the plaintive cry of the fish eagle, the distorted howl of the blown speaker. The catamaran took us scuba diving off the nearby island and then on to the hippo pools round the bay. We saw three *mvuus*, the local name for hippos, passing within metres of a fisherman perched in his precarious dugout. They watched our progress, heads poked above the surface, regarding us with that aloof, quizzical look hippos have perfected.

We returned to Chembe just in time for sundowners. Usually, as the sun dips beyond the waterline and the sky starts turning the colour of a bruise, I stop writing and play a game of *bawo* with Saulo. *Bawo* is that game of calculation played in a hollowed-out wooden board with seeds for counters. Various forms of the game are found throughout Africa.

Then it's time for dinner. Max takes out the drum and beats a rich tattoo signalling to the guests that it's time to eat. Dinners at Chembe Lodge unfold around the long communal dining table. Max fusses round each diner, making sure a fresh flower has been placed amid the crisply folded napkin in each wine glass. Food at the lodge is innovative, especially as cuisinal variety is close to impossible here in Malawi. But Kelvin the chef once made me a magic chicken mexicali pizza for lunch. And each night an array of chicken and fish curries, vegetarian dishes, even desserts such as mangoes, peaches and custard pour forth from the kitchen. The table talk is spirited, and the mosquitoes are thick and dance about our ears. The paraffin lanterns attract swarms of midges, which frequently nose-dive into the food – protein supplements. Nali – the hottest peri-peri sauce known to man – is always lurking on the table, ready to fell unwary diners. How hot is Nali? The label on the bottle says, 'Friends, take care'. On the top of the bottle, red-and-white warnings flash, 'Very Hot!', 'Dynamic!', 'Abale Samalane!'. These warnings should be taken seriously.

During dinner the generator will click off, and the hum from the fridge dies to be consumed by the deafening quiet of a Malawian night. The cicadas chirp, competing with the soothing lap of lake on sand. The night skies here are astounding. Ink black, pollution free and vivid. Clusters of stars appear so close you might reach out and grab a fistful. It's as if someone's run amuck in the darkroom with a silver spray-gun.

I was in Cape Maclear when South Africa took on Malawi in a World Cup qualifier at Blantyre a year or so back. There was great excitement in the village, and most of the locals had plenty of kwachas riding on the game. As I walked through the village 15 minutes before kick-off there wasn't a soul to be seen. I joined Moses Banda and his mates to listen to the game on an ancient crackling wireless. Moses is another local I've known since he was about six and who had knocked shyly on our door at Mr Stevens offering to wash our clothes for 50 tambala. We remembered him when we returned to Cape Maclear, and since then we've always stayed in touch. Over the years, a teacher friend called Alistair Stewart and I have tried to set up Moses Banda in a few enterprises. Once we gave him cash to buy a dugout canoe in which to ferry backpackers to feed the fish eagles and to snorkel among the rich seam of tropical fish at Otter Point.

We also tried to get a little pizza restaurant up and running. This venture must have popped into my head after a combination of too much sun, too many Greens and a surplus intake of malaria tablets. The oven proved no problem and was ready in a matter of days with the aid of local builders. The food itself was more of a challenge. At Moses' Pizza Shack, we were eventually forced to settle on a four-item menu: *Chambo* Pizza, *Kampango* Pizza, Chicken Pizza and Pizza Surprise. Pizza Surprise was pizza without *chambo*, chicken or *kampango*. Or cheese. Cheese was the single most pressing stumbling block to the success of our daring addition to Cape Maclear's *haute cuisine* scene. The store at Monkey Bay is 20 kilometres away, and the availability of cheese there is sporadic at best. I suggested making goat's cheese from the village livestock but was shouted down by locals and *mzungus* alike. The only solution was to drive to Mangochi 150 kilometres away, as Oliver at Chembe Lodge does twice a week. This proved highly impractical, and in the end we were forced to resign ourselves to the fact that the pizzas at Moses' Pizza Shack would invariably be cheeseless. Pizza Surprise was indeed just that: a bare wedge of cooked dough decorated with strips of wilting tomato and chunks of onion.

Nevertheless, the market for any type of food other than grit-smeared fish and chips is massive in Cape Maclear, and our young restaurant stumbled gamely along for four months. I'd phone Moses each week or so for an update. This was just after the elders of Cape Maclear had invested in a telephone booth, which stood proudly on the beach front outside Mr Stevens. I'd dial the number from Johannesburg, and the phone would ring at least 20 times before finally being answered by whoever happened to be strolling past. This person would then bellow at one of the kids to run off and fetch Moses, who was usually tinkering at the Shack a few hundred metres away. Moses would arrive breathless and deliver a solemn progress report on the number of meals served and Carlsbergs quaffed.

The phone lasted about three months before it succumbed, an inevitable victim of African attrition, I suppose. Then one day I got a letter from Moses saying that the Pizza Shack had burnt down. Late one night Moses had awoken to shouts of confusion and the sight of bright orange flames licking the sky. The grass walls were consumed speedily by the fire, and in the mayhem all the equipment was looted. Moses suspected that the perpetrators were locals who were jealous of his growing little business, though no one was ever caught.

For that World Cup soccer match, Moses, a few others and I gathered in an open space where the radio was blasting forth in Chichewa. It was frustrating not understanding the commentary, and I was forced to rely on Moses for delayed translations of the action. As a South African I was given plenty of condolences in advance. The consensus was that Malawi would win with something to spare, even if they were up against the African champions. The name on everyone's lips was that of John Maduka, and how this hot-shot Malawian striker would run rings around Mark Fish and company. The beer was flowing freely – Greens as well as the local Chibuku brew, which is potent enough to uncurl chest hairs. Gnarled old men sat on upturned beer crates, impassively absorbing the commentary. Each time Malawi attacked there'd be a ripple of anticipation through the gathering, to be followed by a chorus of clicks and tut-tuts as the attack was snuffed out.

Of course, South Africa won the game, sneaking home by a single goal from Eric Tinkler before going on to complete the job of qualification for the final group phase with a 3–0 win at the FNB Stadium. I was expecting a hard time from the locals after the match, but, with true Malawian grace, my listening companions were highly complimentary of the South Africans and congratulated me as if I had been personally responsible for choosing the team and the tactics.

That night a liquid, late-night raid on The Gap was planned from Chembe. We South Africans celebrated the win, while the locals' defeat was softened under a tidal wave of Greens and Chibukus. By the time we returned to the lodge armed with our torches, we weaved woozy paths. The rain began falling at around three in the morning, and the wind played havoc with the tents. But here at Chembe, I always leave the flaps ajar so that the dawn rays can invite themselves in around 6.30, heralding the start of another delicious 24-hour cycle.

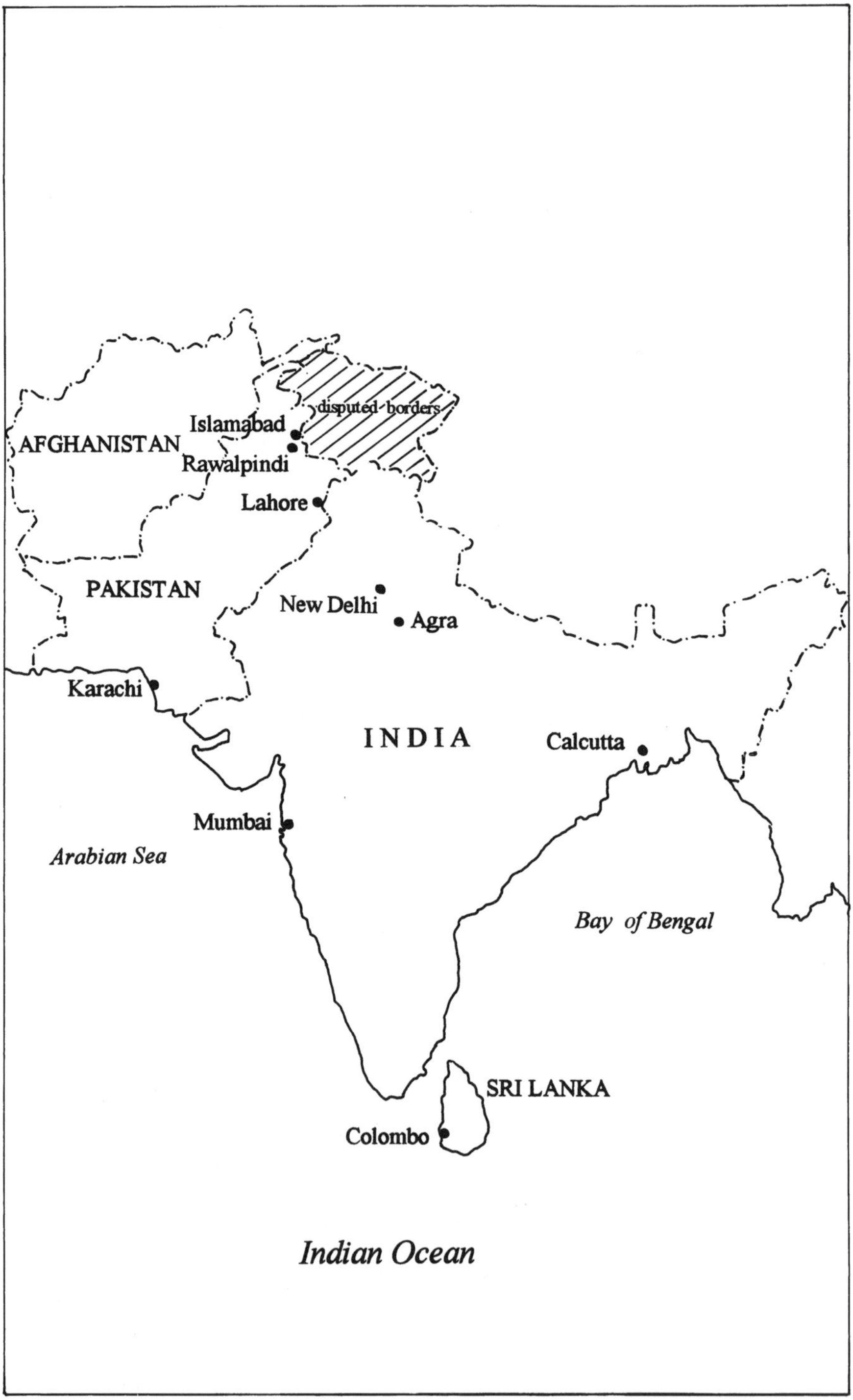
disputed borders
Islamabad
AFGHANISTAN
Rawalpindi
Lahore
PAKISTAN
New Delhi
Agra
Karachi
INDIA
Calcutta
Mumbai
Arabian Sea
Bay of Bengal
SRI LANKA
Colombo
Indian Ocean

CHAPTER EIGHT

'May the Sporting Atmoshphere Prevail'

'IT'S NOT A MATTER of life and death. It's much more important than that.'

Legendary Liverpool manager Bill Shankly was, of course, talking football when he coined the phrase that would become one of the most quoted in sport.

Had Shankly ever witnessed an India v. Pakistan clash, however, he might have concluded that cricket was a sport that could give the round-ball game a run for its money when it comes to rousing passion.

Imran Khan, the former Pakistani captain with a penchant for gorgeous English heiresses, is renowned for his Cambridge-educated reasoned comments. Yet he has described playing against India as like taking part in a jihad, a holy war. To say cricket in the East stokes fire in the breasts of followers is as much of an understatement as saying Sachin Tendulkar can bat a bit.

When it emerged that these sworn foes of the subcontinent would meet in India for the quarterfinal of the 1996 Wills World Cup, politicians in both nations called for the game to be cancelled. The last time either country had toured the other was in 1989, when India ventured to Pakistan. Threats from Hindu militants prevented Pakistan playing in the Hero Cup of 1993 in India, and it had been nine years since Pakistan had played a Test on Indian soil. The teams had sporadic contact abroad in places like Sharjah where, in 1995, players from both sides entered the arena hand in hand to show there was no animosity between the teams on the field. In an attempt to extend the olive branch further, Pakistani batsman Javed Miandad had personally invited a Hindu leader to be his guest at the 1996 World Cup Final in Lahore. This leader's supporters had once dug up the Mumbai wicket to prevent a Pakistani tour.

The root of the bitterness stems from Pakistan's political separation from newly independent India in 1947. Two wars have since been fought over the white-peaked Himalayan region of Kashmir, where Muslim separatists still wage a guerilla war against Indian 'occupation'. Pakistan, which controls one third of the area, disputes Indian claims that Kashmir ever seceded. Political and religious distrust between the two nations has simmered ever since. Kashmiri skirmishes were virtual daily occurrences during the World Cup. The only reason the quarterfinal in Bangalore went ahead, said Hindu activists, was because 'this is an international tournament and we would not like to hurt international sentiments'. Had it been a simple Pakistan–India match, they wouldn't have allowed it to take place at all.

As the build-up to the game intensified, the Pakistani nation was fed a diet of jingoism through its various state-controlled newspaper and television media. One premise was that Pakistan would win because one Pakistani (Muslim) soldier was equal to ten Indian (Hindu) soldiers.

Before the match, the Pakistan team complained of feeling vulnerable because they were playing in India. The game ultimately went ahead amid a security presence of more than 2 000 police, who had been drafted in to supplement units of India's border security force. India won, and the result meant the Pakistanis had much more reason to feel vulnerable upon returning to their own country. The torrents of abuse, gushes of vitriol and waves of despair that flowed in the wake of Pakistan's defeat were startling to behold.

Wild rumours gathered as most people in Pakistan refused to accept that their defeat may just have been because India were the better team on the day. Influential captain Wasim Akram had not been able to play because of injury. Many Pakistanis, however, were convinced the skipper had been bribed to stand down. Others swore the team doctor had been paid to jab Wasim with a pain-inducing injection instead of a pain-killing one. A journalist claimed the Pakistani twelfth man had carried instructions to stand-in skipper Aamir Sohail telling him to throw the match, because the Pakistani team had received death threats in their dressing room while Sohail and fellow opening batsman Saeed Anwar were flaying the Indian attack early on. Another writer said the players had been given drugged snacks at lunch that had dulled their reflexes. The racy start to Pakistan's innings was explained away by pointing out that the drugs obviously needed time to start working. The most lavish theory was trotted out by Pakistan's opposition party mullahs, who accused the government of losing any 'divine advantage' the team might have enjoyed by allowing 'obscene and un-Islamic' cultural shows on stage and television.

Acrimony persisted for days after the match. Javed Miandad, who had come out of retirement for the tournament but performed badly, was savaged in print. 'Miandad's pathetic display, which so cruelly revealed his slowed reflexes and his weakened wrists, was another reminder that in Pakistan, sportsmen do not retire any more readily than politicians or bureaucrats,' bugled one newspaper. A daily columnist wrote that a friend from London had phoned to ask him to confirm a rumour that Wasim Akram had been shot.

The dismay reflected in the media was as intensely felt in the streets. One fan filed a lawsuit against Wasim 'in the public interest'. He demanded that Wasim, Sohail, Waqar Younis and Aaqib Javed be 'tried under the war crime treason law' for losing to the enemy. The judge, being of sober temperament, recommended the lawsuit be withdrawn, saying the petitioner should accept Akram's explanation about his fitness problems 'if Wasim was prepared to swear on the Holy Qur'an that he hadn't faked it'. In Lahore, a group of youngsters burnt an effigy of Wasim in the marketplace. Readers of one newspaper recommended public flogging for Wasim and coach Intikhab Alam, a tactic that certain Gauteng Lions rugby fans might be tempted to propose for coach and captain after their team's mediocre campaigns of late.

Even Prime Minister Benazir Bhutto, who had helped coax Miandad out of his two-year retirement, added her five rupees worth, though to be fair, it was an attempt of sorts to pacify. 'A game is a game and we should accept the result with good grace. It was a chance that we lost the toss and then Wasim Akram was not well. Cricket is a game of chance,' the premier reasoned.

The South African team would probably have agreed with the Pakistani prime minister's sentiments. Hansie Cronjé's team started the World Cup like greyhounds bounding from the trap. They blitzed through their round-robin phase unscathed to set up a clash with the ailing West Indies in the quarterfinals. The Caribbean side were still wandering round in a daze, trying to absorb their humiliating loss against Kenya. South Africa had won seven matches in a row. The Windies would surely be blown away.

The South Africans had proved during the opening round that they were one of the most accomplished sides in the Cup. But the law of averages dictated that sooner or later they must lose a game. Some squad members had actually hoped they'd get beaten just once in the preliminaries, to alleviate the pressure of going through the entire event unbeaten. But one-day cricket, as Ms Bhutto noted, is indeed a game of chance.

I arrived from South Africa early on the morning of the South Africa–West Indies game in Karachi, preparing to chart the side's progression to World Cup glory. By the end of the day, South Africa had been beaten and the squad were heading for home. I'd been in Pakistan for less than 24 hours, and the team were heading in the opposite direction. It was like we were contestants in some Afro-Asian Boeing 747 relay.

In the quarterfinal, South Africa had gambled on playing two spinners – Pat Symcox and Paul Adams – at the expense of strike bowler Allan Donald. The experiment was neither a conclusive success nor a disaster. As it turned out, the South Africans were beaten by a combination of Brian Lara's magic and their own frailties with the bat. For Donald, it was the worst day of his eminent career.

'That to me was the most emotional moment,' Donald would later tell me in an interview. 'Being told by Hansie that we had decided to go with two spinners. I suspected it because three days before you could just sense the vibe wasn't right. I was devastated. We had a team talk where we discussed the tactics, and the adrenaline was surging and we were talking about just two games to go to the Final. But then came the decision and when Hansie asked me to contribute to the meeting, I couldn't. I was shattered and went to my room.'

The Wills World Cup thus ended on a doleful note for one of the world's best fast bowlers, but the tournament confirmed that the Jonty Rhodes phenomenon is as powerful on the subcontinent as it is in KwaZulu-Natal. Throughout India and Pakistan, vast billboards showing Rhodes in horizontal diving mode were used to promote the tournament. In Karachi, a club pavilion had been named after the acrobatic fielder. His was the name the crowds chanted when the South Africans appeared in a new town. I also uncovered another obvious sign of Jonty-fever at a small, makeshift shoe shop in a crowded corner of New Delhi's endless sprawl of bazaars. This outdoor store, wedged between the Malhotra Silk Store, Anand Crockery Emporium and Grasim Gwalior Suiting, proudly displayed a hiking boot with a Jonty Rhodes signature burnt into the leather. Jonty's agent might wish to follow this up, as there may be royalties due.

Someone once asked me what single word best described India. Of course there are the smells, the squalor, the colour, the teeming humanity, the dust, the heat. But above all stands the noise. To be in India is to be in the eye of an aural storm. The cities are a clamour of roaring trucks, parping tuk-tuks, whining diesel lorries, humming scooters, belching minibuses, howling taxis. People shout. Hounds yip. Cows moo. On returning to Johannesburg, death-quiet by comparison, I kept looking over my shoulder, wondering where everyone and everything was.

India is also synonymous with spirituality, but in that country I underwent no alteration of the mind. Unless you count the dangerous bottle of Thunder Rum (42,2 per cent alcohol content) bought on a whim one night in Delhi. That was the evening I wandered from my hotel, taking care not to bother the sacred cows at rest in the middle of a gridlocked traffic circle, flagged down a tuk-tuk and asked the driver to drop me at a disco. These tri-wheeled taxis of the East have two speeds – park and breakneck. Their minimal height above ground enables passengers to inhale an optimum amount of lorry exhaust smog. Taking a tuk-tuk is also a good way to enjoy a near-death experience, as laden trucks belt past inches from your elbow bone, and motorcycles threaten to remove kneecaps, which tend to stick out of doorless tuk-tuks because these vehicles aren't designed to contain 6-foot-3-inch bodies.

But tuk-tuks are a cheap, quick and exciting way of getting round places like Delhi. They bob, swerve and weave through traffic like Baby Jake Matlala in the ring, and seem to have been granted the freedom of the road in India, much as Gauteng taxis have at home. It's a challenge of Manhattan dimensions, however, to find a driver who speaks English. My driver misunderstood the disco request and took me to the Blue Star strip club. That's my excuse anyway. I wasn't even aware they had such things in India. What the heck, I'd have a beer there before moving on.

Take a cab anywhere in the so-called Third World, and you have a friend, if not for life, then at least for the rest of the evening. No matter how long you linger in taverns, your tuk-tuk or taxi driver will be there waiting patiently when you stagger into the night air ready for home. My Delhi tuk-tuk driver tagged along into the Blue Star to make sure no one else would get my rupees that evening. I offered him a beer, but discovered alcohol was not for sale. Not even Kingfisher lager, which is as common to India as Castle is to South Africa. Kingfisher's motto is 'Most thrilling chilled'. Perhaps the cabaret club owners took to heart the other slogan that appears on Kingfisher cans – 'Consumption of liquor is injurious to health'.

By the time I'd worked out there was no beer to be had at the Blue Star, the 'exotic dancers' had emerged from the wings. They did a strange thing. They came and shook hands with every single patron in the room.

While they did so, some guy chanted mournful poems from the rostrum in the manner of my former biology teacher explaining mitochondria. The girls finally completed greeting their customers and took to the stage. One elderly Sikh in a turban was to disgrace himself by attempting a lecherous lunge at one of the dancers, who smiled as she deftly evaded him. The patrons cheered the Sikh wildly.

On a more cultured note, I journeyed to the fabled Taj Mahal in Agra. The 'highway' from Delhi is single lane each way and progress is stately. The 250-kilometre trip took five and three quarter hours in a decrepit yellow-and-black Ambassador taxi hired from Quick Travel Company on Connaught Place, the hub of Delhi, where three concentric circles of whitewashed, colonnaded buildings stand among eight radial roads. I found out the hard way that the vehicle lacked shock absorbers while I tried to cat-nap in the early morning sun. We shuddered and bounced over the highway's many ruts and divots. Drivers in the Indian countryside were as laid-back as the urban motorists were suicidal. The rears of packed lorries all bore colourful signs on the left and right extremities. These signs usually read 'Horn Please'. The idea is to hoot violently at such trucks upon reaching passing range, and the lorry will then pull into the soft shoulder to let you by. Very cordial and un-Gauteng like. This isn't to say accidents are infrequent. They just happen in slow motion. I saw three trucks tipped on their sides during the drive to Agra.

The Taj Mahal is, of course, the immortal creation of the Mughal Emperor Shah Jahan, built in memory of his favourite wife, Mumtaj Begum. It's said to be the most photographed building in the world, and is certainly impressive. The Taj Mahal apparently changes hue at different times of the day. Full moon in October is said to be the best time to visit, when the Taj shines silvery white at night, pinkish red at dawn and with a golden glow at sunset. The marble structure and esplanade is offset by an equally imposing 'guesthouse' in chocolate-coloured marble. The silvery Jamuna River lies behind and villagers splash in its waters. Semiprecious stones stud the interior 26-metre-high dome of the Taj Mahal. There is Qur'anic verse on the wall of the mausoleum as well as a lattice work of ornate flowers. These are made from costly jewels imported from exotic lands, and they illuminate if your guide lifts a cigarette lighter to them. Always assuming you've paid your guide sufficient rupees to spur him into doing this.

My guide was as stubborn as a camel. I had to cross his palm with rupees far too often for my liking. In fact, the entire Taj Mahal experience

– magnificent though the structure is – smacked of grubby commerce. At the ticket office is a sign warning of pickpockets, and they don't mean the guides. Then comes the charge involved for leaving your shoes outside the mausoleum, a fee for a guide to the interior, and a tip needed for someone to show you the river. There are also a host of overpriced stores selling inferior quality knick-knacks just inside the confines.

The Taj Mahal is memorable too for the chancers roaming its sprucely manicured gardens offering trick photographs of the monument. If you stand at a certain vantage point on a raised marble platform with the reflecting pools and the Taj Mahal in the background, and, under guidance from a camera-toter, hold the thumb and forefinger of one hand together, the resulting photo looks as if you are lifting the fabled relic between your fingertips. There is no shortage of photographers eager to press this classy reminder of one of the world's great wonders into the palms of us gullible tourists.

To complete the feeling of being fleeced, the outlying shanty areas of the town of Agra also house hardened young bargainers who have honed their powers of persuasion on a billion simple Westerners. The eight-year-olds here will flog you books of kinky Kama Sutra postcards faster than you can say 'trick photograph'.

I wouldn't say I was disappointed by the Taj Mahal, but, as my travels have tended to confirm, there is always the danger of being more excited by the idea of a place than being at the place itself. Imagination is the ultimate pair of rose-tinted spectacles. I remember Sunday afternoons spent happily engrossed in travel guides at Exclusive Books – plotting courses, imagining journeys, dreaming up trips. When reading of, say, the Taj Mahal, one's mind is filled only with pristine visions of immaculate edifices, smiling locals, soothing conditions.

In my experience, however, the reality of journeying to these icons of global wonderment is often different. Take the Taj Mahal. The trip ultimately spiralled into something of a trial by hustlers. In the end I was mopping the sweat from my brow while flicking at flies in the searing heat as I tried to evade the hustling gimmick salesmen that barged past the sweet-looking beggar kids who were actually trying to pick my pocket before I could get to my wallet and pay the insistent guide who'd led me 800 metres on foot to have my photo taken round the back of this marvel. All so I can take out the picture at a Melville coffee shop and boast to my friends what a cleansing spiritual moment this was.

It was a relief to get back to the taxi. Until I remembered there was no air conditioning in the car. One pothole later my kidneys were reminding me never again to take shock absorbers for granted.

Air travel is the most painless way of traversing the subcontinent. But flying in India is as unpredictable as the dollar–rand exchange rate. Planes are usually late, delays common, connections within a few hours rare. I flew from Delhi to Calcutta for the World Cup semifinal between India and Sri Lanka. I arrived at the airport at noon. The departure time was 2 pm. We eventually took off at 8.45 pm.

On the flight, I was greeted by someone who had noticed South African press credentials round my neck.

'Excuse me,' said the polite Indian, 'but do you know Ernie Els?'

I mentioned that I had indeed interviewed the golfer who put Germiston on the world map, at which the Indian made noises not unlike a teenage boy at a Spice Girls concert. His name was Barun Agarwal, and he was a young golfer ranked in the top ten in his country. Ernie Els was his idol. He insisted there and then that I was to stay in his family's apartment for the few days I was in Calcutta. This was a godsend. As usual, my accommodation plans consisted of a vague notion of bumbling round Calcutta expecting someone to take pity on a confused foreigner and aim me in the direction of a dwelling. Failing which, Mother Teresa's Mission of Charity would surely provide shelter. After all, the doughty Albanian nun runs 81 schools, 325 mobile medical centres, 28 family planning centres, 67 leprosy missions and 32 orphanages in the city. There must be a spare mattress somewhere.

Such thoughts were banished after one look at the seething mass of human beings in the arrivals hall of Dum Dum Airport. Taxi drivers were grabbing wrists and yanking luggage out of hands in order to win customers. Barun, by contrast, was met by his father's driver. Soon he and I were outside a plush apartment block near the Eden Gardens Stadium. I was introduced to Barun's mother who, after greeting me with a formal handshake, bustled off into an adjacent room and minutes later emerged with a steaming heap of Indian delicacies for me to sample. A room belonging to a sister studying in Madras was arranged for the surprised, highly appreciative visitor.

Barun owned a car and over the next couple of days showed me around the Bengali capital city. An Indian poet once said, 'Though Bengal had been torn apart many a time, it is always full of good humour.' It needs to be. Some call Calcutta a city of wonders, others label it a city of processions. Most recently, and probably most accurately, thanks to movies like *City of Joy*, it's known as a city of slums. Yet during the height of colonial occupation, Calcutta was known as the Paris of the East, where opulence, art and culture held sway on a grand scale. The city is still India's literary and free-thinking hub. The Indian philosopher

Gokhale proclaims, 'What Bengal thinks today, India thinks tomorrow and the rest of the world the day after.' Perhaps so, but certainly not as far as sanitation is concerned. Livestock gobble at storey-high stacks of rotting litter. Locals happily wash, launder, brush teeth, greet each other and defecate in the Hooghly River, which runs through the city and is, in parts, the colour of last night's cooking oil.

Calcutta provides striking examples of the squalor and splendour that squat cheek by jowl in India. Barun was a member of the Royal Calcutta Golf Course, which is the oldest such venue in the world outside Scotland. This stretch of clipped-lawn colonial elegance is a tranquil oasis in a city that always threatens to overwhelm. As is the opulent Oberoi Grand Hotel, where World Cup players and journalists stayed, and where the chandeliers are as big as front-room Christmas trees. And the cocktail bar beer prices are positively French – R20 for a Kingfisher as opposed to R2 at the corner shops.

Venture a few metres from the red-carpeted hotel entrance, however, and you're back in the real world – negotiating a swirl of vehicles, pedestrians and gnarled beggars in gritty, throat-searing heat. There appears to be a pecking order among Indian beggars. The more lurid the physical ailment, the more emphatic the request for rupees. Once, a woman pushed what must have been her crippled mother in front of me, unequivocally demanding banknotes. As I boarded a tuk-tuk in New Delhi, someone shoved the handless stump of his right arm under my nose as bait for coins. And, while in Barun's Renault 9 inching through Calcutta's dense traffic at sunset, a blind teenager, eyes opaque like those of a dead fish, scratched against the car window. She had a begging bowl in one hand and a ragged child on her hip whose nose she pushed flat against the glass. Having a vehicle to roam the streets of this sprawling, humid city is a massive advantage, but Calcutta by car is not for the sensitive.

In Calcutta, as in the rest of India, one drives on the left-hand side of the road. Most of the time. If this is not convenient, the right-hand side will do. I'm not joking. I have a vivid recollection of tearing down Calcutta's gloomy night streets, peeping between my fingers like a 'see no evil' monkey charm. Pedestrians whirled past in a blur as Barun hunkered over the wheel. The feeble, watery illumination from the streetlights was what I imagined the gas lamps of London must have looked like during Victorian times. Tramlines criss-crossed the streets like discarded strands of spaghetti. Often Barun would hare off the wrong way down a one-way road. The oncoming vehicle would merely veer out of our path. Not once did I notice surprise or anger on the face of the correct road user. These were customary driving tactics in this city.

India may have won that hi-octane World Cup quarterfinal against Pakistan in Bangalore, but they were also to feel the point-blank blast of their supporters' fury after the semifinal against Sri Lanka.

The Eden Gardens Stadium, where the match was played, is home of the Bengali Cricket Association and is a sporting cathedral of substance. The Dr B.C. Roy Clubhouse is an elegant marble-fronted structure with neatly flowering gardens in front and huge frescoes of cricketers towering over the streets below. The ground itself has a capacity in excess of 100 000, and for the World Cup a swish electronic scoreboard and huge new floodlights had been installed. On the day of the semifinal, the roads within 100 metres of the ground were cordoned off by khaki-wearing Calcutta traffic police who jammed 'No Entry' signs in the road along with notices bearing the message 'We Care for You'. They wore green hard hats and brandished sticks. Fans who queued sedately in the heat were occasionally swatted into line.

The vast press box in the main stand was mercifully air conditioned. Outside our comfort zone, the fans packed into Eden Gardens like battery-farm chickens. An Indian win was anticipated by all but a few hundred Sri Lankan fans. The Mexican wave was in evidence. Spectators wore the orange, white and green Indian national colours plastered in zinc on their faces. They hoisted mis-spelt banners like 'May the Sporting Atmoshphere Prevail'. The temperature was 42 degrees and the humidity close to 100 per cent. Spectators jostled elbows to the fore at the infrequent cold-drink stands.

Somewhere in the crowd was wrinkly rock star Mick Jagger. The still rocking and Rolling Stone was on his way to Lahore to donate money to Imran Khan's cancer hospital and to watch the Final. With Pakistan not able to offer booze and other substances vital to the wellbeing of decadent Western rock stars, the Indian papers claimed plans were afoot for a massive secret party in Jagger's honour at 'an unspecified venue' in Pakistan.

On the field, the sporting atmosphere was being tested. Indian captain Mohammed Azharuddin had won the toss and sent Sri Lanka in to bat on a wicket that traditionally favours spin in the evening. It seemed like the correct decision when Javagal Srinath nipped out two batsmen in the opening over, but the Pearl Islanders fought back and posted a formidable score.

The Indians made a hash of their reply. By the time Sanath Jayasuriya had claimed the seventh Indian scalp, there was no hope of a home victory. The banners that read 'May the Sporting Atmoshphere Prevail' were suddenly being set alight, and around the stadium bright fires sprouted among the heavily peopled bleachers. Life-size posters of Sachin Tendulkar were torched. Then the missiles began raining down on the unfortunate Sri Lankan boundary fieldsmen. South African umpire Cyril Mitchley and his colleague took the players off the ground for a while, but when play resumed, the bottles and stones again arced from the terraces. The match was abandoned and awarded to Sri Lanka. The players needed heavily armed escorts to leave the stadium.

Mohammed Azharuddin came under fire for his decision to bat second on the Eden Gardens turner. Fans burnt posters of the captain in the city after the game, and ignited welcome arches and banners put up for the World Cup. Security men had to be placed outside the home of the Indian skipper in Hyderabad after his family received threatening phone calls. Of course, the Pakistanis celebrated India's semifinal demise as thoroughly as if the result had been a Pakistan win. At the Final in Lahore a number of banners would be waved by locals thanking the Sri Lankans for 'crushing India's dream'.

Calcutta had come to its senses and hung its head in shame by the time dawn broke the day after the match. A local radio station organised a letter of apology on behalf of the entire city to the Sri Lankan captain, Arjuna Ranatunga. The letter read:

> Dear Arjuna
>
> We Calcuttans have over the years earned a reputation for being excellent hosts, who have always received guests with warmth and affection. We are also very proud of the fact that we understand and care for sport better than most. Sadly, we lost our composure and, with it, our reputation last night at Eden Gardens. We are extremely ashamed of our behaviour and wholeheartedly apologise to you and your wonderful team. We congratulate your team on its superb performance.

The sporting atmoshphere had been rekindled.

I took an overnight train back to New Delhi from Calcutta's body-clogged railway station. Barun drove me to the station. Mrs Agarwal was convinced I would not be able to find anything worth eating in the rest of India, so had packed me a bag full of curried samoosas, piquant meat-balls and savoury tarts. The journey was to last 18 hours, and the smart red-and-white coaches of Indian Railways' sleeper compartments were divided up apartheid-style. Foreigners were lodged together. I shared with two Englishmen who could have stepped straight from the pages of *A Passage to India*, so completely did they resemble the colonial stiffs of that era. A sign in the corridors read 'Please do not spit in the compartments'. Most people obeyed this. Though some passengers had the disconcerting habit of clearing their throats in the clearest, most unselfconscious manner first thing in the morning. Not the greatest sound to wake up to.

As the train chugged onward through the provinces of West Bengal, Bihar and Uttar Pradesh, we listened to the Beatles belting out the 'Ballad of John and Yoko' through scratchy speakers. The four-bed sleeper compartments were full, and in an adjacent cubicle was a man who is living proof that the world is indeed no more these days than a global village. He was a rice salesman from, of all places, Ventersdorp. Talk about trying to sell ice to the Eskimos. The gent in question had smuggled a vast stock of Kingfisher lagers aboard to sustain him through the journey (alcohol being forbidden on Indian Railways, as many signs announced). He offered me one and we sat sipping this booty with ears cocked for the guards, like schoolboys sneaking a smoke behind the bike shed. The rice salesman's tongue loosened greatly as inroads were made into the Kingfishers. He spent most of the trip carping on about how much he missed South Africa – the great roads, the efficient infrastructure, the wide-open, unpeopled spaces, the uncomplicated food.

And all this from a man who, though now residing in Eugene Terre'Blanche's turf, was born and raised in Mumbai.

All Pakistan International Airline flights begin with the same honey-voiced message flooding the cabin: 'Let us commence our journey with a short prayer from the Holy Qur'an.' After a short silence, a recorded extract is piped through and passengers, Muslim or not, are cast in a reflective mood.

Not that a journey on this airline warrants such a wing and a prayer attitude in my experience. All the PIA flights that I took during the World Cup were on time, efficient and my luggage didn't end up in Laos. The only thing missing was beer. Pakistan is a dry country. The only liquor available in the entire nation is at the bar of the international hotel in Rawalpindi. When bringing hard tack into the country, you must produce evidence that you are a certified alcoholic.

Journalists have been known to enjoy the odd tipple, so you can imagine the horrors this situation created for the media pack following the

World Cup circus around. Of course, the only thing worse than being surrounded by a throng of drunken journalists for two weeks is being surrounded by a throng of sober journalists for two weeks. Perhaps with this in mind, the Pakistani authorities did, in fact, relax the alcohol rule slightly during the tournament. I managed to bring in a bottle of rum without a hitch. Other reporters were taking no chances, though, and decanted whisky into shampoo bottles, stuffed tot packs down their socks and used other such inventive methods to smuggle in some sustenance.

If Karachi resembles Johannesburg by the sea – sprawling shanty suburbs, pollution, crime and teeming migrants keen to make a quick buck – then Lahore in the north of the country is like Cape Town – regal, austere, scenically beautiful and with a faint air of superiority in the locals.

Imran Khan comes from Lahore. Although during the World Cup, as far as TV and newspapers went, the man appeared not to exist. Imran was about to enter Pakistan's political fray, and the government saw him as such a threat that he was being boycotted and labelled public enemy number one. PIA's 1996 calendar, which I had glanced at while awaiting my luggage, paid homage to the country's past cricket captains. Yet it didn't mention the nation's greatest-ever skipper. Imran Khan led Pakistan to their 1992 World Cup triumph, but every government-related organisation had been ordered to strike him from the records. Pakistan TV had a Pepsi ad that showed the victorious Pakistan team doing a lap of honour after the 1992 World Cup. Captain Imran had been censored out. The head of PTV, who happened to be the wife of a government minister, made news when she had to plead with journalists to return to a press conference after they had walked out when she refused to answer any questions about the Imran Khan boycott. There was also a ban on any adverts for Imran's pet projects, such as his cancer hospital in memory of his mother.

The World Cup Final was played at the Gaddafi Stadium in Lahore. Imran Khan, happily, was alive, well and present at the game, elegant in his crisp white traditional dress. The Final was between Australia and the surprising Sri Lankans. The Sri Lankans had unveiled a new brand of cricket at the World Cup. Their opening batsmen, Sanath Jayasuriya and Romesh Kaluwitherana, had hit upon a simple tactic. Go out and blast away from the first ball. This ploy had worked more often than not, and had propelled the team through to the Final. Predictably, the Pearl Islanders enjoyed vast support in the packed stadium. As has become standard at sports events around the world, a South African was in the terraces wearing a latex Nelson Mandela mask. Banners also showed that South Africans were not alone in their opinion of the Australian umpire

Darrell Hair, who made some bizarre decisions in the 1993–4 series Down Under. One local held an ungrammatical placard saying 'Without Darrell Hair, Australia go get nowhere'.

The Australians batted first and were restricted to 241 for 7 after threatening a much bigger total. During the dinner break, I found myself in the gents, having drunk eight cups of tea during the Aussie innings. While standing there, I became aware of a burly presence. I turned my head and to my left stood a muscled security man. I looked over to my right and there stood a similarly hefty guard. Next to me was a thin, short, middle-aged man in a shabby, blue pinstripe suit. His jacket was ill fitting and wrinkled. As he turned to leave, the two hulks followed him, and I finally recognised the man with whom I'd just shared the urinal.

Mick Jagger's enthusiasm for cricket is legendary. When the Rolling Stones toured South Africa in 1995, he was guest of honour in the Transvaal Long Room during a day/night match at the Wanderers. The Rolling Stone spent time in the Lahore press box chatting with the journalists, although I don't think he revealed the location of his secret after-party to the alcohol-starved hacks.

Sri Lanka's Aravinda da Silva was the man who made sure his team would savour victory that night in Lahore. He capped a great tournament by hitting a fluent century. Rotund skipper Arjuna Ranatunga added a calm 40, and the massively popular islanders went home with the trophy.

The World Cup win gave Sri Lanka a rare chance to forget the Tamil separatist war that has ravaged the country for more than 13 years. It was the Tamil Tigers' Colombo bomb blast that had scared off Australia and the West Indies from playing any group games in Sri Lanka. Yet reports in the following day's newspapers said that rebels and government forces had all hunkered down in front of TV sets for the Final. The fact that Muttiah Muralitharan was the lone Tamil in the side did nothing to dampen enthusiasm for the national team in either political camp.

Sport, once again, proved more important than life and death.

North
Sea
UNITED
KINGDOM
Manchester
London
Windsor
Berlin
Dortmund
GERMANY
Munich

CHAPTER NINE

Sleepwalking Through the Theatre of Dreams

THERE'S AN ADVERTISING hoarding outside the Manchester United Megastore at Old Trafford that just about sums up the passion that is poured into following this most famous of football teams. The ad features a big close-up of a howling baby. The infant wears blue, strangely enough. Underneath is this slogan: 'I name this child Paul Stepney Irwin Crerand Pallister Stiles Best Cantona Giggs Law Robson Smith.'

Those names, of course, have been culled from the litany of legends who have worn the famous red jersey. Who strutted the green grass of the 'Theatre of Dreams', the rather dramatic title that the red half of the city of Manchester has bestowed on Old Trafford. These players' names are never forgotten, and some of Manchester's babies are christened accordingly.

You see the effect Manchester United Football Club has on the city the moment you alight at the city's Piccadilly train station. Here a host of signs claim 'It's Magic in Manchester' and implore visitors to 'enjoy a great outing and see Manchester's top attractions'. One of the photos is of the Rover's Return pub from Britain's longest-running television soap, *Coronation Street*. The other picture is of a ruddy-cheeked tyke decked out in Manchester United football kit.

To get to Old Trafford from Piccadilly, you take the MetroLink light-rail – the Altrincham line – through Mosley Street, St Peter's Square, G Mex, onward to Trafford Bar and Old Trafford itself. It'll cost you R8 for a one-way ticket. At Old Trafford station, alight and slip under the walkway on to Warwick Street, passing the ground of Lancashire County Cricket Club. Then it's on past the headquarters of Kellogg's Great

Britain, and the football ground is a two-minute walk from there. You know you're close when you glimpse the Trafford Pub and a row of fish and chip shops. These include the Red Devils Traditional English Fish 'n Chip Shop and Lou Macari's Fish and Chips, named after the United midfielder of the Seventies.

Manchester United Football Club is possibly the best example on earth of how to market a sports team. Juventus officials, whose team reached two successive European Champions' League Finals in 1996 and 1997, have admitted that the Italian giants are nowhere near achieving the kind of global recognition that the brand name Manchester United enjoys. The club was one of the first teams to be floated on the London stock exchange. They rake in tens of millions of pounds from the sales of Manchester United merchandise. The 'House Full' sign invariably hangs outside the Theatre of Dreams for each home game.

On the west side of Old Trafford is the vast Manchester United Megastore. This is not to be confused with the Manchester United Superstore in the main car park. Both stores trumpet the club as the 'Heart and Soul of Football' and are crammed to the rafters with Red Devil memorabilia. More money is made from the sale of souvenirs here than from ticket sales. Manchester United replica shirts retail at around R250. Each season the team shirt design is modified slightly. There is a home shirt, an away shirt and a third shirt. Yet fans still rush out to buy the updated strip. Modifications to English soccer kits are monitored as closely as the spring collections of Parisian fashion designers. At the stores, both Mega and Super, you can also purchase Manchester United T-shirts, keyrings, underwear (male or female), socks, slippers, mugs and ties. Or Red Devil deodorant at R16 a tin. Perhaps aftershave, or a wash and shine kit for the car. Shaving razors, windcheaters, party packs of designer paper plates and cups, bath mats, dressing gowns or the Manchester United isotonic sports drink (citrus or tropical fruit flavour). I was tempted to ask the assistant if she had the Leeds United home shirt, size XL, but thought better of it. Leeds fans are not entirely welcomed with open arms in Manchester.

Beyond the Old Trafford north stand is the Red Café, an up-market à la carte restaurant with neon signs and massive back-lit photos of United goal celebrations. The room was aswirl with Manchester United emblems, logos, totems and badges. The napkins bore the United emblem. So did the little sachets of ketchup. I went to the gents. Those little mothball-type things that deodorise the urinals, and which Free Staters sometimes mistake for peppermints – each and every one bore the Manchester United logo.

Actually, I'm joking. Free Staters would never confuse rest room accessories with mint imperials, though I do remember once seeing a bloke from Welkom try to tune into M-Net on a cigarette machine. And no, the little sanitary balls didn't have the United logo. Not even Manchester United plc goes that far. Thankfully, the owners of the Red Café have also resisted the temptation to name the dishes after players. There was no Keane lamb chop or Beckham biryani. Instead, the restaurant cashed in on the meals themselves. The burgers at the Red Café cost R53.

In the Megastore, the TV played a recent interview with Eric Cantona. A knot of gathered fans stood hushed like mourners at a wake. Most of the talk in Manchester that week was still about the retirement of the great Cantona. The news had hit the city like a death in the family. The two United stores did a brisk trade in 'Gone but not forgotten' T-shirts. 'Bring back Cantona' campaigns were also under way in the city. Much was being made in the press of the fact that, although Manchester United had chalked up four Premiership titles in five years, the season they missed out had been the season when Cantona was absent, banned for his kung-fu tangle with a Crystal Palace fan.

Cantona had subsequently managed to cloak the red half of Manchester in a cocoon of blind devotion. He was portrayed not only as a supreme footballer, but as a Renaissance man who loved the poems of Rimbaud, appreciated fine art and dabbled with paintbrush and easel. He was always more revered in England than in France. In his home country, whispered the cynics, Cantona was little more than a Provençal peasant.

It's not all hype, flash and profit margins at the best marketed football team in the world. A walk around the Theatre of Dreams reveals more about the heart and soul of Manchester United than any megastore trinket can convey. Outside the stadium, in front of the main car park, there's a bronze statue of Sir Matt Busby, the former manager who shaped the famous Busby Babes, the team that took Europe by storm in the Fifties. Sir Matt gazes into the distance, right hand on hip, left hand cradling a football. Above him is a plaque in the shape of a football field. It reads, 'In memory of the officials and players who lost their lives in the Munich Air Disaster on 6th February 1958.'

The Manchester United museum is tucked away to the left of the statue. In the ground floor trophy room, finely polished silverware is on display – the spoils of United's domestic and foreign campaigns. There are sweaty bits of apparel worn by United stars of past and present, safely stowed behind glass. Here lies the unfamiliar white shirt worn by Steve Bruce when United won the 1991 European Cup Winners' Cup. Also

Brian Kidd's 1968 European Cup Final strip. This is also an alien colour – blue – and the shirt is still stained by white touchline markings.

The club museum is reached from the trophy room up a spiral staircase. The most arresting display in the museum features a series of blown-up newspaper front pages from the past. The first one is from the *Manchester Evening Chronicle* of Thursday, February 6, 1958.

Among the front page stories that day was the tale of an 81-year-old baronet who paid £40 a week to keep his model mistress. The millionaire baronet (63) had met the girl (23) in an air-raid shelter. He was a married man, yet the pair fell in love and he set her up in a London flat for 15 years, all the time paying her £40 a week to keep the tryst secret. In those days, this was both a fortune and a scandal. Also in the news was the report of a 36-year-old window cleaner who crashed 30 feet to the ground from a Salford flat, yet still managed to limp to the hospital.

But the headline story that early February Thursday in 1958 was one which was to plunge the soccer world into mourning. It read, 'United Plane Crashes – Some Feared Dead – 15 Survive 60 foot death plunge.'

The story reported in thick black type that the Elizabethan Airlines plane specially chartered to carry the Manchester United football team had crashed shortly after take-off at Munich airport. There were black-and-white pictures of a charred aeroplane fuselage. Details that day were sketchy.

The next front page display was dated Friday, February 7, by which time the entire story had unfolded. Manchester United had drawn 3–3 with Red Star Belgrade in a European Cup match, and were settling into their seats for the flight home from Germany. The plane had been delayed once and there was talk of holing up in Germany for the night. Then came the news that the flight would go ahead. The plane received take-off clearance, rumbled down the runway and then rose to 20 metres. Suddenly it dipped and then plummeted into the ground just beyond the runway.

The *Manchester News Chronicle* and *Daily Despatch* from that Friday confirmed seven players had died, along with a number of officials and journalists. It gave updates on the condition of survivors. Manager Matt Busby still lay critical in a Munich hospital.

Busby was the man who had been appointed manager of United back in 1945. The team had enjoyed sporadic success and won the League title in 1952. But when United found themselves at the bottom of the League six months later, Busby risked a policy that was to change the face of the football club. At the beginning of the new season, he left out ageing, established stars and drafted in five of the reserve team. This team won a friendly against Kilmarnock 3–0, and that day the legend of the Busby Babes was born. It was two years before the plan bore fruit, but in the mid- to late Fifties the Busby Babes swept all before them in England, landing League and Cup titles aplenty. The Red Devils' next mission was to conquer Europe, and that plan was unfolding steadily before fate stepped in on the snowy wastes of Munich airport.

Busby's youth policy of 1952 would be repeated 43 years later by Alex Ferguson. In 1995, Manchester United finished second in the Premiership behind Blackburn. Ferguson, a Scot like Busby, decided to ditch a number of top stars like Steve Bruce, Andrei Kanchelskis and Mark Hughes. He entrusted the team's fortunes to pimple-faced youth in the guise of David Beckham, the Neville brothers, Nicky Butt and Paul Scholes. United lost their first game of the season 3–1 at Aston Villa, and the critics questioned Ferguson's approach.

Yet, unlike the legendary Busby Babes who had to wait for success, Fergie's Fledglings won the League and FA Cup double that same season. They repeated their League triumph 12 months later. In 40 years from now, the team that Alex Ferguson has assembled will surely be spoken of in the same reverent tones as the Busby Babes are today.

The Manchester United museum houses a tribute to Sir Matt Busby, who eventually recovered from his injuries, led United to their only European Cup triumph, in 1968, and died a fêted hero in 1994. This tribute featured framed messages from fans: 'Sir Matt, Simply the best'; 'Goodbye Sir Matt, Father of the Babes'; 'Sir Matt, you were such a kind, selfless gentleman. It's so comforting to know you went away happy after the success of 1993.' There's also a teddy bear dressed in a white Manchester United shirt. Pinned to it is a message on a plain sheet of paper: 'Sir Matt, father of Manchester United. Finally reunited with the Busby Babes, from David (13) and Chris (8) of Bolton.'

Bafana Bafana had a date at the heart and soul of football, at the history-steeped Theatre of Dreams, on May 24, 1997. It was a big sporting Saturday for Britain. On the same day, England hosted and belted the Australian cricketers in a one-day international at the Oval, and the British Lions kicked off their ultimately victorious tour of South Africa with a win over an Eastern Province invitation team.

There was more fanfare in the British press about the cricket and the rugby than about the international football match. In the build-up, the newspapers that did focus on the game were more interested in the origins of South African players' nicknames than their ability. According to the tabloids, 'you have to be pretty good or pretty tough or both to survive, never mind thrive, in football if your name is Linda.' They were talking about Innocent Linda 'Mercedes-Benz' Buthelezi, the hard man of the South African side. The tabloids loved the irony that, in fact, Buthelezi drove a BMW, and told their readers this stood for 'Black Man's Wheels' in South Africa. The papers also focused on the return of the new slim-line Paul Gascoigne to the England side, and that captain Alan Shearer would be jeered at Old Trafford because he'd joined Newcastle instead of Manchester United when he left Blackburn.

The Manchester public were eagerly snapping up tickets for the game, however. By the morning of the game 43 000 seats had been sold. Although the South African team would like to have taken much of the credit for this healthy interest, the truth probably lay in the fact that the England team were venturing from their traditional Wembley home for only the second time in 31 years. It was the first full England international at Old Trafford since the home team had put seven past Northern Ireland in 1938. A rare chance for northerners to host the national team. The official poster for the match said, 'England at Old Trafford – smaller venue, bigger lung capacity'.

In the souvenir stalls lining the roads to Old Trafford, Springbok rugby scarves were for sale. The local gizmo makers had mostly done their homework. They spelt Bafana Bafana correctly and had not printed the new South African flag upside down. Though one of the flags on sale was a strange-hued black, green and lime combination.

Most of the South African fans gathered in the bright spring sunshine at the main car park. There was a surprisingly large turnout. The bulk of the fans were white *uitlanders* now living in London. Many of them were hardly soccer fans but had felt obliged to journey north and holler on their countrymen. 'Shosholoza' was sung lustily, although the whiteys showed no particular mastery of the lyrics. One fan, draped in an SA flag cape like a multi-coloured Superman, held aloft a huge cardboard fish. There was a roar when the team coach pulled up. The players responded with waves.

Inside the stadium, these Bafana fans sat in the south-east corner of the ground. It was surely the first time white South African faces had outnumbered black ones at a game involving Bafana Bafana. There was a party atmosphere at Old Trafford, and the South Africans huddled in a sea of flags and responded with vigour to the stadium tannoy's invitations to sing along to 'Rocking All Over the World' and the England football anthem from the 1996 European Championships, 'Football's Coming Home'.

When South Africa took on England at Old Trafford, they'd lost only 3 of their previous 29 matches, and boasted draws against Germany and Argentina and a narrow 3–2 defeat against Brazil. But, like a boxer whose lofty world ranking is due mainly to a string of tardy opponents, the South Africans still had a few doubters. Their away form was particularly poor. There was plenty to prove against England, a team who were below South Africa in the world rankings of 1995 and early 1996.

Nevertheless, Clive Barker's pre-match hype championed the unique blend of footballing styles that South Africa offered. They had, said Barker, the physical presence of the British married with the skill of the Brazilians. New captain Lucas Radebe emphasised the shop-window opportunities that the game offered. A good display at Old Trafford by South Africa's best could have major European teams fumbling for the cheque book, said the Leeds defender.

Just as all good things must come to an end, so must all bad things start. The game was miserable. The South Africans looked awed and England never moved out of second gear. South Africa sleptwalked through the first half hour, and were finding it hard keeping their feet on the slippery turf. Only Mark Fish, to the fans' chants of 'Fiiissh', played the Theatre of Dreams without fluffing his lines. A flat-capped fellow near me was none too impressed with the ball wizardry of Doctor Khumalo. 'He's a bigger bum than two arses,' he yelled as the South African again failed to keep his footing while trying to beat his man. Khumalo was the man who found himself floundering at left-back when a deep cross from Teddy Sheringham found Phil Neville on the half hour. Neville passed to Rob Lee, who fired through a cluster of players to put England 1–0 up.

'You're not singing, you're not singing, you're not singing any more,' came the jeers from the England fans. They were aimed at the South African followers, most of whom were not well versed in English soccer chants. They looked bemused and a little hurt by these taunts.

The fans had something to cheer just before half-time, however. John Moshoeu, who was heartened to hear the familiar chants of 'Shoooeees' each time he touched the ball, capitalised on an error by England keeper Nigel Martyn. He aimed an acrobatic bicycle kick at England's unguarded goal, and Phil Masinga headed the ball over the line and into the empty net. 1–1.

The goal prompted South Africa's most spirited play in the match. England backed off, but South Africa lacked the penetration to take advantage. They dithered in midfield, were too slow in creating attacks and Masinga fought a lone battle up front. South Africa hardly fashioned a worthy chance in the second half. Ian Wright finally scored England's winner, with the aid of an arm, but no one could argue that England didn't deserve to win a listless game.

The atmosphere almost compensated for the mediocre match. The crowd somehow lacked the spite and aggression so often associated with English soccer. Fans from both sides were out for a good time. At the end of the game, the stadium announcer led a round of applause for the 'fantastic' South African fans. A veteran English journalist declared it was the first time he'd ever seen the home fans cheer opposition supporters.

'Could you explain one thing?' the man from *The Times* asked Clive Barker at the post-match press conference. 'Why were the South African fans booing some of their own players?' It took a while to fathom out that the hack had confused chants of 'Shooees' for boos and 'Fiiiish' for hisses of derision.

The English press, though, were more concerned about the tackle on Paul Gascoigne by Linda Buthelezi. The Sundowner had come on as substitute with a minute left, and his only contribution to the game was to flatten England's golden boy with a clumsy challenge.

'There was no malice, no reason to be any malice,' said Barker. 'I went to see Gazza, he's got a bit of knock but he's all right. We won't apologise. That's part of football.'

The updates on Gazza's injury received reams of press coverage in the following few days. A couple of the tabloids printed quotes from Buthelezi saying he would have broken Gazza's leg if he had really wanted to hurt him. Gascoigne himself has, of course, hardly been a stranger to headlines over the years. His England career almost ended when it was revealed that he'd once beaten his wife, Sheryl. In the week after the match, most of the tabloids, in their eagerness to crucify 'Mercedes-Benz' Buthelezi, missed the irony of Paul Gascoigne, alleged woman-basher, being scythed down on the football field by someone called Linda.

The eight Manchester United survivors of the 1958 Munich air disaster were invited to the 1997 European Champions' League Final the following Wednesday. The game was to be played at the Munich Olympic Stadium and would doubtless rekindle emotional memories. The match was between Borussia Dortmund, who had put Manchester United out in the semifinals, and Juventus, the reigning European champions.

At 9.30 on the morning of the game, fans from both teams congregated in Munich's central square, the beautiful Marienplatz. Most hung around to watch the touristy puppet play outside the New Town Hall do its thing at 11 am. This little display recreates the wedding celebration between Wilhelm V and his bride in 1568. The blue-and-white Bavarian knight won the joust against the Austrian in red and white. He won again when I wandered back at noon. It must be fixed. Perhaps Don King is the promoter.

A disabled Juventus supporter in a Brazil strip entertained the gathering masses in Marienplatz by juggling a football on his crutches. Groups of Dortmund fans, in their noxious neon-green-and-black shirts, sat at wooden tables in the Viktuelin Market, knocking back lager and bellowing songs. Lyrics included 'Drink bier something something' to the tune of 'Go West'. They draped soccer scarves and caps on the statues in the square. A bunch of Juventus fans wandered by and responded with some Italian ditties from their own repertoire. The supporters were in a buoyant mood and posed for photos with each other.

The Munich Olympic Stadium was of a futuristic design when it was built for the 1972 Olympic Games. It's still an arresting piece of architecture today, a sunken bowl below ground level so that green treetops peek over the lip of the stands. The designer who dreamed up the spider web-like roof of the stadium presented the idea to the town council by stretching a ladies' stocking over some twigs. Gunter Besnich had been studying architecture while he was a prisoner of war in Britain. He wanted to build a stadium with a roof like the vast tented cities he'd seen in deserts. The Munich Olympic Stadium duly became the largest tent in the world.

The white Plexiglas roof covers only half the stadium, and a few of its panels have begun to show evidence of decay. They are a shabby grey colour. It's as if a giant has been flicking cigarette ash on that giant spider web. Refurbishment is imminent. This will include roofing the other half of the stadium and constructing corporate boxes. Munich's stadium must be the only major world arena where the corporate suits have to sit in the cheap seats just like your average sports lover.

I watched the Champions' League Final from behind the goal where the Juventus supporters were sardined. When the gates opened at 5.30 pm, three hours before kick-off, fans dressed in black and white raced to take up their seats and passed their elaborate banners to security men, whose sole official task that evening seemed to be laying out those banners on the athletics track and then rolling them up and returning them to their owners after the game.

One fan had brought his camcorder into the ground and was heckling his girlfriend to film him. He linked a microphone to the camera and gave a five minute 'I was there' eyewitness report for the benefit of his mates back in Turin. Others had their cell phones at the ready, waiting to receive or make calls to Franco and Gianluca back home. Their replica shirts spoke of heroes. No. 21 – Zidane, the new French star. No. 10 – Del Piero, the boy wonder who some say is in danger of being a has-been at the age of 22. Two fans unveiled one of those massive 30x30-metre banners that are draped over an entire terracing like a crimplene duvet. They let it flutter down, helped by the breeze and hundreds of pairs of hands. I briefly wondered how many of the Juventus fans around me were there, or had relatives or friends present, on that black night in Belgium in 1985. The European Cup Final that year was held at the Heysel Stadium, between Juventus and Liverpool. The English supporters had stormed a wall at the crumbling Belgian ground. The wall had collapsed, crushing 39 Italian fans to death. English clubs were afterwards banned from Europe for five years.

As in Manchester four days earlier, there was no aggression on the night of the big game in Munich. Again the atmosphere was celebratory. A 30-piece band waited to fill the stadium with tinny Europop. Meanwhile, the sound system played the Beatles, Tom Petty and a jazzed-up version of Strauss's Blue Danube. Here, many Juve fans took the opportunity to waltz in the stands with their friends. There wasn't much English spoken that night in Munich, but the fans proved a dab hand at the choruses of 'Living Next Door to Alice' as well as 'Na Na Na Na Goodbye'. They filled in the rude bits appropriately, albeit with heavy accents.

The last time Juventus had met German opposition in the European Cup Final they'd lost, 1–0 to Hamburg in 1983. This time they were firm favourites. Danny Blind, captain of the Ajax team who had lost to Juventus in the 1996 Final, said before the game that the Italians were 'a team from another planet'.

Juventus were confident. The fans expectant. When the team sheets were read out, the stadium announcer said each player's first name and let the fans bellow the rest: 'Alan…' 'BOKSIC', 'Christian…' 'VIERI'.

It took less than half an hour for Juventus to have their bubble of invincibility pricked. Dortmund had four former Juventus players (Juventus rejects, the Italian fans would tell you) in their team. In typically purposeful German fashion, they set about tactically neutralising the Italians, and then counter-attacked with slick thrusts.

Juventus went behind to a goal from Karl Heinz Reidle, a striker in the autumn of his career. Five minutes later, Reidle struck again, powering home a header from a corner. 2–0 down, the Juve fans were stunned mute. The Italians surged forward, and Boksic hit a post. Then they had a goal by Vieri disallowed. It was too much for the guy next to me, who flung his banner and cap 30 rows down in disgust and then stormed out of the stadium.

At half-time Juventus coach Marcello Lippi brought on Del Piero. The gamble worked. Just before the hour, Boksic ran on to a ball threaded through by Zidane and crossed low from the left for Del Piero to tuck it home. The Juventus fans were at the opposite end of the field and didn't have the best view, but once they saw the net bulge, there were wild hugs and kisses all round. The consensus was that the equaliser was a mere matter of time. After 70 minutes, however, Dortmund brought on midfielder Lars Ricken. He'd been on the field only seconds when he ran on to a long through ball. His first touch of the game was to lift an exquisite chip from 25 metres over captain Peruzzi in the Juventus goal.

The goal settled the game and many Italian fans drifted immediately towards the exits. In 46 games leading up to the European Champions' League Final, Juventus had conceded more than two goals just once, when they inexplicably lost 3–0 to lowly Udinese in the League. This was a bad time to concede another three. At the final whistle, the Borussian underdogs collapsed in a neon-green heap near the centre circle. A cascade of fireworks erupted behind the stands, only serving to illuminate the despair of Juventus. As the players went to collect their losers' medals, a song from Monty Python's *Life of Brian* boomed from the speakers. 'Always look on the bright side of life,' advised Eric Idle as the players in black and white took to the podium.

Among the Italian fans, there was no rancour in defeat. No nastiness. The Juventus fans who stayed for the trophy presentation applauded the Germans, and later hailed their own team who ran over to acknowledge the fantastic support. Such small gestures go a long way to satisfying fans who spend so much time and money following their sides. Bafana Bafana failed to go over and acknowledge their enthusiastic supporters in Manchester, and this rankled with many of the fans I spoke to afterwards.

On the packed trains heading back to the Marienplatz, fans from both sides mingled with no trace of trouble.

The Dinisi bar in the Marienplatz was where the exultant Dortmund fans went to celebrate. They sang 'Michael, Row the Boat Ashore' with, I'm sure, appropriately triumphant German lyrics. I drank a few cloudy, orange *weiss* beers. This beer is made from wheat, not hops, hence it has the colour of a jaundice victim's urine sample. Nevertheless, it's delicious.

I had to catch a plane back to London at eight the next morning, so I left the revelries shortly after midnight. When I headed towards the Hauptbahnhof train station at 6 am the next day, weaving knots of fans in their radioactive green Dortmund shirts were still reeling and slurring their way back to various city hotels. The vivid hues of their replica shirts were surely doing their heads no good at all.

Back in England, I met up with an old friend who always makes space for me in his Fulham flat when I'm in London. Richard Gloster had invited me down to Windsor for a cricket match that I had been looking forward to for months. Gloster, a South African who has been living in the English capital for nearly a decade, had over the past couple of years put together a South African expatriate cricket team called the Cavaliers. They play regular fixtures against teams like London Australia, London Kiwis and London Caribbean.

The side is competitive enough and often gets to play at some of the better cricket venues in the country. That May day, I was lucky enough to be part of the Cavaliers side that did duty for land and *volk* against the Royal Household Cricket Club in the grounds of Windsor Castle.

For the Queen of England, Buckingham Palace is the office. And Windsor Castle is her 200-hectare weekend getaway in the countryside. In this green and gentle part of the country, the only sounds are the birds and the distant rumble of jet planes taking off at Heathrow. The castle nestles right beneath one of the busiest flight paths in the world. Planes take off on average every 75 seconds. You get to know these things when you spend long periods on the boundary at the Royal Household Cricket Club oval.

Concorde flew over twice while we played – first the British version, and then, after tea, the Air France plane. The noise from Concorde was more like the controlled explosions associated with a space shuttle than the whine of Rolls-Royce jet engines. The constant howl of aeroplane activity must be the only downside to living in the beautiful town of Windsor. One feeble-minded American tourist was once heard to ask, 'How could these guys build a castle under such a busy flight path?'

The RHCC oval is flanked by high green trees, which yield the faintest glimpses of the castle beyond. Adjacent to the oval is the paddock where the queen's horses gambol and break wind with uninhibited abandon. Security is high. The public is not allowed into the Windsor Park grounds. We had to get special permission to reach the oval.

The oval's pavilion is panelled with wood. Framed pictures of Queen Elizabeth and the Duke of Edinburgh guard the entrance to the dressing rooms. Among the photos and trophies in the pub is a bat donated by the former Australian prime minister Bob Hawke. It is awarded to the winner of the annual game between the RHCC and the Crusaders, an Australian team similar to the South African Cavaliers.

One of the players later told me of the time the queen came down to pose for photos with the players from both sides. The RHCC president at the time was a gentleman named John Taylor. He had been the queen's personal page for more than 30 years. The Australian captain of the day was cut from the Crocodile Dundee mould. He was a bit short on finesse. When the Aussie skipper got up to make his speech, he began by saying, 'Er, first of all, ladies and gentlemen, I'd like to thank John Page, the queen's tailor.'

This blunder apparently had even the usually grim-faced monarch all atitter.

The queen was spending the day in Balmoral when we Cavaliers were in town. She obviously hadn't been told about the game. John Taylor was there, however, and made a short speech after the game had ended in an honourable draw.

The team we played against were all somehow connected with the smooth running of the castle. Some were security policemen, others were sons of people who lived and worked in the grounds. One policeman was a fellow by the name of Stan. He'd provided one of the highlights of the day when his bat slipped from his grasp as he aimed a mighty heave over mid-wicket. The flying willow nearly beaned the square-leg umpire.

Afterwards Stan told stories about security at Windsor Castle. A favourite trick among bored cops is to adjust the security cameras to home in on some of the young female employees who like sunbathing topless on the roofs. Stan also spoke of some of the more simple-minded tourist visitors to the castle. Most of these tales featured Americans.

For instance, in preparation for the royal family's Christmas church service a false wall is erected in the castle to accommodate the television cameras that capture the queen on her way to church. According to Stan, if you were unfamiliar with the castle, you wouldn't know this wall is false. A day or so after the service, an American tourist in a ten-gallon hat came on a tour of the castle. He was mouthing superlatives.

'Gee, it's a wonderful castle this, Blanche. You know, we got nothing like this in the States. They're all plastic and fibreglass back home,' he told Stan.

So Stan said to him, 'Well, this is just a fibreglass castle too.'

'Don't give me that bull, buddy,' retorted the American.

'Okay, go over there and tap that wall,' suggested Stan.

Of course the American did just that. He turned in horror to Blanche. 'Oh my God, I thought this was the real thing!'

He was probably the same guy who thought Heathrow Airport was built before Windsor Castle.

Another opponent that blue-sky day was Julian Mitchell. He was the son of the Dean of Windsor, on whom the queen leans for a weekly dose of spiritual guidance. Julian cracked a fine half-century in the match and also entertained us afterwards with a few royal snippets.

He said gin and Dubonnet is the monarch's favourite drink. Julian would know. Each Christmas, the royal family visit the dean's house for a brief drink and a chat. The queen is apparently pleasant in these situations, without being too chatty. She will linger long enough to let you feel your presence is valuable, but not so long that you can slip into babble mode. Julian had been told to fix the queen's drink. He'd been instructed how to mix it just right, and his efforts proved successful. He thus left the bottle of Dubonnet safely in the cupboard for the following year's royal visit. Next Christmas, he mixed a precise replica of his previous year's attempt and handed it to the queen. At this exact moment, a royal aide came over and told Julian that the royal party had just been to visit elsewhere on the estate, and the fool there had given Her Majesty a gin and Dubonnet made from the previous year's bottle. This clod didn't know that Dubonnet went off once opened, said the aide, shaking his head at the depths of ignorance in which some monarchical employees wallowed. Julian choked on his lager and eyed the queen just as she lifted her glass to take a sip. He held his breath. Yet the queen carried on chatting away, seemingly satisfied with her tipple.

Our evening continued in similar vein until around 10 pm when the first streaks of night began dappling the sky. Beer glasses were refilled with draught poured from a watering can. Then it was back to the M4 motorway to jostle with the returning weekend traffic.

I hadn't quite met the queen, but at least I could say I'd been something of a bit player in another of England's Theatres of Dreams.

CANADA
UNITED STATES OF AMERICA
Colorado R.
North Pacific Ocean
see map below
MEXICO
North Atlantic Ocean

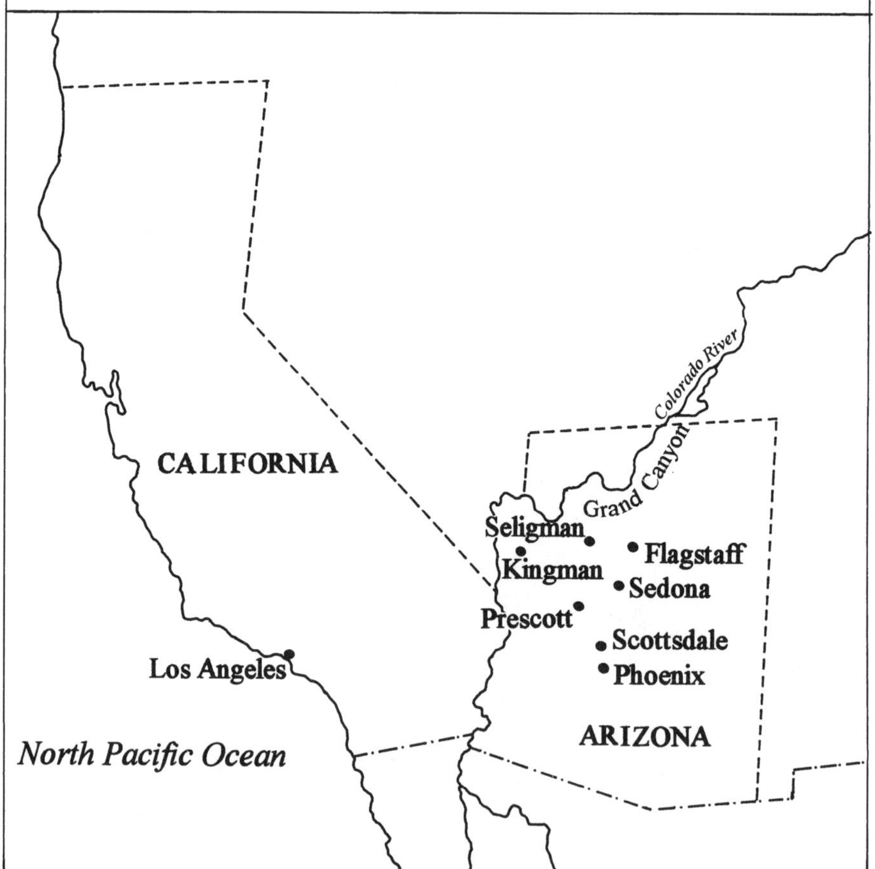
CALIFORNIA
Colorado River
Grand Canyon
Seligman
Kingman
Flagstaff
Sedona
Prescott
Scottsdale
Phoenix
Los Angeles
ARIZONA
North Pacific Ocean

CHAPTER TEN

Bells and Whistles, Stars and Stripes

THERE WERE TWO THINGS that made me feel right at home, as a Gautenger, in the Hollywood Hills of Los Angeles, and they were neither the pall of pollution draped over downtown nor the mild winter weather.

First, the little blue notices jammed on every gatepost in the suburb warning potential intruders that Westec Armed Patrol was just a panic button push away.

Second, a dinner story about a friend's brother who'd been in a furniture store in the suburb of Brentwood (O.J. Simpson's luxury hunting ground – in more ways than one) on a Sunday morning. A hooded gunman followed him in, waved his .357 revolver around and in his best *Pulp Fiction* voice bawled, 'Don't anybody move, this is a robbery!' He then grabbed the manageress, jammed the gun in her mouth and demanded cash. She wriggled free and ran into the street. Her attacker chased and fired three shots. The brother dialled 911. And the cops took 15 minutes to arrive, shattering any illusions of instant rescue that one might have had from watching Captain Kirk's TV show. Of course, I felt obliged to respond with some belters from the modern anthology of Jo'burg crime tales myself, and to judge from the slightly miffed hush that fell on the group, it seems Gauteng easily surpasses Los Angeles in terms of violent crime one-upmanship.

This story was relayed while we dined at LA's flavour of the fortnight restaurant – Fusion at PDC just off Sunset Boulevard. Apparently this was the new watering hole, feeding trough and preening pit of the stars. There were two actors from the *Thirtysomething* show at the table next to us. They were pointed out with due reverence, but don't ask me who they were. The place was more like Central Casting, with every waiter and waitress potential bit-part players in the next season of *Baywatch*.

Our waitress, however, was an embryonic stand-up comic. She made fun of the way she looked and made fun of us and made fun of her musician husband who was idling at the bar minding his own business. She summoned him over to meet us. We chatted and he produced a demo tape from his pocket when one member of our party admitted a tenuous connection with the record industry. In this city it really is nothing ventured, nothing gained.

I was in town for the thirtieth edition of American football's Super Bowl (like rugby's Currie Cup Final, but on steroids) in 1996. For the past few years, the biggest event in Stateside sport has only been awarded to those cities with pleasant winter climates. Makes sense. There's $187-million worth of business generated during Super Bowl week. You don't want people staying home freezing when they could be out buying fridge magnets and loud-coloured team hats.

The Super Bowl was actually taking place in Arizona, one state to the east of California. But I had taken the opportunity of spending a couple of days in Los Angeles before the big game to see if the city really is as bizarre and soulless as many people maintain.

I started with what in most cities would be called parks, but which in LA are the beaches. And the Central Park of Los Angeles is undoubtedly Venice Beach. Renowned for its tawdry boisterousness and let-your-hair-down vulgarity, Venice Beach's carefully nurtured hippie reputation is encouraged, even by the police who are no doubt well aware of the town's commercial significance.

Located just south of Santa Monica, Venice has over the years developed into the location of choice for the Bohemian élite, if that is not a contradiction in terms. Rebel actors like Dennis Hopper live here in sight of the boardwalk and Muscle Beach, where bulging iron-pumpers flex their biceps under the sun.

Venice has a colourful history. Way back in 1892, a businessman called Abbot Kinney first dreamed up the idea of an American version of the romantic Italian destination. His money, derived from cigarettes and property deals, had bought him a rather undesirable tract of marshy shoreland. Undeterred, Kinney carved out 24 kilometres of canals, which he then dredged and bridged, and gondolas were shipped in from Italy to ply the waterways. This urban experiment lasted until 1912 when the authorities decided the stagnant canals were a health hazard. So Kinney transformed Venice into a more conventional pleasure resort of piers and rollercoasters and laid on free transport to publicise his playpark.

Mid-January is hardly the best time to view Venice in all its finery, and the promenade was almost deserted on the blustery day I ventured there. The legendary boardwalk is one long street between the rows of houses and the beach itself. It's a collection of Korean-owned knick-knack kiosks and an outdoor theatre for those with an exhibitionist streak, to whom Venice is a powerful magnet. At least 20 stalls trade in sunglasses, and there are specialist leather shops, typical beachware outlets selling T-shirts with dim slogans, smutty postcards, metal badges and sew-on patches. Nearer the beach are cubicles and tables manned by readers of palms and decipherers of tarot cards. There are also ear-piercing emporia, tattoo parlours and a place catering for New Age lovers of wind-chimes – 'everything from cathedral bells to Nu-wave'.

The street artists who have done so much for Venice Beach's reputation were largely hibernating in anticipation of better weather, although there were a few diehards to treat us handful of visitors. A turbanned rollerblader swayed down the boardwalk jabbing at a muffled electric guitar. Further down the promenade, a limbo routine featured a lithe West Indian balancing a glass of water on his head while he dipped beneath the bar. He soon made it clear he wasn't entertaining for fun.

'Talk to me. You want the bar lowered? Talk to me!' he yelled in strong Caribbean tones. So we clapped and hollered and he lowered the bar to little more than 30 centimetres off the ground. 'I share my culture with you,' he continued, 'now you share your culture with me.' He rubbed his fingers together so that we wouldn't miss the point, then placed plastic buckets in each corner of his space.

'C'mon guys, make my day. Let's see those tens and twenties. Keep it coming.'

A similar level of hustling occurs in Hollywood. These days, the worldwide icon for wealth, stardom and glamour is little more than a tawdry grid of boulevards beneath the famous hill sign. Drug pushers flourish amid the tacky souvenir shops and the star-engraved sidewalks. Not that there's much merit in being nominated for the Walk of Fame these days. If the money's right, you can buy your very own personalised pink pavement star.

Mann's Chinese Theatre on the corner of Orchard Road and Hollywood Boulevard is the epicentre of Hollywood tourism, and is also home to the hand- and footprints of the famous. The handprints of the stars are housed in a recessed courtyard in this movie theatre complex, a powerful draw card for tourists and people who enjoy harassing them.

A bunch of jokers, uniformed like police, were loitering here frightening Japanese tourists, or at least distracting them from the standard Japanese tourism protocol of snapping endless photos of lamp-posts and fire hydrants, by sidling up to them and saying, 'Did you see that sign?' At which the nonplussed tourist would falter, 'What sign?'

'Right above you, sir. You can't do that here. I'm going to have to cite you for not smiling.'

The guy would then delve into a bag and pull out smile stickers and US flag pins. 'They're worth $20 but are yours for just a $5 donation towards homeless kids.'

There's not just one fool but many born every day, judging by the number of tourists I saw happily parting with their cash.

On the next corner, a daily tour was being offered that sums up much about LA. Grave Line Tours is a pun on the Gray Line Tours coach trips that offer sightseeing junkets in most American cities. This particular tour features a ride in a convertible black hearse that stops at the sites of famous killings in the Los Angeles area. Celebrity slayings on the route included the Cielo Drive residence where film director Roman Polanski's wife Sharon Tate and four others were brutally put to death by deranged disciples of the cult leader Charles Manson. There is also a stop at the Chateau Marmont hotel on the Sunset 'Strip' where comedian John Belushi was found dead in his bungalow from an overdose of heroin and cocaine. The O.J. Simpson murders have provided the Grave Line tour with a wealth of new destinations, including the Simpson mansion in Rockingham Avenue and Nicole Brown's condo on South Bundy Drive.

While in Los Angeles, I stayed in the Hollywood Hills – the natural habitat of the Range Rover, Jeep Cherokee and other trendy 4x4s; the home of body-conscious licence plates like 3JOG547. From my bedroom window, I could glimpse the high-rise structures of the city centre far away in the valley. Early morning smog would blur the skyline made famous by the opening credits of *LA Law* as I set forth along Sunset Plaza Drive, which meanders steeply downhill into Sunset Boulevard, for a coffee and a blueberry muffin.

One drizzly morning, while reading the *LA Times* (which will always have a special place in my heart for providing the African Cup of Nations scores), I discovered, tucked away in a small corner beneath reams of college basketball results, that two of the best teams in world soccer were set to meet at the LA Coliseum that afternoon. Brazil and Mexico had won through to the final of the Concacaf Gold Cup, a tournament played between nations from the Americas. It's not every day you get to see Brazil in action, even if they had sent a sub-par team, and I gulped my remaining coffee and headed downtown in streaming rain in search of the venue for the 1984 Olympic Games.

The car parks around the Coliseum were packed with drenched Latin Americans surging to snap up the last few tickets available. The queues were too vast and muddy to contemplate joining, so I sought out the press office, flashed my South African credentials and was soon being ushered through to a sumptuous free lunch along with 400 other hacks.

The third- and fourth-placed play-off featured the Americans against Guatemala, and the home side ran out comfortable 3–0 winners. After the match I had the chance to interview Alexi Lalas, the American defender. Lalas is one of the most recognisable of footballers, with his bright orange locks and matching goatee beard that make him look like he's auditioning for a guitarist's role with ZZ Top. Yet in America Lalas can enter supermarkets unrecognised, dine unmolested and go to a movie anonymously.

Despite the massive success of the 1994 World Cup in the United States, soccer has hardly entered the consciousness of the general American sports fan. Lalas had become the first American player to sign for an Italian Serie A club, and was mobbed wherever he went in Italy. He is his nation's foremost soccer player. The equivalent in basketball would be Michael Jordan; in baseball it might be Emmitt Smith of the Dallas Cowboys. These two command multi-million-dollar salaries and are instantly recognised wherever they go. For Lalas and his American soccer colleagues, however, it's a case of slogging away for recognition, which may be a long time coming.

The success of the new professional Major League Soccer, which now has Lalas in its ranks as well as former Italian star Roberto Donadoni and South Africans Doctor Khumalo and Shaun Bartlett, will go a long way in determining the future market value of American players. The early signs are promising. The MLS debut season in 1995 attracted crowds in excess of most European leagues. They might want to work on some of the team names, however. Dallas Burn sounds like an arson attempt, and trying to bellow 'We love you New York/New Jersey Metro Stars we do' to the tune of the popular English footballing refrain might well leave you with lockjaw.

The Brazil–Mexico match was severely marred by the torrential rain that made the ball stop dead in vast puddles. Skilful football was impossible. The Coliseum provides little cover for spectators, and the capacity 80 000 crowd was forced to huddle in waterlogged clumps among the bleachers. This didn't prevent the huge Mexican support from baying their team through to a surprise 2–0 win, however.

Los Angeles by night offers something for everyone. For free, I could have stayed home and watched the jets stack up over LA International, their lights resembling a nocturnal join-the-dots puzzle. Seeking more structured amusement, one evening I walked down to Sunset, past the Viper Room (infamous for the drug-induced death of River Phoenix outside its doors) and dropped in at the Comedy Store. This is the mecca of stand-up comedy and the place where stars like Robin Williams got their first break. Five separate theatres were devoted to comics.

It was novices' night, so anyone from anywhere was entitled to get up and do their thing. There were some riotous acts. The first performer would have given Eddie Murphy a run for his money, if not in the form of snappy one-liners, then for his torrent of four-letter words. The next aspirant broke off midway through her performance to answer her cell phone. 'I'm expecting a call from the producers of *Married with Children*,' she explained. Each and every amateur act was polished and proficient. It was amazing to think that such adept performers were on the lowest rung of showbiz's precarious ladder to fame.

Then again, that's part of LA's pull. Everyone in the city seems set on having their moment in the spotlight. For example, while having a Michelob beer at a bar in Santa Monica, I got talking to a girl called Penny. She was built like a *Playboy* centrefold, hourglass figure, artificially-enhanced chest and flaxen hair falling straight and long. As we chatted, it appeared her main goal was, in fact, to *be* a *Playboy* centrefold. Though it later transpired this was only her secondary ambition. She had her heart pinned on being a firefighter. When I pointed out, after the fourth brewski, that the *Playboy* option seemed wholly more realistic, she launched into a detailed explanation of what she would like for her nude shoot. The set would be brash and lavish and contain a vintage car over which she would be draped. Strategically placed stacks of gold coins would complete the scene, and the title of the spread would be 'Penny's from Heaven'. She confided she wasn't getting very far with her proposal, but she did admit to no shortage of 'glamour' photographers willing to fatten her portfolio.

When I told her there was a *Playboy* magazine in South Africa (well, there was at the time), Penny's eyes widened. She dashed to her car and returned with a sheet of tremendously fetching slides. Would I look them over and tell her what I thought? I spent a few minutes in mute contemplation. I tried to sound analytical, and said I'd be happy to recommend them to *Playboy*, SA. At which she kissed me and entrusted me with her dream. It was at this point I decided I could really get used to LA.

Arizona is the Grand Canyon State. It says so right there on the licence plates. As marketing strategies go, this one didn't need a boardroom full of ponytailed ad execs brainstorming bumper-sticker slogans. Entice the world's travellers into the yawning red mouth of the canyon, Arizonans realised, and they'll no doubt bump into a few of the state's other wonders along the way.

These are plentiful. For example, just to the west of Phoenix CBD is Sun City. No glitz and roulette, fake waves and indifferent staff here. Instead a retirement village for the mega-wealthy. And each retiree has his own private golf course, by the look of it. Arizona is also a playground of eerie sandstone formations, lush forests, cowboy history, ancient native cultures and forbidding desert. And in the midst of this cowboy and cactus country has sprung the artificial scenery of the tourist highway – the Flintstones Experience, polka-dotted tepees, Indian relics and weeping Jesus statues.

Phoenix is flat like a Mexican tortilla, dry and unintimidating. As orderly as a suburban mall and about as enticing. Climatically speaking, Phoenix is severe. Summer temperatures routinely rise above 35 degrees – days so hot that even the patio furniture stands on one leg, as someone once put it. In keeping with such a rugged state, the police ride mountain bikes in downtown Phoenix. Not that the forces of law in this state are any less gung-ho than their mirror-shaded colleagues the world over.

I was driving on Squaw Peak freeway one dusk, admiring the Camelback Mountain, which was bathed in rosy tones by the setting sun. I was on my way to meet Christy, the friend I was staying with, who was putting on a street concert in Scottsdale ahead of the Super Bowl. Street map unfolded over the steering wheel, I peered into the Arizona gloom, intent on not missing the turn-off. Again. Suddenly, like Richard Dreyfuss in *Close Encounters of the Third Kind*, I became aware of too-bright headlights filling the rear-view mirror. Thinking the pushy driver wanted to overtake, I floored the gas pedal to pass a car blocking the inside, then switched lanes.

The bright lights followed, this time accompanied by a whirl of red and a whining siren. A megaphone voice bawled at me to pull over. In a mild panic, I tried. But forgot which side of the highway was the slow lane, and lurched into the express lane.

The patrol car was up my exhaust pipe like Schumacher tailgating Jacques Villeneuve. I eventually scooped up my thoughts and rolled to a stop in the right place. The pair of troopers nimbly vacated their vehicle and dropped into snipers' kneeling positions, the crosshairs of their weapons focused no doubt on the back of my skull. With one cop covering me thus, his partner, expecting surely to apprehend a wired Colombian dope peddler, approached with stealth.

It took a while to explain myself. To complicate matters, I'd left my driving licence back at the house, so I figured playing dumb was the best way out. I muttered something about being South African and confused. Then I remembered my Super Bowl press credentials in the cubbyhole. This soothed Poncherello and his partner somewhat. Finally, I was booked for 'erratic braking' and, despite my wanly offering free board and lodging any time the pair were in Gauteng, was presented with an impressive fine.

The Tuesday before Super Bowl Sunday is a day devoted entirely to the media. At the Sun Devil Stadium in Tempe, where the Dallas Cowboys–Pittsburgh Steelers showdown was to unfold, signs around the stands indicated where each player could be interviewed. The entire playing roster from either side had to sit there in the baking sun until the media hounds had their fill of pithy quotes and telling sound-bites. The bigger the star, the greater the media huddle around him. Where the truly galactic held court, their arrival was anticipated like the appearance of a rock idol. Like 'Neon' Deion Sanders, whom I had seen in Florida the year before as part of the San Francisco 49ers winning team. The Cowboys defensive back drapes eight pounds of gold jewellery round his neck, ears and fingers. He also wears green boxer shorts with white dollar signs. (This was the lead story one day in the *Arizona Republic* sports section, I kid you not.) Sanders is as colourful as Joseph's dreamcoat and has depthless arrogance. Sample excerpts from the day:

Q: 'Is it true you turned down a role in the movie *Showgirls*?'

A: 'As the leading character? No, man, but you know I can dance.'

Q: 'Tell us about your new $35-million contract.'

A: 'Hey, if it don't make dollars, it don't make sense.'

Q: 'Will you one day pursue an acting career?'

A: 'I'd be good at that. I'm part Wesley Snipes, part Denzel Washington. You don't realise I've been acting all my life. I'm acting now.'

Q: 'What'll you do when you're old and grey?'

A: 'Sitting, fishing, telling lies to my grandchildren.'

I tried to imagine Gary Teichmann or Hansie Cronjé handling an interview in similar style and found myself grinning. The confident swagger with which the average American athlete comports himself is astounding. In the States it's part of the package. In South Africa you'd get a *klap* for being *windgat*.

No one understands, or milks, the value of the media better than American sports figures. As Houston Rockets basketballer Charles Barkley once said when told by a British writer that it was standard practice in the UK to pay the likes of Paul Gascoigne for wit-filled observations: 'That's crazy. When I talk to one of you guys, I'm not talking to you. I'm talking to the kids who're gonna go buy my sneakers. I get my message across through you guys. Without you I got no audience.' South African sportspeople, take note.

The massive Super Bowl media centre in downtown Phoenix was aflutter all week with the musings of 3 000 journalists. It was temporary home to a dozen or more radio stations, and loud sportscasters jawed on about score spreads, guided listeners 3 000 kilometres away in Baltimore through the morning traffic and guffawed loudly at their own corny jokes. Wandering through the thick-carpeted walkways and listening to these guys, it became clear the Cowboys are much like the Gauteng Lions rugby team. Anyone beyond the Jo'burg city limits loves to hate Louis Luyt's moneyed boys. Same in the States with Dallas. The Cowboys may be known as 'America's team', but they have too much cash for many people's liking. And they're too successful. Plus they have their own Louis Luyt. Owner Jimmy Jones – 'Big Daddy' – is renowned for being uncompromising, for throwing dollars at most problems and for having earned not a few enemies over the years. While I was in Phoenix, he was counter-suing the National Football League for $750 million. This after the league slapped him with a $250-million lawsuit for selling the Cowboys name to Nike.

The Super Bowl media centre's 'relaxation zone' was like a movie star's romp room. Laid on for us were banks of video games, indoor putting greens, a golf driving-range net, ping pong and pool tables, and basketball rings where you could shoot hoops while awaiting literary inspiration. It was hardly conducive to work. But if we did grow bored of the toys on offer, we could always resort to some keyboard-pounding in a workroom the size of a car park.

The famed Dallas Cowboys cheerleaders were paraded before the media on one day. In 1996, 319 NFL football players earned $1 million or more as a basic salary, but these girls were paid a paltry $15 a game. Nevertheless, a thousand aspirants still try out annually to get to wear thigh-high boots, hip-hugging hot-pants and halter tops. They must have been inspired by singer Paula Abdul, who started life as an LA Lakers basketball cheerleader. According to the press release issued that day, strict rules 'prohibit cheerleaders from dating players, coaches or club employees to guarantee a professional relationship within the organisation'. However, a few years ago, three sisters who had been with the Cowboys squad revealed a litany of eating disorders, drugs and steamy player liaisons in a telltale book. The book was called *Phallus Cowboys*. (Actually, I made the title up, though judging by the first few pages, it couldn't have been more apt.)

Many people watch the Super Bowl telecast purely to see the multitude of costly new commercials. The annual football final is where new adverts are traditionally showcased – at $1,3 million for 30 seconds. The premier slot is the first quarter of the game. In 1996 Pepsi ran ads throughout the match, the best of which featured a Coke salesman trying to sneak a can of Pepsi from the store fridge and unleashing an aluminium can avalanche. So much for comparative advertising. The ads were rated the day after the game, like critics reviewing the weekend movies. Only in America…

Despite the multitude of diversions available during Super Bowl week (Meatloaf performed solely for the players and press on the Thursday evening), there's a limit to the thrill of lobbing miniature basketballs through hoops in the press room. And the joy of spending every waking hour in the company of 2 999 other journalists and their whines about ego-saturated players and the lack of variety in the hotel room minibars wears thin even more swiftly.

After all, I was in brazen Arizona. So I decided to star in my own personal road movie. Starting from Phoenix, I would nose my rented Dodge Neon north through Prescott, on to the mystical New Age trekkie town of Sedona, through to Flagstaff, on to the Grand Canyon and finally through to the remaining sliver of the legendary Route 66 in the northwestern corner of the state.

To exit Phoenix, take Interstate 17 north. In the same way that Johannesburg's smog-spoiled CBD gives way to the untainted Magaliesberg just half an hour out of town, so the raw beauty of Arizona spins into view minutes beyond its capital. Barrelling north in the Neon, with Alanis Morrisette belting bitchy tunes in my ear from K-Lite 98.7 FM, the countryside took on the quality of a Louis L'Amour novel, or, at the very least, a Tex chocolate bar commercial. This was the dry heart of saguaro cactus country. Cacti loomed everywhere, prickly as a maiden aunt, some as large as a two-storey building. Then came the place names. Bloody Basin Road flew by. Followed by Horse Thief Basin and Bear Wallow Road and Big Bug Creek. And Bumble Bee and Hogwash Creek and The Gap. It was like invading the panels of a Lucky Luke comic strip.

My first stop was at Sedona, a town which was once THE setting for Westerns, as the steep red-rock scenery makes a perfect backdrop to the quick draws and sweaty hombres of the genre. But it appears the only remaining ties to those days are the bronze bucking-bronco statuettes that sell for $1 000 in the air conditioned souvenir shops. Sedona is now the ultimate, sanitised one-stop souvenir shop, where even McDonald's is dressed in pink and lime pastels.

It's also a magnet for New Age theorists, so I stopped off at the New Age Information Centre to investigate. There I found enough brochures and fliers to submerge the Seychelles. Channelling, energy-field therapy, rapid-eye processing, astral projection, reflexology, vision quests. Name your favourite self-help quack philosophy and Sedona will access it.

I took a Jeep tour while in Sedona, with Earth Wisdom Tours. I drank in the drama of red-rock country while wedged in a 4x4 full of these New Agers, each armed with crystals and sensitive smiles, bearing goodwill to all person-kind and aquiver with intuitive knowing.

At one point, the driver swung off Dry Creek Road and, gazing earnestly, asked us why we thought we were all really here.

'To attend the Super Bowl' was my first thought, but I said nothing as my co-passengers reeled off a list of do-good, life-enhancing clichés. My turn came and I faltered a little under the spotlight, but the serene, encouraging smiles from my fellow Jeepsters saw me through.

'I'm here because I want a more solid centre,' I heard myself saying. This is true. I'm not sure what it means, but it feels true. This appeared to satisfy everyone, and the driver embarked on a short discourse on the kinds of energy centres that native cultures (and New Agers) have discovered around the world. He waxed long on healing sites and fertility sites and said that Sedona is known as an oracular site, 'a place of vision questing and ceremonial importance'.

We arrived at a spot called Rachel's Hill and took a mild hike to the 'medicine wheel' that Earth Wisdom Tours had fashioned from rocks on a slope. We held hands around the centre of the wheel. This kind of intimacy with strangers makes me squirm. I hadn't felt so self-conscious since I attended my godson's christening and the well-meaning vicar commanded the congregation to embrace four strangers within hugging radius.

The guide asked us to close our eyes and, again, ponder our existence. The church-quiet stillness of the Arizona air does coax a degree of warm, fuzzy contemplation. We were told to receive the earth's energy, and, if I didn't quite levitate, I did experience a feeling of intimacy, largely, I'm sure, from standing still on the earth for once and not speeding past it in a 140-kilometre-per-hour Dodge Neon blur.

'It'd be a helluva place to lose a cow' was how one early rancher supposedly summed up the Grand Canyon. You know you're getting close to God's Own Sinkhole when the tepees, dinosaurs and totem poles start materialising. 'Flintstones Land – Yabba Dabba Doo means WELCOME to you' blares the sign welcoming tourists to Bedrock City. This cutting edge sample of roadside schlock is just a 15-minute drive from one of the world's natural wonders. Constantly, America startles.

I hadn't come to the Grand Canyon to become embroiled with Barney and his brethren, so I kept my eyes on the road ahead, bypassed the Grand Canyon Imax theatre, and entered the park.

In winter, as I soon discovered, sightseeing at the Grand Canyon is severely limited, but luckily I had arranged a helicopter flip over the canyon. I drove to the airport, was duly weighed and strapped down in a Papillon Tours chopper with two Texans and a Japanese gentleman with a bazooka-style camera lens. (Pardon the plug. It was a freebie flight.)

As we rose through the chill winter air, the scenery below became increasingly toy-like. Snow-coated pine trees looked like props from a model railway. Deer tracks criss-crossed the milk-white landscape. The sense of anticipation as the lip of the canyon loomed grew tangible. One minute we were whirring 15 metres above the pine trees, the next we were out over the canyon, the ground having dropped away at a dizzying, terrifying rate. Suspended in silence, with only the crackle of the radio and the muffled thrum of chopper blades for company, the full magnitude of the Grand Canyon – 1,6 kilometres deep, 446 kilometres long and two billion years in the making – hits home. The spectacular views of the Painted Desert and the Colorado River, threading like a piece of lavender lace between the towering cliffs, were truly awesome. So were the shuddering air pockets that gripped our chopper every 30 seconds. I spent the entire flight with a strangler's grip on the seat in front of me. And I thanked any almighty listening that the pilot confided only once we had landed that a chopper had smashed to the ground just three months before.

Fortified by the flight, I headed west from the canyon in search of Route 66, the stretch of tarmac that has been rhapsodised, glorified and packaged so thoroughly over the years. Though, in truth, it's hard to distinguish the tarmac there from that of the N1 to Pretoria. And 'The Mother Road' only exists in bits and pieces today. Interstate 40 has devoured most of the original route that took displaced farmers and restless pleasure-hounds through Midwest America.

Route 66 today is a 238-kilometre stretch of road linking Kingman in the west with Seligman in the east. The road from Kingman to Seligman is all open range, deep horizons, sprinting tumbleweeds and little evidence of human habitation. One of the few stopovers is Hackberry, home of the Old Route 66 Visitor Center and Preservation Foundation. The building's interior is enough to make a Route 66 aficionado think he'd died at the wheel of a '48 Buick and gone to heaven. Route 66 books, Route 66 maps, Route 66 videos, Route 66 calendars, Route 66 postcards, Route 66 badges, Route 66 chilli mix. I know they're all there because I'm consulting the list here in my Route 66 notebook, compiled with the aid of my smart Route 66 ballpoint.

Back in Phoenix, Super Bowl Sunday dawned crisp and sunny, and by 10 am the stretch limousines were pulling up outside the Hyatt Hotel like a column of oversized marching ants on the prowl. Each took on board wealthy corporate wheeler-dealers. Super Bowl is like Woodstock for 50 year olds. A week-long party where pinstripe types can dismiss wives with the credit card and get blotto with their buddies by night. Spouses reunite on game day, however. Dallas fans favoured wide-brimmed hats, snappy suits and loud cowboy boots. Steelers supporters waved yellow squares of material called the 'Terrible Towel', a totem that is meant to bring the team luck. The roads to Tempe Stadium were clogged from 11 am. And as the 75 156 fans squeezed into the arena, the airspace above became thick with banner-towing biplanes, choppers and blimps. Fans streamed through the streets, begging for tickets. One waved a banner saying 'Hi drunk. I'm Mom'.

Another placard read 'Super Bowl tickets. Will trade for reliable car or truck'. This year tickets cost $300 but touts were expecting around $2 000 a pop at game time. Fans from either side mixed amiably at the Super Bowl Experience interactive theme-park.

Kick-off neared. In American football, even the coin toss is a show. The Most Valuable Players from previous Super Bowls paraded below us, and hallowed quarterback Joe Montana flipped the specially minted commemorative coin. The game was on.

No other sport analyses itself like gridiron, so I'll spare you the technical intricacies. Suffice it to say, the Cowboys won 27–17 for their fifth

Super Bowl triumph. Only the Cowboys and the San Francisco 49ers have won the game's ultimate title five times. It was one of the better championships of recent years. The big game is often an anticlimax, or, like they say over there in the Valley of the Sun, 'more sizzle than steak'. That's because the Super Bowl is played between the winners of America's two football conferences, the AFC and the NFC. The only problem is that most of the best teams are in the NFC. In fact, NFC teams have won the last 14 Super Bowls. The teams of the moment, arguably the Green Bay Packers, San Francisco 49ers and Dallas Cowboys, are all NFC teams and can thus only meet in the NFC championship game, not the Super Bowl. But in 1996, the blue-collar Steelers pushed the Dallas aristocrats all the way and might have won but for two interceptions that led to touchdowns.

After the game a few of us went to Mingles, a bar in unsullied Scottsdale. Fans from both sides were knocking back vast pitchers of beer. Congratulations and condolences were generously offered and accepted. The lack of aggression among American sports followers is astounding. The thought of deliberately segregating Stateside supporters English soccer-style would be unthinkable. In Britain football 'fans' hurl cold-eyed curses, sharpened coins and oranges with razor blades wedged in the skin. In Holland rival club supporters clash at train stations with maiming uppermost in their thoughts. In South Africa Orlando Pirates followers set fire to the stadium if their team is the victim of a dubious decision.

In America, when the game is done, it's all friendly banter, high fives and belly bumps.

I'll drink to that. In fact, make it a double.

North Sea
Leeds
Liverpool
Irish Sea
UNITED KINGDOM
London

CHAPTER ELEVEN

At Play in the Fields of Lord's

IT'S DOUBTFUL WHETHER Thomas Lord, the Yorkshireman who bought the fertile chunk of north-west London that has evolved into the home of cricket, would have approved. The 4 000 MCC members, in their élite members' stand, most certainly did not nod their aged heads in accord.

But South Africans have a reputation for not caring greatly for ceremony, and in the glow of the sweetest of Test triumphs, they were not going to be denied. The Mexican wave seemed as out of place at Lord's Cricket Ground as fish and chips at a Tandoori, but on that glorious fourth afternoon in late July 1994, as England's second innings batting melted like a choc-ice in the heat, the South Africans in the crowd made themselves seen and heard.

For three and a half days, Kepler Wessels's team had edged into a position of control in the first Test match between England and South Africa for nearly 40 years. Their fans had also been on the receiving end of faintly withering glances when they cheered a boundary too loudly, or bellowed 'Op die Bokke' or fleetingly unveiled a smuggled flag. But as that final English wicket fell, there was no halting the wave. This now old-hat contribution to sports events (but who knows, possibly making its debut at Lord's) gathered enough support to make half-a-dozen fairly enthusiastic circles of the ground. Of course, it died a death upon reaching the MCC members' stand, but fans had anticipated that and filled in the gaps accordingly.

It was a moment of spontaneous joy that was appropriate to the manner and margin of South Africa's 356-run victory in the Test. Captain Mike Atherton and his men had been ruthlessly ground into the dust. That the subject of Atherton and dust would occupy most of the British papers for the bulk of the following week was, in the eyes of some, merely an example of the time-honoured English way of deflecting attention away from the main crisis. In this case, a pitiful performance. Atherton's 'dust in the pocket' incident received more column inches in the tabloids than a visit by Princess Di to the Third World.

Throughout the Test match, visitors from South Africa could have mistaken Lord's for Durbs-by-the-sea, rather than St John's Wood NW8. Each day dawned bright and cloudless, and the city was humid like a sauna. The tube rides home after a day at the cricket became tests themselves. In rush hour, you are obliged to stand packed together in the carriages, arms aloft, grabbing for a strap. If you're really unlucky, your nose gets wedged near the armpit of a Mohican-coiffed punk with a stud through his lower lip. These hour-long ordeals underground were like attending the yearly convention of the great unwashed. A sweltering London day will pierce the guard of those most meticulously deodorised, never mind the average British commuter.

Tight, flat 'Serth Effrican' accents wafted from all corners of Lord's. The figures seen strolling around the venue during the Test represented a *Who's Who* of South African sport, past and present. Barry Richards, Clive Rice, Henry Fotheringham, Peter Pollock, Morné du Plessis, Roy McLean, Jackie McGlew, Jimmy Cook. Business moguls Anton Rupert, Nicky Oppenheimer and Donny Gordon also attended.

Then there were the estimated 5 000 South African fans who either bought tickets months previously or haggled a worthwhile deal from a tout outside the ground. These tickets featured the old South African flag fluttering in the breeze, further proof of another proud English tradition of lagging slightly off the pace.

The Compton stand and the Mound stand (that new addition to Lord's that was partly financed by American cricket lover John Paul Getty, but whose conical white domes rather suggest donations from Saudi Arabian sheiks) were particularly magnetic to clumps of 'okes' wearing slops and T-shirts and with large plastic cups of lager clamped to their lips. An enterprising shopkeeper outside the St John's Wood tube station had the foresight to purchase cans of Castle and bags of biltong, and these home-grown delicacies were quickly snapped up each day.

The scenes at Lord's resembled those at any ground in South Africa. The only difference was that South Africans were standing in long queues, and not making a fuss about it. When in England…

When at Lord's, one must also abide by rules, which are everywhere. Large placards outside the main W.G. Grace gates remind spectators not to bring in flags, banners, alcohol, radios or any accessories that would enhance the day's entertainment and thus make a £27 (R148 at the time) open-stand ticket seem worth the price. Big white signs warn spectators not to tread on the grass. There was also no opportunity to mill around the practice nets adding to an autograph collection, as you can at the Wanderers. And it would probably have been easier to plunder the crown jewels from their Tower of London fortress than get past the doorkeeper to the members' pavilion without a jacket and tie. Archbishop Desmond Tutu tried to breeze past one such doughty gentleman, and almost needed a little divine intervention to persuade the man to let him up to the balconies to wish his boys good luck before the Test.

The members of the MCC appear to have been vacuum-sealed in a time warp dated 1950, spending their days happily chattering away in their little square of England that remains untouched by changing times or altering views. For the privilege of sitting in the convention-drenched members' pavilion, one would have to wait 20 years to reach the top of the application list, and thus qualify to wear the toxic mustard-and-ketchup-hued MCC tie.

Small wonder most of the worthies who finally get to don this neckwear appear to have little time left on this planet to savour the mellow sounds of leather on willow. Cricket in England doesn't seem geared for the young. The England team has long suffered from a lack of youngsters capable of making it in the cauldron of Test cricket. One glance around Lord's offered a possible explanation. Whereas the stands at the Wanderers, Kingsmead and Newlands are normally sardine-packed with banner-waving kids in their replica national shirts, there seemed to be hardly anyone at Lord's under the age of 21. Perhaps high ticket prices were to blame, or maybe the multitude of other diversions shortening youthful attention spans. But Lord's is not a ground that encourages the sweet bird of youth. Cricket in England is, it seems, dying as an extra-curricular activity in all but the smartest schools.

One youngster who did attend the Lord's Test every day appeared each morning dressed immaculately in shining shoes, grey pants and navy blazer with the letters 'MCC' carefully embroidered on to the pocket.

The voice had the slightest traces of a cockney twang, but if you were one of the thousands of South Africans watching the Test match unfold, then you would have recognised instantly that the accent belonged to someone more accustomed to the dusty streets of South Africa's townships than the tree-fringed home of cricket in north-west London.

Young South African left-arm spinner Jacob Malao was over in England for a six-month stint on the Lord's ground staff, and he'd taken to his new surroundings so rapidly that he would lapse into London-speak every now and then. This was a far cry from the day when he had arrived at Heathrow for his first taste of life in a foreign country.

'I just couldn't understand the accent. Some of these guys don't use their lips. It just comes out from the side of their mouths. Now I can understand them better, just every now and then I can't make out what they say. Everybody in the team here goes "Hey mate", and that's getting to me as well. I've been trying to get them to speak a few words in Zulu, and it's a laugh when they try and pronounce words in my language.'

Malao had long been touted as living, breathing evidence of the success of South African cricket's development programme, and therefore carried an oversized burden on his 21-year-old shoulders. His ability as a spinner has already won him a handful of matches for Transvaal B, and he was the first development player to be invited on to the Lord's ground staff – a kind of finishing school for promising talent where 'pupils' honed their skills under the expert eye of coach Clive Radley, the former Middlesex and England player.

A day in the life of a young MCC cricketer consists of cricket, and not a whole lot more. 'We come here at about 9.30 am, not later, check in and afterwards go to the nets where we practise till 1 pm. After that we do some fielding or go back to the nets. We also do a coaching course and learn scoring and umpiring. Here, during a Test match, we'll sell scorecards on one day. Then the next day we'll be on covers duty or help the ground staff to move the sight-screen.'

But extending his on-field abilities was the prime goal for Malao during his stay, and he'd had to modify his southern hemisphere approach to bowling.

'The English wickets are quite difficult to bowl on. I have to keep it up to the batsmen, because the turn is so slow. That's the first thing I've learned. Back home the ball comes on quickly to a batsman, but over here it's so slow. My bowling technique has changed slightly. I'm getting a lot more side-on, and I'm following through better too. My batting has improved as well, though they keep me at No. 11, which is not so great.'

The MCC side flex their muscles against county second XIs, but it was bowling in the nets to the South African team before the Lord's encounter that had provided the highlight of Malao's sojourn.

'The South African players made me very welcome. Bowling to them was great. It meant a lot to me, and I was very excited to sometimes trouble them with a couple of deliveries. Especially because some of my team-mates like to wind me up. Early on, they called me "baker" because they reckoned I bowl pies. They call all spinners "pie-throwers" here.'

We finished chatting and the 'baker' had a fresh batch of scorecards to sell. As he returned to his post behind the Compton stand, he allowed himself a moment of reflection.

'I never ever thought I'd be here at Lord's. It's an opportunity I was given and I hope to make use of it. It would be even better if when South Africa come over here again, I was part of the team. That would be a great day.'

Of that South African team of 1994, Fanie de Villiers was the player who had gained himself a reputation as a travel-hungry tourist. The Northern Transvaaler needs more stimulation than lying in foreign hotel rooms watching videos of upcoming opponents. Instead he itches to mingle with the locals, drink in the sights and immerse himself in the culture.

The day before that first Test at Lord's, Fanie was kind enough to don his Tommy the Tourist hat for the magazine I was working for. I wanted to do a 'Fanie de Villiers tour of London', and the seam bowler was only too happy to put on his team kit and set out for the sights. The shoot showed Fanie feeding an armful of pigeons in Trafalgar Square, posing with policemen outside Buckingham Palace and floating down the Thames on a cruise to the Tower of London. What the pictures didn't show was the effect that the lone South African had on the crowds in the capital. He was recognised wherever he went. At St James's Park tube station, a cockney seller of London's *Evening Standard* newspaper bellowed out to the fast bowler that he was in for a pasting over the next few days. In Piccadilly Circus, he was mobbed by a group of South Africans, who insisted on photos alongside the statue of Eros.

De Villiers loved being out and about, and even suggested itineraries and routes of interest. He remains one of the few professional sportsmen who are still determined to suck the marrow out of sports tours, both on and off the field. In the latter part of the twentieth century, sports tours are business, and no longer offer opportunities for wide-eyed athletes to indulge themselves as in the past. De Villiers, though, always balances his priorities and makes sure that the bigger picture is firmly in focus when abroad.

The final stop we made on that footslog through London was a place to which both Fanie and I had always wanted to go. The Rock Circus in Piccadilly pays homage to all the great names in music. Here, one literally calls the tune by simply looking at the display required. Stereo CD sound is fed through one's headphones as one moves around the exhibitions. Glance at the Jimi Hendrix display and 'Hey Joe' booms forth. Turn your head 90 degrees towards the Beatles exhibit and 'Hey Jude' wafts through the headset. All the musicians' figures at the Rock Circus are crafted by Madame Tussaud's sculptors. Real hair is used on the head – each strand individually inserted.

That trip to the Rock Circus whetted my appetite to fulfil another musical ambition, and seeing as I had a day or two to spare before interviewing South Africa's two newest soccer exports, I motored up to Liverpool, birthplace of the Beatles.

One look at Liverpool, and it's clear that the city would indeed inspire songs with characters such as lonely Eleanor Rigby, that solitary sock-darner. The city contains the re-vamped, up-market Albert Docks, a more modest version of the Cape Town waterfront, as well as some of the most depressingly derelict areas in Britain, where dirty street urchins shout two-fingered abuse.

But I wasn't heading for either extreme. I made my way straight to the Liverpool Welcome Centre on Clayton Street, and joined a lengthy throng of Japanese tourists readying themselves for a tour of the Beatles' Liverpool. Normally I'd regard a tour of this nature as more mysterious than magical. But because I'm a paid-up Beatles maniac, the two-hour pilgrimage proved better than bumping into the girl with kaleidoscope eyes herself. As essential as Mecca is to Muslims. Not that I want to talk religion. The late John Lennon covered that when claiming the Beatles were bigger than Jesus Christ back in the Sixties, the comment that provoked mass burnings of Beatles records in the American Bible Belt and earned the group a banning from the old SABC.

Yet there is something spiritual about Liverpool. Not least when the city cathedral looms large and eerie through a shroud of grey mist, or the ferry foghorn sounds in the murk as it begins its mournful path across the Mersey, as vessels have done since the twelfth century.

For a day in the life of Merseyside's most famous sons, all you need is £5 for the bus that leaves the Clayton Street depot at 2.20 pm each day. Each bus has its own Beatles guide to detail microscopic trivia about the sites where the Beatles lived, hung out and met up. When the guide takes a break, the songs that have sidetracked generations pipe through at full volume. Modern music's most legendary sound was sired and shaped during 292 gigs in a dank, subterranean Mathew Street basement called the Cavern Club. It was here, after an equally seedy secondment to Hamburg, that the four young Beatles toiled and tinkered while waiting for manager Brian Epstein to walk into their lives. Today the Cavern

Club is a shopping complex. A bit of a letdown that. But the Cavern has been painstakingly recreated across the road and upcoming Liverpudlian musicians try to recapture that famous Mersey Beat most nights of the week. Mathew Street is also home to the Beatles Shop and the Abbey Road pub, as well as statues paying homage to the rock quartet.

Onward to Penny Lane, just outside the city, between districts 15 and 16. No nurses selling poppies from a tray here. Rather a bustling traffic roundabout with public toilets squatting in the middle. The adjacent Penny Lane Wine Bar has the lyrics to the famous song adorning the entrance.

None of the Beatles had a particularly affluent upbringing, and their childhood homes are all in blue-collar neighbourhoods. The youngsters of these areas have got to know what time the tour coaches draw up to take a look at the curtains hanging in Ringo's pre-teen bedroom. And they emerge from the alleyways to shout abuse and make unambiguous digit gestures at the busloads of Beatles fans.

Despite his working-class-hero image, John Lennon had the most middle-class upbringing of all the Beatles members. His Aunt Mimi's beige-coloured, two-storey semi at 18 Menlove Avenue is notable only for its ordinary suburbanness. The present occupants have long tired of tourists aiming long lenses at their living room window. The blinds were firmly drawn. Not far from Menlove Avenue, in a leafy-green part of Liverpool 18, the graffiti-scrawled gates of the Strawberry Field Children's Home loom into view. And the haunting opening bars of that song danced through my mind in Dolby stereo.

For some ungodly souls, this trip might be a ho-hum waste of time and pounds. A needless, sentimental pining for an era long lost. Me? I wasn't even born when Beatlemania first bit. But I'd gladly queue up in the Clayton Street cold again. Tomorrow. And the next day. In fact, I could handle that magical mystery tour eight days a week.

Just 70 kilometres or so down the M62 motorway from Liverpool, two other South African sportsmen were tentatively dipping their toes in an alien culture – both on and off the field. Phil Masinga and Lucas Radebe, the Bafana Bafana soccer players, had impressed the English club Leeds United when South Africa played two friendlies in Australia. The Leeds scout's brief had been to watch Masinga, but so highly did he rate Radebe that the club bought them both.

I travelled to the team's home ground of Elland Road, to the club I've supported with a passion since the days I had milk teeth. Leeds first became my team when they reached the 1975 European Cup Final, after having won the League title the year previously. I don't know if the two events are related, but the team has experienced lean times ever since I joined the ranks of fans. The team faded from the forefront of British soccer in the same way Eugene Terre'Blanche vanished from the political scene after the 1994 elections.

They did have their moments in the early Nineties, however. Leeds had been heading for the old third division before former school teacher Howard Wilkinson arrived as manager in 1988. The club was living in the past, consumed by memories of the glory days under Don Revie in the Sixties and early Seventies. Wilkinson's first salvo was to rid the club of the mementos of that golden era, to ditch the portraits of Billy Bremner, Norman Hunter and Johnny Giles, to expunge from the halls all the trumpeting references to domestic and European wins. He then led Leeds to promotion and an unexpected League title in 1992.

They call Wilkinson 'Sergeant Wilko' round Yorkshire way. He's known for not mincing his words. Nor does he dilute his responses for the sake of a visiting South African journalist, no matter how long that writer has been supporting Leeds United.

'How are Phil Masinga and Lucas Radebe shaping up here?' was my first question that morning, soon after the two South Africans had moved from sun-baked Soweto to the smog, the sleet and the slush of this northern English industrial city.

'They'd be doing a lot f...ing better if they didn't have to f... off back to Africa every other week,' was the answer.

Welcome to the Premiership. No sentiment required.

Wilkinson was referring to the disruption caused by the South Africans having to return home frequently for World Cup qualifiers and African Cup of Nations matches. The trips were exhausting and, in his view, often a waste of time.

Wilkinson had further reason to be pacing the Elland Road training pitch that morning like a bear with a sore head. His side had been dismantled by Queen's Park Rangers at the weekend. It had been an abject performance that had the manager in teacup-smashing mode in the dressing room at half-time. For South Africa's innocents abroad, it was an eye-opening experience.

'That doesn't happen back home. In South Africa, if things go wrong they say "hard luck" and forget about it,' reckoned Masinga.

As I was saying, welcome to the Premiership. Where managers are not renowned for their humanitarian approach to problem-solving. Less ego-massaging, more a swift steel-tipped toecap to the ribs. There's a famous story about Manchester United manager Alex Ferguson. The fiery Scot was known for tempestuous half-time chats during his early managerial career at Aberdeen. During one blistering attack on his team, he kicked the laundry hamper. A pair of underpants sailed through the air and nestled on a cowering fullback's head. Too terrified to twitch a muscle, the defender sat bug-eyed through the rest of the onslaught wearing this unorthodox headgear.

Wilkinson, whose name in newspaper articles is invariably accompanied by adjectives such as 'dour', 'taciturn' and 'no-nonsense', is also known for the brevity of his temper. A couple of years ago he brought out his Leeds United side to play in South Africa in the United Bank Challenge. According to one of the women whose task it was to look after the team, Wilkinson was extremely demanding. He carped about travel arrangements, whined about hotel facilities and refused to let his players attend certain functions. When the team flew back to London, Wilkinson's parting shot to the organisers was a dip at the airline that ferried his squad home. The following morning, that lady learned that the Leeds team had landed safely at Heathrow. Wilkinson's luggage, however, had been mistakenly diverted to Miami. The organiser could hear Wilkinson's rants even when she held the phone at arm's length. She allowed herself a slightly indulgent chuckle.

The players who trooped on to the Elland Road training pitch that Monday morning were still reeling from Wilkinson's weekend tongue-lashing. It was all too much for Carlton Palmer, a feisty midfielder for whom the term 'motormouth' might have been coined. He vented his spleen on Leeds coach Mick Hennigan. 'We're married men here. He can't talk to us like that. I'm a married f...ing man. It's coming to something. I'm telling you straight. It's coming to something,' he moaned. The other, less verbose members of the squad hung their sullen heads like suspects at an ID parade, before the coach finally kick-started the session with a few listless laps of the pitch.

After a morning of five-a-side one-touch training, it was lunchtime at Leeds United. How many of you long-distance die-hards of English football, like my own naive self, grew up thinking Premiership athletes were fine-tuned beasts who were fed closely monitored, scientifically formulated diets? On being invited to join the food queue for lunch, I saw an array of limp meat pies, slap chips and baked beans. The players tucked in with gusto. I made patterns with my chips in the HP sauce.

From the training ground adjacent to the stadium, players cross through the Elland Road car park to reach the dressing room and dining hall. The entrance to the dressing room houses a stack of pigeonholes.

Each player has his own mail slot. The team's stars of the time – Gary McAllister, Gordon Strachan, Gary Speed – had wide racks to house their copious fan mail. Masinga and Radebe had slimmer slots, which were nevertheless scoured daily for letters from home. McAllister was thumbing through his correspondence as I entered the dressing room. He sported black eyes from a broken nose gathered in recent combat. The Scotland skipper was impressed with the attitude shown thus far by the South Africans.

'They've shown that they're eager to improve. No complaining. They realise that they've got a lot to learn, and they've shown an appetite to do it. They look like they've got the ability. But sometimes you need more than that to survive here. You've got to be strong mentally. It's really up to them if they want to succeed.'

The manager's office at Leeds United is far from glamorous. It's a crowded nook housing a tidal wave of papers. The desk was awash with notes. On the wall, at least 200 videos were crammed on a crooked shelf. Each contained a complete Leeds game, labelled chronologically season by season. The tapes dated back to 1988, the year Wilkinson took charge of what looked like a sinking ship. In this manager's inner sanctum, where Wilkinson did all his strategising, coach Hennigan spared me a few minutes to offer his views on the South Africans. His responses were shouted in a barely decipherable Yorkshire accent. He talked in pure manager-speak, a language unique to football men the world over, and unintelligible to the community at large. What I got was a watered-down version of Wilkinson's 'out of it in Africa' theme. In short, just as the pair were getting in the groove, they'd be yanked back home for international commitments.

'I really like Radebe, though,' Hennigan confided. 'He's got the lot. Pace, strength, skill, vision. Of t' pair, he's t' one to watch.'

Phil Masinga knew he was in for a fight when he signed for Leeds. To make the team. To adapt to England. To pioneer a path for fellow South Africans ambitious enough to try to take on Europe.

When initially pressed into first team action, Masinga had shone. He scored against Chelsea on his home debut, and, after being ousted by Brian Deane shortly thereafter, had returned to notch some impressive performances, notably a two-goal blitz against Arsenal. His strikes against the Gunners weren't going to trouble the compilers of a 'Golden Goals' video, but a brace at the Highbury fortress is something that not many Premiership strikers have on their CVs. Masinga quickly learned that goals are hard to come by in England. And he swiftly picked up the local phrase which best described his physical state after most games: 'I'm fooking knackered.'

Waves of homesickness clearly ebbed and flowed for both South Africans. But yearning for the sunshine took a backseat to making the most of a golden opportunity. The money was worth braving the chill for.

'It's a lifetime chance I have here. That's what I tell myself,' said Masinga. 'I want to be here for a few years and make myself some money. Then when I get home I'll be smiling. Over here everything from the start is against you. But the more you stay, the better it gets. They said how cold it was going to be in January, but then January came and I could handle it. When you're playing in cold weather, it's no problem. I just wear gloves, and when I run I get warm. It's when you want to walk around town to do some shopping that it is very cold.'

Masinga also spoke of the problems of marrying Premiership ambitions with international obligations.

'If I'm called up for the national team and everything is discussed with the manager here, I'll just have to go, because I have to play for my nation. It's an honour. I know the effect of going back home. I once talked to Clive Barker about this. Even five minutes away from England and you start missing out. But I want to play for my country.'

When Masinga and Radebe first arrived at Leeds, they were accommodated in club digs on the spartan side of town. Most soccer clubs in England have a few boarding houses whose owners are paid to look after the young players and the new arrivals. In the case of Masinga and Radebe, Leeds had followed the example of Italian giants AC Milan – buying at least two foreign players from the same country. Tough times and strange customs seem easier to bear when hardships are shared with a compatriot. The Dutch trio of Ruud Gullit, Marco van Basten and Frank Rijkaard took Milan to unprecedented heights, and the Inter Milan team of the same era tried the same tactic by buying three Germans – Lothar Mattheus, Jurgen Klinsmann and Andy Brehme. Alhough Leeds' ambitions for their South African duo were a touch more modest, the logic was the same.

Masinga and Radebe started off sharing a small bedroom in the semi-detached home run by cheerful landlady Suzanne Humphrey. Phil's half of the room contained a swish new CD player, his Boyz II Men, Keith Sweat and Aaliyah discs, as well as photos of wife Carol and son Siphiso. Radebe, the quieter of the two, had less clutter. Suzanne Humphrey was the epitome of bustling northern hospitality, and made it her daily task to ensure the pair were thoroughly fed and watered. At each memorable mealtime during my stay there, every carbohydrate known to mankind would be piled high on the plates – rice, roast potatoes, boiled potatoes, mashed potatoes and, of course, Yorkshire pudding.

The South Africans had an uncomplicated routine. Their winter days consisted of training, eating, sleeping and talking on the phone. One Sunday night Masinga received a call from Carol in Johannesburg as the opening credits of *Last Action Hero* appeared on the Sky movie channel. He was still speaking when the film ended some two hours later – tracksuited, cap on backwards, foot tapping furiously on the floor while he nattered away.

According to the Humphreys, the South Africans were 'like a pair of hermits' compared to their boisterous predecessor in the boarding house. The Irish fullback Gary Kelly had come over to Leeds at the age of 15 and soon became a surrogate son. Being one of 13 children, Kelly no doubt knew what it was like to have to fight for attention.

The South Africans, meanwhile, had been quick learners when it came to the social scene near the boarding house. The words 'wide' and 'berth' came to mind. The only pub in the area was a dank and shifty place at the bottom of the road. I ventured in one night and found myself in the midst of tattooed, beefy, crew-cut patrons downing pints of Tetley's bitter. All eyes were on me as I ordered a beer in an accent that stood out like a whitey at a Chiefs–Pirates match. I swiftly sank the pint and scarpered.

Generally speaking, Masinga had a low-key social life and got on best with the youngsters at Leeds, such as Kelly, Mark Tinkler, Jamie Forrester and Kevin Sharp. He was, however, trying to teach defender Chris Fairclough to sing 'Nkosi Sikelel' iAfrika'. The tune proved a cinch. The lyrics were taking a bit longer.

Christmas that first year was spent alone at home with Carol in a new apartment. The day was cold. In the evening, it was business as usual at Elland Road – a training session ahead of the Family Day clash with Newcastle. Masinga was nicknamed 'Chippa' at home, but the Elland Road faithful dubbed him 'Waltzing Masinga'. His name appeared in print as Massinger, Massinga, Philomen, Phillemon, and a host of other variations. At least the British commentators are more successful at getting their tongues around Masinga than they are at attempting Radebe or Ndlovu.

Howard Wilkinson always said that Radebe showed the greater potential of the pair and so it proved. Masinga later moved on to St Gallen in Switzerland and then to the Italian second-division team Salertinara and finally to Bari. His international career looked to be over when he announced he was retiring from the national team in early 1997. Masinga could no longer take the insults and threats from the boo-boys in the crowds at home. Thankfully, this retirement was short-lived.

Wilkinson was hounded out of his job when a string of shabby results saw him resign as manager of Leeds in late 1996. George Graham, the former Arsenal boss, arrived to take over.

So, of the three main characters in the Leeds United plot that enabled me to hang out at the club I've long cherished, Lucas Radebe is the only one still at Elland Road. Under the eye of Graham, one of the best defensive organisers in the game, Radebe has become a key figure at the heart of the Leeds defence. He has experienced the magic of a Wembley final when he turned out in the Coca-Cola Cup Final against Aston Villa in 1996. He also has a new three-year contract with the club, and his daughter was born in Leeds in 1997. He is settled.

Leeds United, however, need a little more work. They scored the least number of goals in the 1996–7 Premiership season. By a long way. Their other African player, Ghanaian striker Tony Yeboah, was injured for most of the campaign. Even when he was fit, Graham chose not to play him very often. This led to Yeboah throwing away his shirt in disgust after being substituted in a match against Tottenham. His days at Elland Road are surely numbered.

Yet Graham always maintained that his priority on taking over at Leeds was to plug the leaky defence. He got that right almost immediately. When Graham managed Arsenal, fans called the Londoners boring. But they still won League titles.

Maybe, along with Lucas Radebe, this particular Leeds United supporter might have cause for more celebrations in the near future.

BRAZIL
PARAGUAY
Puerto Iguazú
Foz do Iguaçu
Ciudad del Este
Iguazú Falls
URUGUAY
Colonia del Sacramento
Buenos Aires
Montevideo
Pacific Ocean
ARGENTINA
Atlantic Ocean

CHAPTER TWELVE

Fear of Flying

JAMES SMALL, DENNIS BERGKAMP AND I have something in common. And it's not the fact that I pose for calendars, score goals for Arsenal, date top models or even have brief skirmishes with wave skiers in nightclubs.

Instead, I include myself alongside that distinguished sporting pair because of our shared fear of flying. That gut-tightening sensation of being shot across the skies in a steel capsule at 900 kilometres per hour is something I find highly disconcerting no matter how many frequent flyer miles I log up.

For Dennis Bergkamp, the Arsenal and Holland striker, the prospect of flying creates such panic that he will check out the ship, bus and train schedules whenever his team is playing abroad and take one of these options where practical. Apparently, the main reason Bergkamp chose not to join Holland for their friendly with South Africa in June 1997 was that the prospect of spending half a day suspended at 12 000 metres, with just a thin sheet of aluminium between himself and oblivion, was a challenge too daunting for the Dutch star to tackle.

Fear of flying is not a pleasant affliction, given the hours sportsmen and journalists spend airborne these days. Of course, I've heard all the statistics that prove flying is a less chancy means of transport than aiming the car in the direction of the grocery store. That argument, logical though it is, holds no water with me. Speaking of which, I seem to find myself in an even more agitated state when jetting over oceans. This is irrationality at its best. There's some deep, dim part of me that says if the plane goes down over the Sahara Desert, I'll have a chance. But plunging into the Pacific Ocean at midnight, into vast, inky blackness a million miles wide, would somehow be far worse.

There's a flight simulator at Johannesburg International Airport that, it is claimed, offers comfort to nervous fliers by explaining the intricate workings of aeroplanes. I'm not going near it. Ignorance, in some cases, is indeed bliss. My fear of flying only started after childhood, when I was able to understand fully just how much could go wrong when on high. I don't want to have an intimate knowledge of all those other bits that could be faulty.

This fear of flying is at odds with my passion for travel. Ever since I've been old enough to turn the pages of an atlas, I've had a desire to visit every continent on the planet. And no way will I let this dread I feel when anticipating a flight stop me visiting places I've already been to in my mind. Over the years, I even began to relax marginally the more I flew. But, like a champion football team becoming complacent, relaxing on a plane only lowers one's guard. There's always some palpitation-inducing surprise lurking just around the corner.

I think I can trace the root of these airborne flutters to bouncing around Kenya in a succession of light aircraft a few years back. We were travelling between Mombasa and Malindi. It was just me, my then girlfriend and the pilot. As we reached cruising height on the short coastal journey, the pilot turned to Caroline with a toothy grin and wondered 'if the madam would like to fly the plane' for a few minutes. She readily accepted and was soon in an animated 'what will happen if I push this red flashing button here?' mode. The white tips of miniature ocean waves broke way down below us. The green canopy of trees looked like broccoli. I cringed in the back seat, head in hands, feverishly plotting a fanciful Plan B if the pilot were to have midair heart failure.

Later on that same Kenyan trip, I sat alongside a young American who was piloting the eight-seater plane that ferried us from Amboseli game park to a smaller park within the Tsavo reserve. Also on board were two British tourists who had just got married in Mombasa. As we neared the reserve, I spied the bronzed-earth airstrip on which we were to put down. Gazelles and wildebeest lunched lazily on tufts of grass at the edge of the runway. The pilot prepared to land.

It was clear, from the speed and angle of our descent, that the airstrip was going to be way too short. Beyond the runway, a solid block of jutting rocks waited. It looked ominously solid. Sitting in the co-pilot's seat, I had an unblemished view of the ground racing up to meet us. I glanced sideways at the pilot as we dipped to no more than 50 metres above the airstrip. There was no indication that he intended to reduce speed. Behind me, my fellow passengers shifted in their seats. As the plane's wheels were about to touch the ground, as that solid wall of rock began getting bigger in the windshield, the pilot suddenly jerked back the joy-stick and we lurched skyward once more. The gazelles and wildebeest ambled off into the long grass.

The pilot had forgotten to tell us that it was a customary part of Kenyan light aircraft strategy to buzz the airstrip and thus frighten off the fauna before landing.

The pilot circled the strip once more and this time made a smooth, measured landing. He had been wearing headphones all along, and was, of course, unaware of the panic his innocent animal-frightening actions had wrought. The new British bride had retched impressively on the back seat behind me, convinced that her short wedded career was to end in a heap of twisted metal on a remote bush airstrip. The pilot turned round and shot us a calm 'wasn't that a fun trip?' look, and remained a picture of composure until he saw the results that his buzz had caused in the young honeymooner.

Flying down to Cape Town from Johannesburg in the winter of 1996, we were climbing through 8 000 metres when suddenly the oxygen masks that provide such vivid food for dark thoughts during pre-flight safety drills, dropped from their overhead resting places and danced in front of our eyes. I felt a cold thrill of fear. The pilot came on the line to say there was 'a serious problem with our pressurisation' and that we would have to put on the masks and then drop rapidly. We fell like a stone, leaving our stomachs in the stratosphere. Around me were muffled whimpers and wide eyes peering from behind masks. The pilot reached a safe level, then turned his plane around and we limped the 45 minutes back to Johannesburg like World War veterans. We landed safely enough, and disembarked on unsteady legs. Any relaxing I could do in the skies had been banished for good.

Towards the end of 1996, the Springbok rugby team headed for Buenos Aires in Argentina. This was the first tour the Boks had undertaken after Francois Pienaar had been axed in that unthinkingly callous fashion by coach André Markgraaff (remember him?). We left Cape Town under fine, blue spring skies. On approaching the South American continent, however, a capsule of foul weather followed us into the Buenos Aires airspace. The pilot began his final approach as lightning streaked the sky and rain sheeted down.

The plane's wheels prepared to kiss South American soil, thus giving me my long-cherished dream of visiting all continents (bar Antarctica). Suddenly, the pilot made a move that called to mind that Tsavo bush pilot. He jerked the plane heavenwards, back into those forbidding, leaden, rain-lashed skies. I was with a group of none too sober journalists and Springbok rugby fans, and so felt obliged to maintain an exterior of humorous bravado. I chortled and jeered along with them, while the frantic timpani drumbeat of my heart betrayed mounting panic.

The pilot circled the airport once more and tried to touch down again. This time the wheels bit into the tarmac. Ironic applause filtered through the cabin. We then reached that moment when you realise how truly fast the plane has been travelling; that instant just before deceleration when it appears the back end of the craft is set to overtake the front. This time there was no slowing down. As spikes of rain slewed past the windows, the plane fishtailed sideways, lacking control like a novice skater on an ice rink. We thundered onward down the runway, and then showers of red mud and clumps of grass began flying past the windows.

You know it's time to worry when the stewardesses start wearing expressions like startled owls. No one told us to brace, but I had my head down in that emergency position quicker than a tortoise sensing peril. The plane skidded on, and at last, amid a tortured grinding of brakes, we fishtailed once more and finally ground to a halt in shin-deep mud.

The pilot came on line to say this was 'an emergency situation' and that we should remain where we sat. Twenty minutes later we left the plane, some passengers down the emergency chutes, others down the landing steps that had eventually been wedged into place. We had overshot the runway by about 100 metres. The plane had come to a halt less than 50 metres from a massive bank of runway lights. Had we careered into them, the resulting eruption would surely have shamed American Fourth of July firework displays.

Like that British honeymooner whose wedding celebrations were so nearly cut short in Kenya, I was convinced my first taste of South America would also be my last. James Small, of course, got to hear about the incident. He decided to drive the six hours to Mendoza for one of the midweek games rather than join the rest of his team on the charter plane.

I eventually recovered my South American land legs with the help of large doses of Quilmes beer. That night we strolled the broad, bustling *avenidas* of the capital. Buenos Aires resembles a European city and is often called the Paris of South America. This comparison probably holds true, only there's far less dog crap on the streets of BA, and the girls are far more beautiful and chicly dressed than the French pretenders to the fashion throne. I was expecting all Argentinian ladies to be swarthy Gabriela Sabatini clones, yet the majority who strolled down designer streets like Calle Florida appeared to be blonde, olive-skinned goddesses.

Buenos Aires is also home to Avenida Nuevo de Julio, the widest street in the world. The city squats on the southern bank of the River Plate, the widest river in the world. And the restaurants and *parrillas* of the city produce the thickest, juiciest cuts of steak anywhere. The only problem with Buenos Aires is that your money disappears faster than an apartheid hitman appeals for amnesty. It has the sophistication of Paris and the buzz of New York, but the prices of Tokyo.

Luckily, if you need to escape the peso-dwindling temptations of the Argentinian capital and relax in a less pricy location, there's one close at hand. Buenos Aires is just across the River Plate from Uruguay. Montevideo, the Uruguayan capital, is a two-and-a-half-hour hydrofoil trip from BA, while Colonia del Sacramento is just 50 minutes away.

Fellow sports writer Mark Keohane and I had tired of hanging around the swanky Springbok team hotel waiting to see if players would tear themselves away from their Walkmans long enough to deliver meaningful sermons on how the tour was proceeding. So we decided to check out Colonia, and arrived early one morning at the riverside port of Darsena Norte, where the hi-tech Sea Cat ferries ply their way across the waters of the Plate. The R150 return ticket is worth the price solely for the receding view of Buenos Aires as the ferry chugs towards Colonia. The vast waterfront edifices stretch for kilometres, testimony to the status of surely one of the great capital cities of the world.

Colonia might be less than an hour away from BA, but the difference between the two settlements could hardly be more pronounced. To visit Colonia is to step back in time to an era of narrow, cobble-stoned streets, whitewashed stone houses and old men with time on their hands sunning themselves in the midday heat.

Many visitors to Buenos Aires take a day trip to Colonia for the same reasons that we did. The result is a great number of homely little hotels and restaurants. In fact, for such a small town, there's almost an overdose of eye-catching inns – nearly 30 in the old town, or *barrio historico*, alone.

The restaurants are no less profuse, and we retired to a fetching little *parrilla* called the Mercado del Puerto just off the main waterfront in San Gabriel Street. We expected to hear no word of English for the rest of the day, until the waitress turned up the sound system, and the sounds of John Lennon wafted through Colonia's ancient streets. Munching on the chicken and downing drafts of the local beer, we were soon agreeing that this was how life should always be – no traffic, cell phones, deadlines or pollution. These dreamy observations were enhanced by 'Imagine' booming out at maximum volume, and before our mushy frames of mind led us to start checking out the local real estate prices, we decided to move on.

To be frank, there's not much else to do in Colonia other than sit around. It's a place to come and soak up old-world atmosphere and chill out over a beer or three.

We bumped into a dreadlocked Colombian in the main street. He overheard our English and came up to declare us his long-lost brothers. He was sharing a massive bottle of beer with his two mates, and insisted we also swig heartily. The fact that the rain which had threatened all day was now streaming down was of no concern. So we stood there in Colonia's main thoroughfare swallowing beer and chatting while the rain plastered the hair to our scalps. Soccer remains the world's greatest conversational ice-breaker. I recited the names of a couple of Colombian World Cup stars to our new chum, and our status as blood brothers was reconfirmed. After discussing the abilities of Carlos Valderrama, Rene Higuita et al., we told him we were visiting Argentina for the Springbok rugby tour. The Colombian gave us a lively interpretation of what this odd game meant to him. He began tackling his friends with gusto, backing them savagely into shop walls and bowling them into tree trunks. He finally concluded, with a broad smile, that whereas soccer was a cerebral game played by artists, rugby was only for *el stupidos*.

After a protracted, emotional farewell to our Colombian brother, we still had a couple of hours to kill before returning to the ferry. So we entered a bar that was like stepping into one of those television commercials favoured by the makers of posey products such as wraparound sunglasses or trendy American bourbon. You know the kind of designer remoteness and chic backwardness I'm talking about. In this Uruguayan tavern, ancient men sat alone at wooden tables nursing the dangerous local brew. All had skin wrinkled like molten bronze, and they gazed with vague curiosity at us gringo patrons. The bar owner was bent over an antiquated, crackling transistor radio, listening to horse-racing. Every so often he'd stand up and rub his hands together, cackling happily. One stubbled drinker came up to us and implored us in passionate, beer-breath Spanish to follow him. From what we could make out, he was offering to take us to a snooker hall where there were lots of girls. This latter fact he communicated by rubbing his fingers on his ear to denote earrings. He winked at us, beckoning us along, but all we wanted was to hang out and drink a beer or two.

We ambled along to the ferry, and within a couple of hours found ourselves back in bustling Buenos Aires. Back to chicly dressed girls, speeding taxis, glitzy nightclubs and designer boutiques on spacious boulevards. Colonia, 50 kilometres across the River Plate, was an entire world away.

James Small and myself have something else in common besides a fear of flying. He probably won't remember this, but the first time I came across the bustling Bok winger was when he and I were both serving crêpes and cappuccinos at Café Royale in Johannesburg's Hyde Park Corner shopping centre.

He was an embryonic rebel who occasionally attended class at Greenside High, just down the road. I was a student at Wits. Back then, one word leapt to mind when first encountering Small, and that was *windgat*, the expressive Afrikaans word for 'arrogant'. He was clearly very pleased with himself, had never had an idea he didn't love, flirted with every waitress and showed no special dedication to his serving duties.

Someone once mentioned the standard nine pupil's sprinting prowess, I remember. Small was already as capable of running a sub-11-second 100 metres as he was of sneaking off for a smoke behind the bike sheds.

The next time I heard the name James Small was via a couple of mates who were bubbling about the dynamic performance of the Greenside High fullback in the big schools match against King Edward's. This guy James Small was apparently a dead cert for 1987 Craven Week selection and might even knock on the SA Schools door. Could this be the same flash strutter in the pink shirt and bow tie?

Down the years, many people have made snap judgements about James Small. Often they've been proved wrong. Although he sometimes does his best to shoot himself in the foot, Small has generally proved as hardy as the pink bunny rabbits in Duracell ads. He appears to be one of the few South African sportsmen aware of the value of making himself available to the media, even though he's often lived to regret this generosity with a telling quote. He knows how to showcase himself and manipulate the press to his own advantage. And there's nothing wrong with that. We're all sales reps in the vast used car lot of life, and there are few institutions as manipulative as the mass media.

What has emerged during my interviews with Small is that there are a number of distinct personalities that go into making up rugby's favourite rebel without a pause. James Small the patriot is the man to whom the Springbok jersey means everything. The man who pleaded for an anthem, any anthem, during the days, just after isolation ended, when the Springbok team shuffled around, hands in pockets, while their opponents received massive adrenaline injections from hearing 60 000 countrymen in full voice. When an anthem did arrive, Small was the player on whom the TV cameraman would linger. Eyes tightly shut, chest heaving with emotion, Small craves national pride like a junkie needs his next fix. Natal and ex-Springbok coach Ian McIntosh, with whom Small has not always seen eye to eye, says, 'He's a very intense man, but he's also an incredibly loyal person. He's very emotional too. I remember in New Zealand when André Joubert was left out of the second test in 1994, James had tears in his eyes – he was reacting for André.'

Then there's James Small the rumbler. The nightclub skirmishes, acrimonious brushes with the press – sectors of the Kiwi media once dubbed him a 'smack-head' and a 'nutter' – the urban legends about altercations with Bok team-mate Brendan Venter in New Zealand, of a Natal team-mate having to restrain him in a Cape Town pub as he sprayed customers with beer. Everyone whose life has rebounded off Small's, however briefly, has their own stories to tell. And the result is sometimes an image of an uncontrollable lout reeling from fracas to fracas.

But another dimension to James Small is as a lover of children. Many tears flowed from the man when Small was named godfather of Natal centre Jeremy Thomson's baby. And I remember he once sat through an interview jiggling the baby of ex-Natal coach Andy Keast on his knee. Small received bulging sacks of hate mail after he'd been kicked off the Springbok squad in 1994 for that nightclub altercation with a Springbok wave skier. But he also received petitions of support from many kids. Yet Small is not altogether happy with his undoubted status as a role model, and he echoes the sentiments of basketball bad-boy Charles Barkley.

'I didn't ask to be anyone's hero. I didn't ask to be anyone's role model, and I don't see why I should be put under any pressure to try and live up to it. I love kids. I'll be great with any kid I'll ever meet in my life. But don't tell him to look up to me. He must look up to his parents. He must do his own thing, live his own life. Obviously, I come from a different planet from some of the other guys in the team. My whole mindset, lifestyle, would probably give heart failure to some of the guys. But that's the nice thing about rugby and about travelling around the world. That you can get different opinions and different influences. It's how you sort your differences out that makes you a good person, a good team. I've never just walked away from someone because I don't like them. I've always confronted them in my own way.'

The James Small that toured Argentina in 1996 appeared, for the most part, to be in the mellowest of moods. He'd been given a long leash by management and responded by not letting them down. He'd huddle in the hotel, Walkman on head, happily retreating into his own world.

The entire tour of Argentina, France and Wales was, according to pressmen who had followed the Springboks since 1992, the most relaxed trip since isolation ended. This was perhaps surprising, as the furore over Francois Pienaar's sacking was still fresh in most South Africans' minds. Yet the Springboks played with freedom in the two Tests at the revamped first-division soccer stadium of Ferrocarril Oeste. For both Tests, the stadium was three-quarters full. Soccer may be the game of choice in Argentina, but the locals knew how to get behind their side. They also knew how to treat the visiting reporters. Half an hour before kick-off, a bewhiskered old gentleman appeared in the press box bearing a tray of champagne-filled crystal flutes.

The local radio commentators were whipped into a frenzy in the opening minutes of the second Test when the Pumas managed to score first. Argentinian soccer commentators are renowned the planet over for their prolonged, melodic roars of ecstasy whenever a goal is scored, and it was clear that their rugby counterparts were determined not to be outdone. Unfortunately, from a local perspective, these celebrations were infrequent. The Springboks played poised rugby and scored comfortable wins in both Tests.

The post-match press conferences were probably more difficult for captain Gary Teichmann and coach André Markgraaff than the games themselves. The Pumas had enlisted the services of a suave local beef magnate as interpreter. The man knew his rugby, but, sadly, the nuances of the English language defeated him. Many reporters' questions were lost in a labyrinth of misinterpretations. Some of the local press were more adept at English than the man chosen to decipher, and hurried the shamed man into vapid explanations of whatever the Springbok brains trust said. The conferences tended to end with uncomprehending shrugs all round.

After the Springboks had flown on to France, I boarded a regional Lapa flight from Buenos Aires for the town of Puerto Iguazú, the gateway to the Iguazú Falls on the border of Brazil and Argentina. This stretch of raging cataracts is mightier than Niagara and more varied than Victoria. Also, the falls are photogenic enough to have provided the backdrop for the movie *The Mission*. Yet they remain a relatively undervisited destination for South Africans. Perhaps with Victoria Falls so close, the type of South African likely to visit Iguazú has overdosed on the pleasures of gazing at sheets of water cascading over a river's edge. However, ever since Robert De Niro and Jeremy Irons tussled above the abyss in *The*

Mission, the Iguazú Falls have hovered near the top of my must-see list of global destinations.

I was still in a fairly fragile state after my rocky entry into South America, but the flight to the falls, mercifully, passed without incident. We were deposited two hours later at an airport straight out of the pages of a Paul Theroux novel – a dilapidated wooden building with a single, creaking luggage carousel leading through to the muggy arrivals hall. Here, the first vestiges of a tourist magnet that draws more than two million visitors a year reveal themselves. Television screens showing the video of a flight over the falls compete with tour guides soliciting sightseeing business and throngs of taxi drivers fighting for the 15 pesos needed to take you downtown.

I had no accommodation booked, and my few days in Buenos Aires had bled me of the bulk of my currency. Luckily, the town of Puerto Iguazú has lodgings to suit many a pocket. I stayed at a tiny establishment called Lilian's Place. No one spoke any English, but the diminutive room had a spotless shower and a ceiling fan. A positive snip at $12 a night. Just round the corner was a little *parrilla* that served great steaks and great flagons of foaming beer. On my kind of budget, this was my kind of hotel.

The Iguazú Falls were discovered, as we Westerners would have it, by a Spanish conquistador called Alvar Nunez Cabeza de Vaca (literal translation: A.N. Head of Cow). He christened them the Salto de Santa Maria. The first records of the falls were made by Jesuit missionaries (no, not Robert De Niro and Jeremy Irons) who settled in the region and made it their life's work to educate and convert the indigenous Guarani Indians. So successful were they that they attracted less scrupulous pioneers who exploited the Guarani, sold them into slavery, and caused the Jesuits to be expelled from their missions in the late eighteenth century.

I prefer the local Indian story of how the falls came about. A god of Guarani beliefs was due to marry one of the local tribe's girls. The señorita, however, was having none of this. She and her earth-bound lover decided to elope one stormy evening. They were apprehended by the god who, in his wrath, split the earth above the River Iguazú, sending the shamed pair, along with several billion kilolitres of water, tumbling over the abyss, where they have remained trapped ever since.

To fully appreciate the magnitude of the falls, which stretch in a roughly horseshoe shape for more than 3 kilometres across the rivers Iguazú and Paraná, it's best to set aside two full days, and thus see them from both the Argentinian and Brazilian sides. The Brazilian side offers a more panoramic view, while on the Argentinian side, it's feasible to walk among the brilliantly sited array of catwalks, where the white-water tumbles and broils metres from your head.

I began by taking a day trip to the Brazilian side (where the Portuguese spelling of the falls is 'Iguaçú'). Fortunately, no blizzard of bureaucratic paperwork is necessary to cross the border from Argentina. Anyone going to Brazil merely for a falls day trip is rapidly ushered through. After entering the national park on the Brazilian side, it's about a 15-kilometre trip to the falls themselves, which begin in front of the Hotel das Cataratas, a spectacular pink stucco edifice that has breathtaking vistas straight into the heart of the water.

As at the latter-day Victoria Falls, locals on both sides of the border have cottoned on to the money-spinning potential of the asset in their midst. While there are no white-water trips or bungee jumps at Iguaçú, the Brazilians have concluded that seven-minute, $50-helicopter flips over the falls is what really floats el turistos' boats. Hardly a minute goes by without the incessant droning of these giant metallic dragonflies swooping overhead and drowning out the thunder of the waters. Argentinians are firmly against such mechanical exploitation of the falls, claiming that the choppers meddle with the delicate ecological balance of the territory.

The Brazilian side of Iguaçú features winding walkways leading down to wide-angle views of the falls. Some of the catwalks jut perilously out over the river, leading the brave-hearted through a misty veil of spray directly over the churning foam. And free enterprise has even made its mark among this most natural of wonders. There's a souvenir store, for instance, built smack under a thundering chute. Here you can sit and sip Coke or snap up cheap keyrings while the full-throated rumble of white-water plays havoc with your eardrums.

On the Argentinian side, you can get within touching distance of any number of truly terrifying cataracts. Here, a stroll along the *paseo superior* (upper walkway) leads to a striking vantage point above Salto San Martín, a lyrical curtain of water where one can stand gazing for hours. The *paseo inferior* (lower walkway) takes the more intrepid visitor down a sheer set of steps right down to the river's edge. A short free boat trip leads to the Isla San Martín, a green wedge of land stuck in between the two main sections of the falls. As befits the flora and fauna of such a lush, tropical region, there is plenty of wildlife to stumble across. Like multi-coloured lizards and tame bandicoots. The latter are small cute mammals the size and shape of an anteater, whose purpose in life is to rummage through rubbish bins in search of ice-cream wrappers and boiled-sweet remnants.

Visitors can take another boat trip, one which tugs at the adrenaline gland like few other tourist attractions on earth. Sleek little motorboats are laden with jittery passengers at the base of the falls. These then roar back up river, through churning water, to within metres of the Salto San Martín Falls. Needless to say, occupants are drenched within seconds, and the less hardy among us surely aged a few years when the driver decided it would be a fine joke to cut the boat's engine. The flimsy vessel was sucked closer and closer to the raging torrents beneath the falls. The driver tried the ignition. There was a moment of brief but nonetheless high terror as the engine failed to catch, before the grinning pilot successfully engaged his vehicle and thundered back up the river to safety.

Two days of staring at lashings of falling water finally start taxing the attention span, so I thought I would sample a fourth South American country and head over to neighbouring Paraguay.

Ciudad del Este is a border town. Though 'border' is an inappropriate term. There appears to be little or no immigration control. Hence there's a non-stop barrage of cars, scooters, trucks, pedestrians and donkeys traipsing across the Amizade bridge that separates Brazil and Paraguay. Any car with Paraguayan, Brazilian or Argentinian licence plates is waved through. Must be paradise for smugglers. In a way, the lack of control is a good thing. The bridge is clogged with humanity at the best of times and when people are humming through the border at the rate of a thousand an hour, it's a small mercy that no paperwork is needed. It's not often one fails to find a single redeeming feature about a destination, but Ciudad del Este – Eastern City – has an atmosphere and bearing that not even a mother could love.

As well as displaying the usual desperate traits of your average border town, Ciudad del Este markets itself as a fifth-rate South American facsimile of Hong Kong. All manner of cut-price consumer goods are up for grabs here, as the town has evolved to take advantage of the tourist money brought into Argentina and Brazil by the falls. Every conceivable make of fake Far Eastern gadget, dicey electronic appliance, counterfeit timepiece and bogus perfume is for sale on rickety, health-hazard kiosks. Each and every inhabitant is out either to hustle a buck or to pick up a bargain piece of hi-tech gadgetry. Then disappear back over the border, to Brazil or Argentina, where they conduct their real lives.

To be fair, there's one decent building in the town – Mercado Bom Bom Shopping Asia, a valiant attempt at replicating a multi-storey shopping arcade. Otherwise, trash piles high on the fetid pavements, all manner of sewer seepage froths around your feet, and the stall-owners adopt strong-arm vending tactics. I was reminded of the Intergalactic bar scene from *Star Wars*, where all the weirdos of the universe descend to drink, hustle and scuff each other about the head. The only difference between this Paraguayan town and the bar that Luke Skywalker visited is that the Ciudad del Este hustlers don't have three-feet antennae growing out of their heads.

When in Ciudad del Este, you can either beat it, or join them. So I decided to add my bit to the Paraguayan economy by picking up some Ray-Bans for $4 and a Tag Heuer watch for $10. You don't have to tell me they weren't the real thing, but I have a friend who bought a genuine Tag Heuer for $1 600. His watch has barely gone a day without giving him hassle. Mine is still ticking gamely. Albeit, as I write these words, I can't help noticing that my Tag says its 3.30 pm while the oven clock reads 5.15 pm.

Oh well. At least I didn't succumb to the persuading powers of the Chanel No. 5 vendors. I watched one blonde-haired gringo buy herself a splendidly packaged bottle of this stuff from a Ciudad hawker. She was pretty proud of her purchase, until she opened the box to find her Chanel was merely green-coloured water. She scanned the thronging pavements, but the seller had already melted into the crowds.

I'd had enough. It was about 5.30 pm (if my Tag could be trusted). Rush hour, or more accurately, exodus hour, as a surge of people abandoned Ciudad del Este to head back across the borders. It was the wrong time to leave. We travelled about 200 metres before becoming wedged in a four-lane traffic snarl. Crazed drivers competed for non-existent gaps in the traffic, kids sold Cokes from dirt-smeared cardboard boxes, buyers tottering under the weight of televisions quarrelled with uniformed border police. Eventually we edged back across the bridge into Brazil. I looked in the rear-view mirror at the rapidly retreating skyline of Ciudad del Este. It was the best sight I'd seen all day.

If ever some shifty tour guide sidles up offering a day trip to Ciudad del Este, make sure you mutter 'No speak Spanish' in firmer tones than usual.

Back at BA's Ezeiza Airport, I psyched myself up for the long-haul flight back over the terrible Atlantic by downing two Quilmes beers as quickly as possible. I picked up a copy of the local English language *Buenos Aires Herald* in the departure lounge. The lead story was the midair collision over New Delhi involving a Saudi Arabian jumbo and a Russian cargo plane. The near disaster with which I'd entered the country was still fresh in my thoughts and dreams. I realised I needed another intense psyching session. I called for a third Quilmes. Then another. And one more, just for luck.

HONG KONG
South China Sea
MALAYSIA
BRUNEI
Sabah
Kuching
Sarawak
BORNEO
(Kalimantan)
Sumatra
INDONESIA
Java
Indian Ocean
AUSTRALIA

CHAPTER THIRTEEN

Borneo to Be Wild

ONE THURSDAY AFTERNOON, in October 1996, a friend in the travel industry phoned to ask me if I wanted to go to Hong Kong for the weekend. He offered the trip as casually as if he were suggesting an overnight stay in Warmbaths. There was a travel fair in the soon-to-be-ex British colony, he said, and someone was needed to hand out brochures. He didn't have the time. Would I go and dish out the flyers instead? All hotels, meals and airport transfers would be paid for. Also, a second person could tag along for the ride for just R800.

'Let me think about it,' I said. Three seconds later, I asked him what time I needed to be at the airport.

I then phoned an old cricketing mate, Tancred Melis. I asked if he wanted to spend 48 hours in Hong Kong, in a similar 'weekend-in-Warmbaths' tone of voice. He pondered the question even less than I did.

And so, 30-odd hours after that phone conversation, we found ourselves rubbing sleep from our eyes as our Cathay Pacific 747 commenced its descent to Hong Kong's Kai-Tak airport. The landing here is probably the most vivid in the world. There's precious little room for pilot error, as the single runway juts out into the South China Sea. A China Airlines jumbo discovered this a few years back when it slid off the runway and into the ocean. Planes must bank steeply and then approach the runway through a canyon of skyscrapers. As the plane rushes to meet the ground, jet passengers are treated to the sight of tower block occupants going about their wake-up rituals.

If the world's your oyster after one night in Bangkok, as Murray Head sang in the musical *Chess*, then a weekend in Hong Kong must mean the globe's your crayfish thermidor lightly sautéed in a chilli and garlic sauce. Washed down with a bottle of Dom Perignon.

This miniature splotch of land on the southern tip of mainland China is more than a little overwhelming. With just hours on the ground, there were places to see, bargains to harvest, prawns to devour, beer to swill. We arrived at our Kowloon hotel at 9 am. We were heading home the next evening. Tedious things like sleep, jet lag and credit card balances could wait.

We started with the places. The travel expo had laid on a morning tour of the island. First port of call was Repulse Bay. Despite the name, this is the best bit of beach in Hong Kong, a fetching stretch of white sand set below dramatic green hills. Repulse Bay is known locally as Excuse-me Bay due to the crowds in summer. Everyone has to step over everyone else to get their toes wet. Property prices here, as in the rest of Hong Kong, are high as a Greenwich Village crack dealer. Basic two-bedroom flats, admittedly with stunning sea views, fetch R6 million. The blocks themselves seem to have been haphazardly jammed into the hillside, like estate agents' signboards on a suburban street corner.

One multi-storeyed building overlooking the bay had a vast gap in its centre. The legend goes that there's a dragon that lives in the hills behind these flats. The developers were told that their project would block the dragon's view of the ocean and this would bring untold misfortune. So they left a 12-apartment-size hole in the middle. A space that, had it been filled with flats, would have added around R78 million to the project's coffers.

Superstition plays a large part in Chinese culture. One local property tycoon had recently purchased a number plate for his newest Rolls-Royce. The number eight is considered lucky by the Chinese. So the tycoon hedged his bets for future prosperity in this life and the next by choosing 8888 for his vehicle. It cost him R2,8 million.

Victoria Peak is the best place in Hong Kong to observe what is surely one of the most impressive marks that man has thus far left on this planet. If you're a fan of reflective glass and towering cement, that is. Perched 500 metres above the concrete jungle of Hong Kong Island and, across the bay, Kowloon, one has a dazzling perspective on the growth that Hong Kong has undergone in the past 50 or so years. Victoria Peak is reached via a winding, vertiginous drive and at the top are a number of restaurants with locations designed to maximise the vistas, particularly at night, when the entire island is a wild mass of light.

By the time we'd finished ogling the Victoria Peak views, we were itching to let rip with the credit card, so our host wisely drove us from Hong Kong Island across to adjacent Kowloon. All roads on a Hong Kong shopping binge lead to Nathan Road, a 2-kilometre, neon-smeared, north-to-south boulevard that is the equivalent of London's Oxford Street or Singapore's Orchard Road. Here teem electronic shops, big name consumer stores, bargain stalls, mahjong emporiums, massage parlours and shady characters offering wristfuls of fake Rolexes.

For homesick South Africans, there's the 'Van der Merwe' electronic shop on the corner of Nathan and Mody Roads, opposite the Holiday Inn. This store first sold camera equipment to South African Airways crews about a decade ago. The South African connection strengthened through word of mouth. Eventually, business was so good that the owners changed the name of their shop to Cape Town Audio and Video Co. (Van Der Merwe Shop). The business card of salesman Ringo Ling, who sold me some cameras for a third of the price I would have paid at home, had 'Beste Prys! Beste Diens!' printed under the store's logo. Our consumer appetite had been whetted and we went on a spree. I bought a laptop computer. Tancred got himself a printer, a video camera and an armful of Rolexes. Hong Kong is a dangerous place for jet-lagged South Africans wielding Mastercards.

The fish market, into which we blundered around dusk, offered a bizarre array of livestock for sale and slaughter. As well as the more conventional fruits of the sea, vendors bellowed the virtues of creatures as off-putting as Madonna in fishnets. Thick, metre-long eels sliced in two, but still break-dancing on the slab, cages of scaly lizards, plastic bags filled with locusts. Also basketfuls of frogs. The French might enjoy frogs' legs, but Cantonese favour the whole package. Tancred filmed one customer buying ten wriggling amphibians. The vendor took the cleaver to the poor creatures with practised relish. She first chopped their heads off, then split their stomachs to extract the entrails, de-skinned the still-thrashing creatures, then twisted back the skin and sliced off their back feet. Each frog was dressed in about ten seconds flat. The customer left with his plastic bag full of skinless, headless, footless, organless frogs still twitching.

Dinner beckoned. We took the metro to Wanchai. Apart from Singapore's spotless marble and glass underground, the Hong Kong MRT must be the only metro in the world where people queue as tidily as an accountant's in-tray for the rush-hour train. This might have something to do with Asia's orderliness, if that's not a politically-incorrect generalisation. It's surely no accident that this part of the world is experiencing such an economic boom. The work ethic of South-East Asia's inhabitants is legendary. Each and every person appears motivated, goal-oriented, purposeful. There is no such thing as loitering. Begging is a cultural embarrassment. A delinquent Hong Kong kid is one who didn't get an A for his maths homework. And no angst-ridden teenager would think of defacing the train station or spraying graffiti on the wall. The money isn't good enough. I suppose some people might now quote the suicide rate in Japan as the downside to all this industrious beavering. At least the Asians have the cash to erect buildings worth throwing themselves off.

We were out for dinner with two young women from a Randburg travel agency. It was their first trip abroad. We ordered a smorgasbord of seafood at the Broadway Seafood Restaurant in Wanchai. Curiously, the waiter brought the prawns to us live and kicking on a plate. These shellfish bucked and wriggled like pre-teen Olympic gymnasts before we pinned them with chopsticks and popped them in the fondue pot on the table. But not until a couple of them had flipped towards us like menacing Parktown prawns, causing one of the travel ladies almost to back into the neighbouring table's bird's nest soup to avoid the gallant critters. Needless to say, our attempts provided ample live entertainment for the rest of the diners. One of the local patrons was gracious enough to come over and offer tips on snaring live prawns. Not that it helped.

From the Broadway restaurant, we moved on to sample the rest of Wanchai's nightlife. Joe Bananas is the nightspot that has achieved legendary status among the droves of rugby fans who storm Hong Kong for the Sevens rugby tournament each March. We had a brief yet notable altercation with the doorman who wouldn't let me in as I was wearing a T-shirt. We had to fork out R200 for a Joe Bananas polo-shirt.

And there we sat, contemplating our orgy of capitalist excesses as the clock crept towards 4.30 am. A combination of jet lag and San Miguel beers left us in a vaguely euphoric state. On a whim, Tancred ordered cigars. The waitress brought the box and we selected a pair of Cuba's finest. R800 worth of toxic smoke was sent billowing on to the strobe-lit dance floor as more strawberry daiquiris appeared.

One evening in Hong Kong. Kings of the planet for a night.

That mad 60-hour sortie to Hong Kong sharpened my appetite for the Far East. Dangerous, wriggling foodstuffs notwithstanding, I hoped to visit that thriving part of the world many times in the future. Fortunately, soccer's Under 20 World Championships were held in Malaysia in June 1997. It seemed a great excuse to spend some more time in the exotic East. Even better, the South African team had qualified for the finals, becoming the first national team to reach the finals of a world soccer tournament at any level. The United Warriors, as they were known, were to be based in Kuching on the island of Borneo.

The South Africans had reached the final of the Under 20 African Championships in Morocco earlier in 1997. On the way, they had beaten fancied opposition like Zambia and Ghana. The Ghanaians routinely turn out world-beating junior teams, but the South Africans had eliminated the West Africans in the semifinals before losing 1–0 to Morocco in the final. A lot of talk had focused on the exciting South African striker Benedict McCarthy, a youngster from the mean streets of Hanover Park in Cape Town, the Bronx of the Mother City. A clutch of international club scouts had attended the Under 20 African Championships, keen to discover and latch on to young talent that might become the next George Weah, Tony Yeboah or Finidi George. These days there's big money to be made unearthing African soccer gems. Benedict McCarthy had made his mark in Morocco. He scored five goals in the tournament. The scouts scurried to alert their clubs.

Sobering signs greet arriving passengers at Malaysia's Kuala Lumpur airport. All over the landing hall are posters reminding desperados and fools that 'Drug Trafficking Carries a Mandatory Death Penalty in Malaysia'. This airport is not a good place to loiter with unlocked bags. I spent the day in Kuala Lumpur before connecting to Kuching, the capital of Sarawak. KL, as the locals call the Malaysian capital, resembles nothing so much as a giant building site. Such is the economic flourish in this part of the world that new glass-faced buildings are erected at the speed of a time-lapse nature film. The Malaysian attitude is encapsulated in their 'Vision 2020'. They aim to be a 'fully developed' nation by that year. Huge department stores squat alongside swish hotels and giant banners remind the world that the Commonwealth Games will he held in KL in 1998.

Some Malaysian traditions haven't succumbed to the march of modernism, however. For instance, dinner. As dusk fell in the bustling Chinatown district of the city, roads were busily cordoned off by police in preparation for dinner and the nightly street market. Vendors fired up portable gas cylinders in their food carts and began bawling their edible wares to passers-by. Much was made of the fruit available, some of which is unique to the region. The most bizarre is the durian – the biggest, worst-smelling fruit in South-East Asia. This offering is the size and shape of a football clothed in a spiky green shell. Eating a durian is like swallowing crème caramel in a blocked toilet. Its pungent whiff has caused the fruit to be banned on the underground in neighbouring Singapore. Though the stench is awesome, locals munch the sticky yellow flesh with relish, believing the fruit has rejuvenating powers. Far more nasally friendly than the durian is the small, hairy rambutan. Burst open the fruit's red skin and three segments of juicy flesh pop forth, firm like a litchi. I also sampled the mangosteen, which looked like a smooth grenadilla, and the watery star fruit.

I met a Canadian girl by the name of Victoria. She was from Victoria, Vancouver. Victoria from Victoria. We nurtured our main-course appetites by roaming through the narrow lanes of market stalls, haggling for the fake R30-Rolexes, imitation Lacoste and Benetton shirts, and pirated videos.

Wandering from stall to colourful stall, tempting aromas wafted from exotic blends of Malay, Chinese and Indian dishes. It was time to eat and we chose the alfresco delights of the Ngan-Kee restaurant. This establishment's most popular item was the 'steamboat', a Chinese-Malaysian variation on a fondue. Skewers of bamboo were brought out on which a myriad of meats had been impaled. These we cooked in a sunken pot of boiling water in the middle of the table and then dipped them in an array of piquant sauces. The bill was calculated by totting up the number of used skewers. I made a note of the delicacies that rapidly disappeared from the table – quails' eggs, abalone, prawn, sea snail, pork and fish balls, cuttlefish, spring rolls, mushrooms, chicken and won ton (a fish and meat combo). Happily, none of the food was still wriggling.

Onward to Kuching in Borneo, a 90-minute flight across the Malaysian peninsula and the South China Sea. Borneo is the world's third largest island, after Greenland and Papua New Guinea. It comprises two Malaysian states – Sarawak, where part of the Under 20 World Championships were taking place, and Sabah. Between these is the oil-rich kingdom of Brunei, home to the Sultan, one of the world's richest men. The southern area of the island is Kalimantan, the Indonesian part of Borneo.

Borneo is the island where the ruthless Dayak head-hunters plied their trade decades back. The 'Wildmen of Borneo'. So go the romantic notions. Of course, I'd entirely dismissed thoughts of such goings-on persisting in the twilight of the twentieth century. This would have been as silly as small-town Americans thinking lions still stalk the pavements of Gauteng. Then I read an article in *The Malaysia Star* while on the plane. It told of 4 000 people being killed in riots in a remote part of West Kalimantan. The report said many victims had been 'decapitated or had their hearts torn out in an ethnic war of scarcely imaginable savagery, fought according to the ancient principles of black magic'.

As the plane descended, the thick jungle terrain of the island was interrupted only by a wide, cappuccino-coloured river snaking through the emerald foliage. The wilds of Borneo attracted a wad of intrepid British adventurers from the colonial era. One of these doughty Brits, James Brooke, became Rajah of Sarawak in 1841, and a succession of 'white rajahs' reigned for more than a century before Sarawak finally seceded to the British crown after World War II. Independence followed in 1963.

Many tourists travel to Borneo to spend a night or two in a longhouse, a traditional local village under one roof. The longhouse is a collection of individual family dwellings built side by side but sharing a communal veranda. Some of these longhouses can harbour up to 100 families. Though longhouses have been modernised to satisfy the coddled needs of Western tourists, some families still cling to ancient mores. A handful of them keep the head trophies collected by ancestors from head-hunting forays.

Unfortunately, most of the longhouses are mere tourist traps these days. So much for the Wildmen. Instead of bones through noses, expect modern Dayak headgear to be a Chicago Bulls cap worn backwards and a pair of bogus Ray-Bans. It was no different down by the river. No ominous wooden canoes disgorging painted warriors in loincloths. The locals seemed to prefer jet skiing in wetsuits along the Kuching waterfront.

The stadium that hosted Group B in the Under 20 World Championships was also a monument to modernism, with its hi-tech scoreboard and Citi Golf colour schemes. South Africa's young team had the misfortune to be grouped with powerhouse teams Brazil and France, as well as South Korea. The tone of their tournament was set when they could only manage a goalless draw against the Koreans. With the mighty French and heavily fancied Brazilians to come, they needed a win over the Asians to have any chance of progressing. The second match, against Brazil, saw the United Warriors play their best hour of football in the tournament. They matched, even exceeded, the boys from Brazil, until 15 minutes into the second half. Then two defensive errors were seized upon, and the Brazilians went home 2–0 winners.

The South African No. 9, Benedict McCarthy, was finding the going a little tougher than at the Under 20 African Championships. Then again, the Capetonian's life had changed massively in the space of just a few months.

While in Morocco for the African tournament, McCarthy had diligently phoned his agent to tell him that European club scouts were filling his head with stories of fabulous signing-on fees, CEO salaries and fame untold. The Dutch sides Feyenoord and Ajax seemed most interested, but Monaco, AC Milan and Paris St Germain were also sniffing around.

McCarthy's agent is Rob Moore, the Cape Town publisher of a batch of sports magazines. Moore had entered the money-soaked world of contemporary soccer back in 1994. He had long dreamed of owning a soccer team and so founded Seven Stars, which played in the national second division. Benedict McCarthy, then 17, had come along for trial matches at the end of 1994. When the goats had finally been shooed from the playing arena, and the trial game got going, it was clear McCarthy was several cuts above the rest. Moore signed the teenager for two sets of playing kit. McCarthy went straight into the first team and ended up joint top scorer in his first season with 28 goals. He also became an Under 23 international in his first year with Seven Stars when he played for Mich D'Avray's side against Manchester United's youth team.

In 1996, his second year with the club, a local agent went to the press saying that Inter Milan were after McCarthy. Moore smelt a rat and asked to see documentation. Nothing was received. The rival agent was clearly trying to drive a wedge between the player and his club, to gain control of the player's mind. Once a player starts thinking that his future lies in Milan, and here's his manager and agent telling him to carry on dodging the goats during practice, it can lead to tension. The week after the Milan rumours surfaced, McCarthy was sent off during a game for dissent. His mind was clearly elsewhere.

McCarthy remembered those fake Milanese overtures when he was being seduced by scouts in Morocco. He turned every inquiry over to Moore, who sensed the time was ripe to launch his prodigy on to the global stage. A young player can set himself up for life these days by making a prudent first foray into the moneyed European leagues. Moore was aware that his player was currently on a hot streak. Hot streaks don't last forever. It was time to cash in.

'When he came back from Morocco,' remembers Moore in conversation with me, 'I said we'll go over to Europe and spend one week at a time with a few different clubs. It was a case of not wanting to lose all that momentum he'd built up in Morocco. We had a month or so to get a definite contract. The pressure was on him to perform. The strategy was high risk but with the potential for high rewards.'

When Moore and McCarthy left South Africa, there were four top European clubs keen on the boy from Cape Town – Monaco, AC Milan, Feyenoord and Ajax. The Ajax air tickets came through first. The pair arrived in grey, cloudy Amsterdam one Friday morning in April. That afternoon, McCarthy was plunged into his first training session. The following Tuesday night, Ajax set up a trial match against top amateur club Quick Boys. On the morning of that game Moore told his prodigy that their strategy would be one of pressurising clubs into making a decision. Of not sticking around too long. McCarthy had to shine that night.

The game kicked off. McCarthy's first touch of the ball came with his back to goal. He leapt in the air to meet a knee-high ball, and flicked a back-heeled pass through his legs down to the winger. Moore sat in the stands wondering how someone in such a stressful situation could produce such deft magic with his first touch. Two minutes afterwards, McCarthy hit the bar. Thirteen minutes after that he scored his first goal. In that first half he had three or four certain goals stopped by the keeper. No matter; by the time the ref halted the game, McCarthy had scored twice and laid on two other goals.

Moore and McCarthy sat happily in De Toekomst club bar after the game. Things looked promising. Moore reached down to his bag for his cell phone to call home. His bag wasn't there. The leather holdall containing cash, air tickets, camera and passports had been stolen from the bar of one of Europe's most prestigious clubs. Red-faced officials rushed about. The bag was never found, but the problems were swiftly sorted out. Club directors refunded the money and put a car and a driver at the South Africans' disposal to sort out their travel documents.

The following afternoon, there was an assessment of the previous night's trial match with Martin Oldenhof, general manager of Ajax. The club's new coach, Morton Olsen, had made a special trip down to see McCarthy play. By half-time he'd told the Ajax scouts that McCarthy had to be signed.

Moore had prepared his demands in typically thorough fashion. Number one was the basic salary. Two, the length of the contract. Three, the bonus structures. Four, the signing-on fee. There were also queries about how much money his parents were going to get, the transfer fee, and air tickets for McCarthy's parents and Moore to visit during the period of the contract. At the end of the meeting the Ajax officials tabled an offer. 'You won't get a better deal in Holland,' they said. But they wanted an answer by Saturday. There would be no chance of going to Feyenoord for a week, or moving on to Milan and Paris.

McCarthy hadn't attended the negotiations. Moore came out of the meeting and the young footballer didn't even ask him what had happened behind those closed doors.

'So I left it. I wanted to see how long he would stay cool for,' recounts Moore. 'I actually had to say, "Don't you want to know what happened in the meeting?" All he asked me was if they wanted to sign him. He wanted to know nothing else. Nothing about money. So I said, "Yes, they want to sign you for five years." His face lit up. I then told him how much money was involved for him personally. I don't think those kind of numbers really sank in.'

After that meeting with Ajax, Moore phoned Feyenoord and told them they needed to talk. On Friday morning Moore sat down with Feyenoord's Hans Hegelstein.

'We sat and negotiated for four hours. They were very keen to get Benni. Hegelstein went back three times to his computer to run out new copies of the contract, and eventually, when we walked out of there, we had a deal that was 80 per cent better than Ajax's offer. It would really have put Benni among the top earners of Feyenoord. They had to wake up the president of the club in Chicago at 6 am to get approval on certain aspects of the contract they hadn't anticipated. But throughout they were brilliant, and when we walked out of Feyenoord, I said to Benni the deal was unbelievable. He said, "Fine, it's up to you where I play," but later in the day I could sense that he loved Ajax the club, the atmosphere, the facilities. Everything.'

As soon as Moore got back to Amsterdam he phoned Ajax. It was 3 pm on the Friday afternoon. He told the club if they wanted an answer by Saturday, they would have to talk as there had been some major developments.

Moore again sat down with Oldenhof. 'You told me you offered the best deal in Holland. You'll think I'm bullshitting you, but here is the written offer from Feyenoord. Now I want to bring it on to a footballing decision. You have to up your offer substantially. I don't want to get into a Chinese auction situation where I go back to Feyenoord, because Benni wants to play for Ajax from a footballing perspective. But we have to reach a situation where he doesn't turn round in a few years' time and say the deal was better at Feyenoord, maybe I should have gone there.'

An hour and a half later, Ajax offered a deal worth double the initial one made 48 hours earlier. The contract was signed. Benedict McCarthy would be transferred to Ajax Amsterdam.

Moore, like most who dabble in the lucrative field of buying and selling footballers, is cagey when it comes to revealing the dollars and cents of the deal.

'All I will tell you is that even if he never makes it at Ajax, never kicks a ball in the first team, he'll never have to work again in his life. I don't want to mention figures, because if people in South Africa know how much he is earning and he goes to an international camp, there might be a bit of animosity, so I shield him. But I tell you one thing, it was interesting to see the Bafana Bafana squad contesting their R7 000 win bonus before the friendly match against England. For players in the Ajax first team, in any league match the win bonus is R45 000. And it doesn't take a genius to know Ajax is going to win about 15 to 20 games a season. This excludes the Dutch Cup and European money. That gives you an indication of the kind of money involved, and that is only the bonuses.'

Ultimately, said Moore, the Ajax legacy for developing talented youth settled the dilemma of which club to join.

'Also, signing for a club like Ajax, with the racial harmony in Amsterdam being probably the most relaxed in the whole of Europe, was, for a young coloured kid from Hanover Park, a major part in our deciding to go with them. But the key thing in the deal was Ajax's record for finding youngsters and turning them into superstars. If you look at the Milans and Paris St Germains of this world, those clubs buy established stars. They're looking for instant success. A young guy trying to learn his trade would probably be on the sidelines for too long. Ajax is very good beyond soccer because they educate you about life, patience, mental requirements. So he couldn't wish for a better club. They look at your overall make-up and work on whatever they need to make sure your feet stay on the ground.'

The celebrations that night were put on hold. They came later. The next morning, McCarthy went shopping in the main street of Amsterdam. He bought himself some jewellery and some presents for his family. He blew R17 000 in an hour.

The next step was to organise suitable digs for Ajax's newest recruit. McCarthy could have bought his own apartment, but Moore warned him against it. 'When it's the seventeenth week in a row that you are playing in the second team, and it's cold and snowing, and you come home to an empty flat with no friends, you are going to be in trouble.'

The club thus set McCarthy up with a local family who would be able teach a wide-eyed youngster about Amsterdam and provide him with company while he busied himself establishing a network. McCarthy is staying in the suburb of Diemen with a couple in their early thirties who have a young child. They both love football and are knowledgeable about the city. The South African youngster is in good hands.

The final chapter in the Benedict McCarthy fairytale came soon after the Ajax deal had been clinched. National coach Clive Barker called him up to the Bafana Bafana squad for a friendly, ironically against Holland. He thus became the first South African player to represent his country at three different levels in one year – Under 20, Under 23 and senior international. His debut was rather muted. He came on with 15 minutes to go. South Africa were being given a lesson in possession soccer by the skilful Dutch. McCarthy didn't touch the ball for the first ten minutes, but when he did get some touches in the final five minutes, he didn't give it away. What was important was that he was in the shop window. In South Africa and in Holland.

Contemporary soccer is littered with hot talent that swiftly burns itself out. These days, the challenges are as much mental as physical. Moore, untypically for one with a vested interest, is confident that McCarthy's mental make-up is of the right stuff.

'He's a confident youngster without being arrogant. Very passionate, but very level-headed.' He's also prone to lapses, though, which Moore puts down to the 'exuberance of youth'.

When McCarthy scored the winning goal against Zambia in the Under 20 African Championships, he celebrated by running to the corner flag, stripping off his shirt and performing an ecstatic hip-shuffle. As he ran back to the halfway line, the referee asked who had scored the goal. 'Me, ref,' said McCarthy, thinking the official was unsure whom to credit the goal to. Instead the referee took out his yellow card and flashed it at McCarthy in a theatrical fashion. He'd been booked for over-exuberant celebrations. Two bookings in a world tournament mean an automatic one-match suspension. McCarthy would be on thin ice in the semifinal against Ghana. Sure enough, he was booked in the semi. He would thus miss the final of the Under 20 African Championships. It was a bitter pill to swallow.

McCarthy had a disappointing Under 20 tournament in Malaysia. As did the entire South African side. They scored only two goals in their campaign and were eliminated in the opening round. In the final group game, a 4–2 defeat against France, McCarthy was as subdued as he had been throughout the event. He did make the first goal for his side, however, rising to flick on a cross from the left into the path of Junaid Hartley who buried the half-chance.

In the second half, McCarthy was caught offside more times than he would have liked. He had a great chance midway through the second half, but scuffed a tame shot into the goalkeeper's hands. He was then booked for taking a shot at goal after the whistle had gone. He was substituted soon afterwards, and further admonished by the fussy Jamaican referee for taking his shirt off on the bench. There will be better tournaments in the future for one of South Africa's band of rising soccer stars.

Just as Benedict McCarthy lit up the African Under 20 finals, so the rave player in the Under 20 World Championships was the Brazilian Adailton. At just 19 years old, he was being called the new Romario or the new Ronaldo. Adailton scored six goals against South Korea and had one disallowed, as his side romped home 10–3. Just as McCarthy was swamped by signature hunters in Morocco (for contracts, not souvenirs), so the full glare of the spotlight bathed Adailton in Malaysia. Telephone-number transfer fees and massive salaries were bandied about in the newspapers.

It takes a supremely clear-headed teenager to cope with the demands of the modern game. The harshly critical soccer world will be monitoring every move of the likes of Adailton and McCarthy over the next few years. Good luck to them. They'll need it.

CANADA
UNITED STATES OF AMERICA
Las Vegas
MEXICO
North Atlantic
Ocean
North Pacific Ocean

CHAPTER FOURTEEN

Crocodile Tears at the Bite of the Century

THE CROCODILE WAS BITING as he swaggered through the Studio B conference room of the MGM Grand Hotel in Las Vegas. The Crocodile was bitin' and he was bawlin'.

'We gonna send the heavy arsenal in. We gonna fight this time. We ready to go to war. Right now. TWO DAYS AND A WAKE-UP! That's all. Two days and a wake-up. And Mike Tyson will again be the heavyweight champion of the world. GUERILLA WARFARE! And whoever don't understand guerilla warfare, that mean HAND TO HAND COMBAT! Two days and a wake-up. We want a knockout. We gonna take it from the root to the fruit. The last time Holyfield, he fought Mike. This time, he's fighting IRON MIKE TYSON! And there's no man in the heavyweight division that's gonna beat him. Mike Tyson will regain the heavyweight championship of the world. Mystique is a powerful force. Remember that, mystique is a powerful force.'

Crocodile wore olive-green, Vietnam-style battle fatigues, an olive-green bandanna and black-lensed designer shades. He had biceps as big as sweet melons and wore an inch-thick gold chain round his close to non-existent neck. It was almost like Crocodile's head had been welded directly to his shoulders. The veins in this virtual-neck throbbed and pulsed while Crocodile hollered. There was a tattoo on his left forearm, a variation of Rodin's 'Thinker' crowned by the slogan 'Team Tyson Rules'. 'Take a good look at that, fella,' he told me as he sidled by.

'LOVED BY FEW, HATED BY MANY, RESPECTED BY ALL!' screamed Crocodile. 'That's Mike Tyson. You media guys ask why's Mike always so mean. But when a guy get ready to do battle with another man, he ain't supposed to be smilin'. You get ready to go to war, you ain't going, "Hi man, how are you?" Come on, fellas, come on. It's war! You look at some of them old fighters, Dempsey and all o' them guys, they were way more vicious than Mike. Way, way more vicious. Anyways, you can't cook wi' cold grease. That's why I'm here – to heat it all up. TWO DAYS AND A WAKE-UP!'

Crocodile was surely heating up the 800 or so media types gathered at the MGM Grand Hotel for the final pre-fight press conference ahead of the Sound and the Fury. The rematch between Evander Holyfield and Mike Tyson for the heavyweight championship of the world was being hyped as the fight of the century. Crocodile, who'd spent time in jail for manslaughter, was one of the assortment of hangers-on who littered the Tyson camp. His designation in Team Tyson, he said, was that of Master Motivator. 'Whatever he needs done to do the job, I do,' said Crocodile.

Team Holyfield, the pristine half of the ultimate clash between good and evil, entered Studio B. Mike Tyson, the self-styled 'baddest man on planet earth', was up against a deeply religious Christian crusader. Crocodile had a message for Holyfield when the world champion emerged. 'You won the first fight, Holyfield. But you can't win this one. We comin' for that second fight, baby. Guerilla warfare. HAND TO HAND! I wanna tell you, you're not the only one with the blood o' Jesus Christ, baby. We comin' at you. You know it. You woke us up, baby. You gave us a wake-up call. That's all it was. Three minutes is a heavy round. Perpetual motion is coming at you. PERPETUAL MOTION! And don't go talkin' about your heart after this, Holyfield. Don't start with that, you hear me. We got your ass. We got the nuts. I'M BITIN' MAN!'

At no stage during his lengthy tirade did Crocodile mention ears.

Born and raised in the hard-core ghettos of Cleveland, Ohio, legendary fight promoter Don King has long been famous for his adage 'Only in America'. As in his oft-quoted theme tune: 'Only in America could a Don King happen. America is the greatest country in the world. I love America. I'm a patriot. What I've accomplished could not have been done anywhere else.'

What King has accomplished is to stage some of the most memorable fights in boxing history. He got his initial break when staging the 'Rumble in the Jungle' between Muhammad Ali and George Foreman more than two decades ago. His American backers pulled out of that fight at the last minute, so King brazenly approached Zaïrean dictator Mobutu Sese Seko. He persuaded Mobutu to stage the fight in Zaïre, and the bout that spawned Ali's famous 'rope-a-dope' tactic went down as one of the greatest in history. The equally epic 'Thriller in Manila' between Ali and Joe Frazier followed, and King, as he is never shy to recall, was on his way.

'There's always the beginning. As there is with the word of Jesus Christ. The alpha and the omega. The first, beginning and the end. George Foreman signed seven blank sheets of paper in order to accommodate the contract I'd already had signed by Muhammad Ali, and those two guys were giants and must be respected. So I'm just very happy to have known two athletes, two African Americans named Muhammad Ali and George Foreman who opened the door to the land of opportunity. The rest is history.'

Of course, King and his spin doctors conveniently omit any references to the time King spent in jail for manslaughter. In 1966, while he was running the numbers game, King kicked a man to death on the streets of Cleveland. They shrug off mention of how he uses then discards boxers like spent cigarettes; they ignore the fact that King is constantly tap-dancing around the taxman. Nevertheless, King's unique flair for generating hype, not to mention dollars, has found a special niche in the tainted world of boxing. In 1994, America's *Sports Illustrated* magazine named him one of the 40 most influential sports figures of the last 40 years. A week before the Tyson–Holyfield rematch, King had been inducted into boxing's Hall of Fame.

King's eccentric, vertical shock of white hair makes him look like he's been plugged in to Las Vegas's main power source, but it's his voice that electrifies. It's impossible to replicate in print King's rapturous manner of speech. He's part charismatic preacher, part desperate politician, part stand-up comedian, and he still imparts his own distinctive spin by making up his own words. He spoke to me of a boxer's 'instinctuitiveness'. You won't find that word in any dictionary, but coming from King's motormouth, it works.

In the week's build-up to the fight, Don King was talking to anyone who would listen to him. He'd swan into the vast media tent adjacent to the MGM Grand Garden Arena at various times of the day, paunchy in a black polo-shirt, black shorts and black alligator shoes, fingering a cigar the size of a mealie cob.

When I asked him about the fight ahead, he launched into familiar three-ring-circus speak. 'Every pub, every barbershop, every restaurant, every cab driver, from every lumpen proletariat to the élite presidents, kings, dictators – they're all on the edge of their seats,' he railed. 'That's the measure of its greatness. It will be seen by three billion people. From the shock of Evander Holyfield's win on November 9, which resounded and reverberated around the world stunning people into shock and amazement at an upset victory, now comes the devastating fury. It is only two great gladiators that can cause this type of excitement around the world, live from the MGM Grand Garden Arena strictly for your viewing pleasure. Say, where you from, young fella?'

When King heard I was from South Africa, he was interested.

'Well, I want to say hello first of all to Nelson Mandela. He's my hero and please let him know that I love the people of South Africa and I love Nelson Mandela. I would love to come to South Africa. Nelson Mandela has extended an invitation to me and I'd love to be able to accept that invitation, so nothing would please me more than to put on a great boxing event in South Africa. I think it would be something that would be a crowning achievement and I would be certainly proud and pleased to do it. Meantime, let us all sup at the table of brotherhood on this one. Set up your parties in South Africa and get ready to see boxing at its best when the Sound and the Fury comes to you, live via satellite.'

I asked King whether there was anything in boxing he still wanted to achieve, and received a typically convoluted, if not unenthusiastic, reply.

'You know, I'm a legacy of Muhammad Ali, the heavyweight champion of the world three times. Every knee must bend, every head must bow, every tongue must confess that thou art truly the greatest of all time, Muhammad Ali. I'm a legacy of him. So every boxer that comes in close proximity to me, that has benefited in this court of boxing, is an extension of the great one himself: Muhammad Ali. He opened the door for me in spite of the fact that door was nailed closed. I'm very proud and privileged to be an African American in that another African American by defiance, by instinctuitiveness, by overcoming the hobnobs and fighting for principles and convictions, has opened the door for me to practise my skills and talents. Likewise it is incumbent on me that I should do the same, and that is why I stick around in this sport of boxing hoping I can touch someone in the same way Muhammad Ali touched me.'

Don King has a habit of naming all his big fights in over-the-top terms. Stand aside 'Rumble in the Jungle' and 'Thriller in Manila'. Saturday, June 28, 1997 was the 'Sound and the Fury'.

'When I made this fight, I couldn't think of a name,' said King. 'And so, me in my spirituality, I called on Ernest Hemingway. I called up Ernie and I said, "Ernie, do you have anything in your re-per-toire that could identify a fight where a man was destined to lose, but he upset and shocked the world, and then he goes back into a rematch with the baddest man on planet earth?" And Ernie said to me, he said, "Wait a minute, Don." He paused a moment and then he said, "No, Don. I don't have anything. But let me plug in Bill Faulkner." So he plugged in Bill Faulkner, and we reiterated our story: we got a fight that shocked the world against the baddest man on planet earth, and now they're about to do it again. Well, I want to find something that could be significant, that could be related to and identified with.

'Bill Faulkner paused and then he said, "I think I have just what you need, Don. Ernie, let's call it the Sound and the Fury." And so, the Sound and the Fury was the name came by, and Bill said, "This is taken from 'To Be Or Not To Be,' which is *Hamlet*, a question out of Shakespearean theatre."'

Once, not so long ago, King had dismissed Evander Holyfield as a fighter of such limited appeal that he 'couldn't attract flies to shit'. This all changed when the 'Real Deal' had dumped 'Iron Mike' Tyson on the seat of his trunks in that first fight. Holyfield was now worthy of a $35-million purse. King's fawning introduction of Holyfield at that final pre-fight press conference rambled on longer than speeches at a political convention and had more twists and turns than a Vegas rollercoaster.

'Before the first fight with Tyson,' King began, 'they all wanted Evander Holyfield examined, and then they wanted the examiners examined. They wanted everything tested that never heretofore had been tested on a boxer. They would call us up and say have two ambulances at the side of the arena door. They were saying, this man here, you are threatening him with borderline murder. What are you doing? All of these things they were saying beforehand. But The Man was on board with Holyfield. Evander Holyfield serves the righteous Man, the Prince of Peace and the peace of principalities, my Lord and Saviour Jesus Christ.'

King's references to the world champion's devout Christian faith weren't about to end there.

'Yet I know He also had to let this fighter know about the Philistines and the tinkling cymbals. You know what I mean? About how they were all going to jump on board the gravy train after the victory is yours. But this man came this far by faith, trusting in the Lord, leaning on the Lord. He's never failed him yet. He isn't directed by others. He dances to his own drummer. And I have to applaud him and respect him for that brilliance.'

Evander Holyfield sat through this monsoon of lavish praise with a broad grin. 'Don, he's really something,' he said afterwards. 'It's really entertaining to see him getting it on. When you hear one of those, you don't soon forget it, do you?'

King was no less verbose when launching into a bizarre, blatantly false introduction of Mike Tyson. Tyson had strolled into Studio B 20 minutes late. He was at least a head shorter than the phalanx of brawny guards surrounding him. Shaven-headed, Tyson wore a polo-shirt in yellow, navy and green stripes and an expression like he was being ushered to the dentist's chair.

'This man is noted for being pound for pound the baddest man on planet earth,' intoned King. 'But more than that he's also a vi-sion-ary. A visionary who will reach out and touch those around him. This is what I wish all our athletes would do. This is something that makes a difference in the chain, not just sitting around supplicate [sic], but doing something with responsibility that demonstrates what America is. And that man goes beyond the realm of a fighter, he goes in the realm of the visionary. A visionary who regardless of what critics or foes and naysayers or doomsayers say, continues to persevere for the betterment of quality of life for all Americans, especially for those who are the disenfranchised – the left-outs, the underprivileged, the downtrodden and denied. I introduce to you the former heavyweight champion of the world – MIKE TYSON!'

During the questions that followed, Holyfield was open and expansive. The current world heavyweight champion is a genial, genuine man. He had time for reporters in the days leading up to the fight, and could often be found hanging out in the media tent. Unlike Tyson, who was hardly ever seen outside his hillside training fortress on the fringes of the garish casino town. Throughout that morning's press conference, Tyson looked alternately irritated and bored. He would grab his head in his hands, like he was trying to lift his neck off his shoulders, then he'd lay his head down on the table.

'It comes down to how you handle pressure,' said Holyfield, when quizzed about tactics for the fight. 'I truly believe that when it comes down to talent, we're just as equally talented in ability and strength. But I also know that pressure decides fights, and I thank God that he's given me the peace of mind in times of pressure to overcome that pressure.'

'How much do you want to win the fight? Can you talk from your heart a bit?' asked one earnest scribe of Tyson. Tyson shifted in his seat, screwed up his face, stared at the floor, then eventually said, 'I'm just looking forward to it. I'm not emotional. I'm professional. I don't get involved emotionally with anything. I've got business here on Saturday night.'

The guy from the *LA Times* asked if Tyson had made any mistakes in the first fight against Holyfield and, if so, how Tyson planned to rectify this now.

'Sure I made a mistake,' Tyson growled. 'I lost. I plan to rectify that by winning.'

It was clear that the entire media process was irksome to Tyson. His surliest response was saved for somebody from an organisation called Christian Broadcasting, who asked Tyson if he had been able to find peace in his life, like Holyfield, and if not why not.

'I'm not going to answer your question,' snapped Tyson. 'I'm all right. I'm okay.'

Just when it seemed there was more chance of winning the $14-million MGM Grand Casino rolling slots jackpot than extracting a worthwhile quote from Tyson, he came up with a revealing follow-up answer.

'We write our own books in life. Most of the time when you receive trouble, you bring it on yourself. That's just from my own experiences in life. You know what I mean? You can't cry over spilt milk. We have to be men and handle whatever comes at us and deal with it.'

Tyson left Studio B engulfed by handlers, who fended off the signature hunters with enthusiasm. They whisked the baddest man on the planet out round the back of the media tent and into a dark green Range Rover, which sped away from the hotel with a shriek of rubber. The hordes of gawkers who had gathered for a glimpse of the fighters returned to the multitude of other diversions in Las Vegas.

Of course, the main reason people come to Las Vegas is to throw money at their problems. And the marketers of this neon-spangled glitter pit in the Joshua tree-studded lunar landscape of the Nevada desert have hit on an effective plan to keep the masses rolling in. If you lodge outside the megabuck resorts, accommodation is cheap. I stayed at the slightly tired Hotel Continental for just $19 a night. Also, food is for the taking in Las Vegas. Everywhere on the Strip, huge electric signs advertise all-you-can-eat prime rib and shrimp buffets for around $5.

But meals and lodging, even championship boxing bouts, aren't what the people come here for. To reach the lobby of any hotel in Las Vegas, you must pick your way through the casinos. At the Continental, any hour of the day or night, there'd be the dull jingle and whirr of coins being spat out to be gathered up by metronomic people. These dull-eyed folk would then feed those same coins back into the slots. Waitresses in bow ties, velvet coats and leotards weaved among the banks of slots dumping complimentary drinks, hoping to score a buck or two in tips. Many of these waitresses had no business wearing leotards. Some sported wrinkles and talked of the battles of single parenthood. It was clear that most of the people in the casinos at the Continental were not exactly moneyed. The giveaway was the acres of polyester clothing in the flared John Travolta disco cut. The seedier hotels in Las Vegas are clearly home to Losers Inc. Pty Ltd. For these people, Las Vegas would seem to be the ultimate Last Chance Saloon, where wages are blown in a desperate hunt for the supreme pay day. Hotels help grease the slippery slide by offering incentives such as 'Free Sirloin Steak with every Pay Check Cashed'.

Nine of the ten biggest hotels in the world are situated in Las Vegas. The vast turquoise and bottle-green MGM Grand is the planet's largest hotel resort. It occupies 45 hectares, has 5 005 rooms, parking for 9 000 cars and cost a billion dollars to build. Across the road is the New York New York Hotel. Here, a rollercoaster encircles the entire block that this hotel consumes, so people plummet earthwards toward gridlocked traffic on Las Vegas Boulevard for kicks. In front of the hotel is a half-sized Statue of Liberty. Other landmark Big Apple buildings have been built in a similarly half-scale fashion, in the cartoon colours of a Batman movie. New York New York is linked to other resorts like Luxor and Excalibur by overhead walkways and moving travelators.

Luxor is an Egyptian-themed resort built beneath a black glass pyramid. The Nile Bar features fake palm trees and there are earth-coloured plaster statues of reclining lions outside the Pharaoh's Pheast buffet restaurant. At the pool area are massage facilities and lolling bathers are sprayed with a fine mist of water, like runners in the Comrades marathon, from neatly concealed sprinklers. They need it. Every day I spent in Vegas, the temperature hovered around the 40-degree mark. The local radio station's weather forecaster would say things like, 'Today in Vegas, hot and sunny; tomorrow in Vegas, hot and sunny. Five day forecast – do you really want to know – hot and sunny. Bob, tell us what's happening in the traffic.'

Las Vegas Boulevard, the legendary Strip, houses most of the big hotels and casinos in town. These venues sport a myriad of entertainers, both cheesy and current. During the build-up to the Sound and the Fury, the two Fields – Danger and Copper – were the top acts in town. Rodney Dangerfield, the pop-eyed one-liner merchant, was at the MGM Grand's Hollywood Theater; David Copperfield, the magician, was headlining Caesar's Palace. Fading stars, apart from the obligatory Tom Jones, included veteran Engelbert Humperdinck and his warm-up sidekick, Zachary Fingernut, who were competing, no doubt, for the title of the 'world's stupidest entertainer alias'.

Las Vegas Boulevard snakes left before reaching downtown, just after the pink Normandie Motel with its 'Elvis Slept Here' signboard. This area is littered with the town's famous wedding chapels. Such as the Little Chapel of the Flowers, which sits smack between a 7–11 corner store and a filling station. And the Chapel of Love, which is next door to the Belmar Hotel, a place that advises in loud neon that credit cards are accepted for rooms showing XXX ADULT MOVIES ON COLOR TVs. Every temptation and vice known to mankind thrive in Las Vegas like bacteria on meat left in the sun. Correct me if I'm wrong, Andre Agassi, but growing up in such a city must be a perspective-warping experience.

The 24-hour drive-up wedding window apparently does good business at the Little White Chapel, a cutesy white wooden building like the church in the opening scene of the *Rocky Horror Picture Show*. Here you can drive up, press the buzzer and be married forthwith. As easy as ordering a quarterpounder at McDonald's and, no doubt, as heartfelt as a 7–11 cashier's 'Have a nice day'. Nevertheless, the celebs seem to love these places. The Little White Chapel trumpets the fact that basketball superstar Michael Jordan and ageing actress Joan Collins were married there (not to each other). Also Bruce Willis and Demi Moore (who did marry each other), Frank Sinatra, Mickey Rooney and Judy Garland. They're all there on a photo wall in the reception.

The Little White Chapel has various wedding packages to choose from. The economy deal costs $139 and includes the use of the chapel, music, photos, bride's bouquet and garter, champagne glasses, 'beautifully etched marriage scroll' and a 'free love recipe'. There are other, pricier options, like the Michael Jordan special at $389 and the $499 Joan Collins deal. I asked the lady at the drive-up window for a brochure. 'Call us when you're ready, honey,' she said. And I will. The day I go gambling at the Vatican.

It's all very superficial, of course, but that doesn't matter in America. After all, here's a nation obsessed with image, fame and surface beauty. Americans possess a craving for the limelight that is almost embarrassing. Inhabitants of the world's quintessential sound-bite society will do anything for their Warholesque 15 minutes of fame. While I drove through California's Mojave Desert to Las Vegas, radio shock-jock Howard Stern quizzed an 18-year-old from Long Beach. She had phoned Stern pleading to get into showbiz. Stern asked the teenager if she'd be happy to sleep with studio executives to get a part in a movie. She answered, 'Sure, why not?' as casually as if she'd been offered an extra lump of sugar for her coffee. Stern went on to say that studio execs tend to be wrinkly fatsos who neglect dental hygiene. Would this bother her? 'No, not at all. As long as they give me a part, they can do anything,' said the wannabe.

Although Americans are weaned on, and aspire to, media images of perfect athletic bodies, immaculate teeth and full heads of hair, suburban reality is horribly different. Americans are, no question, the fattest people on earth. Las Vegas in summertime was Blimp City. No subtlety when it came to attire either. I saw one woman in the queue at the MGM Grand's Oz buffet who could have packed down against the Springbok scrum on her own. She wore stretch shorts and a Spandex bra top. Even though a thousand television talk show hosts try to convince their vacuous audiences that no one is at fault, that excess blubber is due to defective genes and other flaws of nature, it would appear the real bottom line is that the Yanks are far too fond of the Whoppers and the Hostess Twinkies.

While I'm sliding down this trash-the-Yanks tangent, there's another thing someone must explain to me about America (besides the obvious matter of how a country where the majority of the population struggles to locate London on a map becomes the most powerful nation on earth). Upon arrival in the United States, you are given an entry form to fill in. On the reverse of this form, six questions are posed to visitors. The third of these questions is: 'Have you ever been, or are you now involved in, espionage or sabotage; terrorist activities or genocide; or between 1933 and 1945 were you involved in, in any way, persecutions associated with Nazi Germany and its allies?'

I want to go back through every single one of those entry forms since the dawn of time and see if anyone has ever answered 'yes'. Is this how they caught the guys for the Nuremburg Trials? Maybe that's how all those Nazi war criminals got a safe passage to South America in the first place. They were probably ushered happily through United States immigration: 'Mr Mengele, you answered "yes" to question three on this here immigration form. Step right this way, please. Your connection to Buenos Aires will be leaving in an hour. Have a nice day.'

The 40-degree Las Vegas heat is unrelenting on Sound and Fury night. June 28, 1997 is the first time Mike Tyson has ever looked across the ring into the eyes of a fighter who has beaten him before. Tyson knows that many veteran fight insiders are saying that the image of the schoolyard bully, the aura of intimidation that he worked so heavily on his opponents, has largely vanished. That the big early bombs are failing to find their target, and the awesome Tyson power has been withered by his spell in jail and the passage of the years. Lennox Lewis's trainer, Emanuel Steward, says that Tyson's one-dimensional, straight-ahead style won't carry such fighters past the age of 27. They burn out, like Joe Frazier. Tyson would turn 31 two days after the fight.

As fight time nears, a TV shot of Tyson reveals a tense figure in the dressing room. Perhaps Tyson thinks back to the early Eighties. To the days he once sobbed uncontrollably on the shoulder of trainer Teddy Atlas because he was so scared and unsure of himself. This happened during the Junior Olympics, and after he goes on to win the event's heavyweight title he is back to his macho posturing. He tells reporters, 'When I'm in the ring all the nervousness and tension stops, it's not there no more. Because I'm facing reality. I'm not in the locker room thinking, "Oh man, this guy's a killer." As soon as I get in the ring, I'm the killer then.'

Teddy Atlas is a man who believes Tyson always needs a shoulder to lean on, someone to give him a boost, a shot of confidence before he's ready to get into the ring. Atlas could never understand why Tyson would get so emotional and insecure when preparing for fights against opponents he'd already beaten many times before.

The years will show there's much of Tyson's life that defies explanation. Even for the man himself. In the week before the Sound and the Fury fight, Tyson tells a *Newsweek* journalist, 'I really don't know what I am. I just try do the best I know how. Nobody should look to me for anything. People f... you again and again. That's the truth of humanity and I deal with it by accepting it.'

The only thing Mike Tyson trusts is his ability with his fists. To fight and to win. He says he wouldn't know what he would do without boxing in his life. 'What am I going to do?' he asks. 'Be a brain surgeon?'

In that week leading up to the fight, Tyson wears the face of a haunted loner, ill at ease with himself and his entourage. There are no shoulders to lean on. He is openly disdainful of Don King and doesn't even trust his handlers, though he and manager John Horne go back a long way. But he's bound to both King and Horne by long-term contracts. There are pots of money to be made out of Mike Tyson. Over the years, the shrewd, the ruthless and the opportunistic have flocked to the fighter from the tough streets of Brownsville, New York like vultures to a fresh carcass.

Evander Holyfield, by contrast, is in a tranquil state of mind as the Sound and the Fury draws near. Religion is his stability. Whenever the world champ signs an autograph, under the signature he writes a reference from the Bible: Phil. 4.13. The verse reads: 'I can do all things through Christ which strengtheneth me.' Holyfield sways, dances and mimes to gospel songs while building up a glistening sweat in the sanctity of his dressing room. When he enters the ring, he meets Tyson's eye with a steady gaze while referee Mills Lane talks the fighters through the pre-bout ritual. Lane has only been given the fight the day before. The Tyson camp had threatened not to fight if original referee Mitch Halpern was in charge. They got their way.

Seconds after Mills Lane ends the pre-fight formalities with a dramatic 'Let's get it on', the Sound and the Fury is unleashed. Holyfield lands solid shots in the first round, which he dominates. He is similarly in charge in round two. During this round, Tyson is headbutted by Holyfield and a 7-centimetre cut opens above his right eye, the same damage that originally caused the fight to be postponed. Tyson glances angrily at the referee. No point is deducted, as Mills Lane believes the butt to be unintentional.

Tyson comes out smoking for round three. The fighters clinch, again bump heads in the middle of the ring. The referee struggles to part the fighters. Tyson lands heavy body shots that stop Holyfield dead. Again the fighters clinch. Heads lock once more. There are 33 seconds left in round three. Evander Holyfield has won the first two rounds on all three judges' cards, but Tyson is well ahead in the third. The fighters yet again clinch in mid-ring. Tyson throws a wild right, then an equally wild left. Holyfield ducks under both blows. As Holyfield comes up to clinch, Tyson sinks his teeth down hard into the top of Holyfield's right ear. Tyson turns away and spits something out of the side of his mouth. The world champion wheels around and leaps in the air in outrage, showing his mangled ear to referee Mills Lane. While Holyfield's back is turned, Tyson charges, sending Holyfield careering into the ropes.

Many members of the crowd cheer Tyson's aggression. They don't know what has happened. Tyson retreats to his corner. His eyes narrow, nostrils flare and jaw tightens into a sneer. The fight is delayed for four minutes. Holyfield is told by his corner to breathe deeply, to keep concentrating as they try to repair the damage. Mills Lane, ex-Marine, docks Tyson two points – one for the bite, one for the shove.

The fighters come together in the middle. The electricity in the ring has been turned way up. The fighters set about each other with a vicious blur of fists. For 15 seconds, it's a street brawl. They clinch once more, and Tyson bites Holyfield's left ear. The champion is blinded by rage, but this time carries on boxing. Tyson beckons to the champion with both arms, taunting him, 'Come on, come on!' The referee doesn't see the second bite and allows the round to end.

Mills Lane then walks over to the Holyfield corner and sees a second set of toothmarks in Holyfield's left ear. As the swimsuited girl with the round four board starts circling the ring, Mills Lane ends the fight by disqualifying Mike Tyson.

The disqualification triggers chaotic scenes. The girl is swiftly ushered away as the ring is flooded with people. Tyson and Tim Hallmark, Holyfield's cornerman, begin screaming at each other. One of Tyson's handlers shouts that Holyfield has quit the fight. The world champ is a quitter. Tyson charges Hallmark and Holyfield and bowls over an MGM Grand security man. He swings a punch at a policeman in the ring and has to be pulled back by a swarm of guards. One of his handlers tries to restrain him, and Tyson cocks a right fist as if ready to flatten his own cornerman. Khaki-wearing Las Vegas cops storm the ring. Tyson has a bewildered expression on his face. His eyes dart from side to side. Tyson cornermen yell, 'We're all right, we're all right, we got him,' as the cops move in.

Holyfield and his handlers do the smart thing. They leave the ring as soon as possible. When Tyson and his group finally exit the arena a full ten minutes later, they are booed raucously and pelted with plastic bottles from the seats above the walkway leading to the dressing rooms. Security men are again called in to prevent a mini-riot, as Tyson makes a brief attempt to leap into the stands. He swings and misses at several spectators before being pulled away and down into his dressing room.

In the bowels of the Garden Grand Arena, Evander Holyfield prepares to head for hospital to have the piece of his ear re-attached. Given the bizarre turn of events, he is remarkably composed when a microphone is stuck under his nose. 'They have rules and regulations for this. He caught me with a good shot and then bit my ear and spit it out. Look at the bite. I'm missing part of my ear. It doesn't show any courage when you foul and try to get out of it. Fear causes people to do things to get out of it. It was kind of sad. I thought he took the bite because it was an easy way to get out of the fight. All you have to do is foul, and you get yourself out of the fight. If you feel you can whup me, why don't you whup me with the gloves on? This is a boxing match, it's not a rumble where after the fight is over you get brave and then you wanna fight. He had the chance to hit me in the ring.'

Tommy Brooks, one of Holyfield's trainers, says Tyson should be banned for life. 'He should lose his licence permanently. He's a coward, a Jekyll and Hyde. I had a lot of respect for Tyson as a great athlete before. No more. I can't believe what I saw. That's a typical bully move. He had Evander in the ring, one-to-one, man-to-man, and he didn't do anything.

Then, when all of those people are there in the ring, he wants him. Come on, that's bully stuff.'

Tyson's manager, John Horne, a sharp-faced former comedian, is highly agitated. 'A little nick on his ear don't mean nothing,' he yells. 'My fighter had a three-inch cut. Mike has been cut four times in two fights with this guy and neither time by a punch. Holyfield turned it into a street fight a long time ago. There's nothing wrong with Evander Holyfield that could prevent him from performing.'

Tyson is eventually summoned from his dressing room. He's still sweating, though slightly less on edge.

'He butted me in the first round and in the second round again. I saw him. He was holding me and looking right at me,' says Tyson. 'He kept going down and coming up on me. No one warned him, no one took away any points from him. What am I to do? This is my career. I can't get butted like that. I got children to raise. I have to retaliate. I complained in the first fight and nothing was done.'

Tyson's lisping voice rises. He's the schoolyard bully again. 'Holyfield's not the tough warrior everybody thinks he is. He got a little nick and he quit. I got one eye. I'm ready to fight him. Ready to fight right now. He didn't want to fight. Regardless of what I did, he butted me for two fights. I addressed it in the ring. Look at me. Look at me!' he now screams. 'My kids will be scared of me.' Then Tyson walks away before his wrath again becomes unmanageable.

Don King, as usual, is at Tyson's shoulder throughout this brief media interview. King is quietly stunned, like a witness at a bloody freeway smash. He says, 'The correct reaction is not to bite, but I guess when a guy is being butted and he's pleading with the referee and doesn't get consideration, he goes beyond reason. You have two athletes who are highly hot and passionate, and the fight was only beginning. Maybe the referee should have given the fighters five minutes to recuperate so that at least the people out there get their money's worth.'

Two million people had paid $49,95 to watch the fight on pay-per-view television in the United States. Ringside seats cost $1 500 face value and were going for up to $5 000 on the black market just before the bout. There is a whole horde of disgruntled Sound and Fury patrons at the MGM Grand Garden Arena.

Shots are fired in the vast casino as frustrated spectators file away after the aborted fight. Twenty people are injured in a mass stampede to exit the venue. The mood in the hotel resort is taut and hostile. Later, MGM officials say no shots were fired. The sounds people heard were of breaking glass, they claim. Eyewitnesses insist they heard gunshots.

King finally tries to fluff out his tail feathers when he's asked if Tyson should still get his $30 million purse for the fight. 'Yes, he should. They both came to fight. Boxing is unpredictable. That's what makes it so great,' he says in a half-hearted stab at injecting something positive into the fiasco the world has just witnessed.

Great? After Mike Tyson spat on the Marquess of Queensbury's rules, lifted his leg on sportsmanship and plunged pugilism back into the cave era?

Even Don King had no chance selling that one.

The Crocodile, if he's still hanging round Team Tyson, will have to amend his 'Loved by Few, Hated by Many, Respected by All' battle cry. The first two descriptions still hold true, but the last claim evaporated in 30 seconds of madness that hot summer night in Las Vegas.

Postscript: Mike Tyson was fined $3 million dollars and had his licence revoked by the Nevada State Athletic Commission after the fight. He can re-apply for his licence in July 1998. Cynics maintain the punishment was a mere slap on the wrist. Too many people stand to make too much money from a third Tyson–Holyfield showdown in the future.

Acknowledgements

AS ANY SOUTH AFRICAN will tell you, flitting around the world on the rand is not for the faint-hearted. Never mind the exchange rate; most of us have limits, not targets, on our credit cards. Airfare and accommodation form the bulk of travel expenses and, luckily, my global sorties have cost only a fraction of their true worth because of a number of generous people.

So hearty thanks to Cecelia Amory and all at Travel Trends in Northcliff for providing me with so many free and cut-price air tickets to planet-wide destinations.

I'd like to thank the many people who allowed this foreigner to invade their lives for a few days, and who provided a soft bed and, in most cases, a hard night or two on the town: Beth Harris in Cardiff, Christy Sullivan in Arizona, Izabela Tomaszewska in Warsaw, Frankie Deges in Buenos Aires, Tony Graham and Deirdre in Los Angeles, Richard Gloster in London, Barun Agarwal and family in Calcutta, Jan Gregory and family in Derbyshire.

Also thanks to Oliver Reprich at Chembe Lodge in Cape Maclear, Malawi, who put me up for a couple of weeks to get this book going, and saw fit only to bill me for the Greens.

Many people read drafts and advised during the writing of the book. Such as Heather Dugmore, Caroline Hurry and Brendan Templeton, all journalists of note, and none of whom dress like extras in the 'Bring out your dead' scene in Monty Python's *Holy Grail*. (Though, Carrie, those faded leather trousers and mamba-green stockings skate perilously close to the qualifying zone.)

Some of the material in the Jamaica, India, rugby World Cup and Far East chapters of this book appeared as short travel articles in the *Saturday Star*. Part of the Arizona Super Bowl chapter appeared in *Out There*. A portion of the Togo chapter appeared in *Sunday Life*. The 'Champions Past, Present and Future' and 'At Play in the Fields of Lord's' chapters were expanded from articles written for *SA Sports Illustrated*. Grateful thanks to those publications for allowing me to reproduce them here.

I'd also like to thank David O'Sullivan of Radio 702 for putting me in touch with Marga Collings of Zebra Press, who in turn introduced me to Tamsin Shelton, whose expert editing has ridden the book of most of its errors. Any that remain are solely mine. Thanks also to my sister, Penny Roper, for speedily transcribing and diligently inputting so many of the taped interviews. A slew of Barbie dolls for Katie and a truckload of Lego for Marc was a negligible price to pay.

Finally, thanks to the many local journalists, particularly at *The Star*, who were so encouraging when I first got into the game. Heavyweights (metaphorically speaking) such as Rodney Hartman, James Clarke, Denis Beckett, John Perlman, Michael Shafto, as well as *SA Sports Illustrated* publisher Rob Moore and my old cadet teacher, Quraysh Patel.

Modern journalism often proceeds in a cut-throat blur, but people such as these always had time to find spirited words for a novice.